Matthew Mark Trumbull

The Free Trade Struggle in England

Matthew Mark Trumbull

The Free Trade Struggle in England

ISBN/EAN: 9783744662420

Printed in Europe, USA, Canada, Australia, Japan

Cover: Foto ©ninafisch / pixelio.de

More available books at **www.hansebooks.com**

FREE TRADE STRUGGLE
IN ENGLAND

THE

FREE TRADE STRUGGLE

D

... To the Literary Editor of the ...

With compliments of

THE OPEN COURT PUBLISHING CO.

169-171 La Salle Street, Chicago.

Please mail us a marked copy of the paper containing the review.

Retail price

SECOND EDITION, REVISED AND ENLARGED

CHICAGO
THE OPEN COURT PUBLISHING COMPANY
1892

THE

FREE TRADE STRUGGLE

IN ENGLAND

BY

M. M. TRUMBULL

SECOND EDITION, REVISED AND ENLARGED

CHICAGO
THE OPEN COURT PUBLISHING COMPANY
1892

DEDICATION.

TO THE

RIGHT HON. JOHN BRIGHT, M.P.,

THE ELOQUENT FRIEND AND DEFENDER
OF THE AMERICAN REPUBLIC,
THE ENLIGHTENED ADVOCATE OF PEACE AND FREE TRADE
AMONG NATIONS,
THIS WORK IS RESPECTFULLY INSCRIBED BY
HIS FRIEND AND DISCIPLE,

M. M. TRUMBULL.

London
132 Piccadilly
Mar 3. 82

Dear Sir,

I am glad to learn that you are discussing the Question of Free Trade.

If it will be of any service to you, I cannot object to your dedicating your little Book to me.

The American Tariff is so incapable of defence & that Discussion of the charge burdens it lays upon your people can only end in some

great

change of great expense. Such a reform will bring our two great nations nearer together, but the advantage will prove to be much more for your people than for ours.

Free trade in England since 1846 has been of great service to other nations, but of ten times greater service to us, than to them.

So it will be with you. Your people will be the chief gainers, & in a few years after your Tariff has

been

made reasonable, it will be as easy to persuade the United States to go back to the times of Slavery as to the days & the mischiefs of Protection.

I wish you every success in your efforts on behalf of Free Trade,

I am
Very respectfully
Yours
John Bright

M. M. M. Trumbull
Dubuque
Iowa
U. S. America

LETTER FROM JOHN BRIGHT.

132 Piccadilly, London,
August 8, 1882..

Dear Sir: I ought to have thanked you sooner for sending me your useful and very interesting "History of the Free Trade Struggle in England." I hope it may be widely read, and be of much use. But I do not expect your people will copy from us—they will learn from what is passing around them how much they suffer from your present barbarous tariff.

There are persons amongst us who are not anxious for a reform of your tariff. They say you cannot have an export trade, and cannot compete with us in foreign markets; that we have complete control of markets where there is no high tariff; and where duties are considerable, that we can surmount them where you cannot, and that we have a great advantage over you in every market but your own.

Again, in your mercantile marine your condition is miserable and humiliating owing to your protective system, which has driven your ships off the ocean. Surely, there is intelligence enough in your country to perceive this, and it can only require discussion to bring about a change, which would bless every honest industry amongst you. The shackles have been struck from the limbs of the slave, and they cannot remain to fetter the freedom of your industries.

I hope your movement will advance—the world expects it from you. England and America, with free institutions and Free Trade, will lead the world to something better than the past. I am very truly yours,

John Bright.

PREFACE.

In the Spring of 1882 I published a short History of the Free Trade Struggle in England. That little work became popular beyond my expectation, and the edition was soon exhausted. The press comments upon it were very favorable, and a second edition was called for. In preparing another edition of it I determined to revise the work altogether, to make it more copious and more interesting, and especially to show that the moral of the contest is as applicable to the United States to-day as it was to England forty years ago. This must necessarily be so, for the law of liberty cannot vary with climate or geography. One of our most popular statesmen, a candidate for the second office in the republic, intimates in his letter of acceptance a different opinion. He says, "the fact that our form of government is entirely unique among the nations of the world, makes it utterly absurd to institute comparisons between our own economic systems and those of other governments." This is a very serious error. No government is "unique" enough to violate the laws of moral science with impunity. No government ever will be so "unique" that it can justly tax one man for the benefit of another, or forbid its citizens to buy their goods in the cheapest market.

The arguments used by the advocates of the American Protective system in 1884 are all borrowed from the speeches delivered in the British Parliament in 1844 by the advocates of the English Protective system. This proves that the principle of both systems is the same, and that it must be beneficial or injurious to one country as well as to another. I am glad to notice that Mr. Bright has recently expressed this view of it.. Speaking of Mr. Blaine's letter of acceptance he says that it reminds him of the old theories long maintained in England and finally discarded for a system more enlightened and more free. To make this parallel more plain to the American reader is the chief object of this work, while presenting at the same time a fair and truthful history of the Struggle for Free Trade in England.   M. M. T.

CHICAGO, Oct. 1884.

PREFACE TO THE SECOND EDITION.

Since the publication of the first edition of this book the issue between Free Trade and Protection has grown in public interest, and in political importance, while the demands of monopoly for larger privileges have been clamorous and incessant. Growing with what it feeds on, the appetite of Protection, not satisfied with the McKinley Bill, calls for more subsidies, and a larger share of the taxes which the consumers have to pay. The protected interests are willing to allow the government a reasonable share of the moneys derived from Internal Revenue taxation, after taking a few millions out of it for bounties on sugar and subsidies for ships; but all the money derived from External Revenue taxation, duties upon imports, they impudently claim belongs to them. They have therefore inverted an ancient formula and made it read like this: "Tariff for protection with incidental revenue."

To keep this book abreast of the debate, I have revised it, and have given some additional facts bearing on the lesson to Americans which is given them in the study of the Free Trade Struggle in England. Had the English arguments for Protection been preserved in Mr. Edison's phonograph, the unwinding of the machine would not have more faithfully reproduced them than they have been reproduced by the American protectionists in the debates in Congress—excepting this one, "the foreigner pays the tax." In all the debates in Parliament between 1841 and 1846, I cannot find it of record that any member was foolish enough to think that, or daring enough to say it. M. M. TRUMBULL.

CHICAGO, July, 1892.

CONTENTS.

CHAPTER	PAGE
I. The Anti-Corn-Law League	9
II. The Protection Triumph	26
III. A Tory Ministry	48
IV. The Tariff of 1842	60
V. The Horizontal Plan	73
VI. Hard Times	89
VII. American Wheat and the Drain of Gold	105
VIII. Overproduction	120
IX. Wages	133
X. Reciprocity	150
XI. At the Zenith	166
XII. A Surplus Revenue	177
XIII. Nearing the End	189
XIV. At Last, Famine	206
XV. The Reformed System	222
XVI. The New Policy	239
XVII. A Tariff for Revenue Only	256
XVIII. The Fall of Peel	267
Index	281

THE FREE TRADE STRUGGLE IN ENGLAND.

CHAPTER I.

THE ANTI-CORN-LAW LEAGUE.

By the Free Trade struggle in England is meant the campaign from 1838 to 1846, or from the formation of the Anti-Corn-Law League to the final overthrow of the Protective System. Of course there were enlightened persons long before 1838 who doubted the wisdom of crippling commerce by a hostile tariff on imports; but those heretics were comparatively few. They were easily brushed aside by practical statesmen who believed in the blessings of scarcity, and who looked upon abundance as a calamity to be provided against by law. The believers in commercial freedom were told that their doctrines were all very well in theory but would never do in practice, and with this convenient argument they had to be content. No doubt that in the "dark ages" of political economy, when "Protection" flourished in direct proportion to the popular ignorance, there were men in England who saw, clear over the fogs in the valley, the bounteous and beneficial Free Trade sunshine gleaming on the heights beyond; even as Galileo and Columbus saw farther and clearer than the men who called them theorists and doctrinaires. They, too, were told that the sciences they cultivated were theoretically well enough, and good for colleges, but being morally scientific they must fail when tried by the test of practical experiment.

Indeed, more than a hundred years ago, Adam Smith had refuted the argument on which the protective theory was based, and which up to his time had been known by a sort of paradox as the "Mercantile System." Carried to its logical results its effect was to hinder mercantile transactions, and to cripple commerce, by closing ports to international trade. In the time of Henry Clay it was known in this country as the "American System," and in our own day it is called by the captivating title of "Protection to Native Industry." Mr. Huskisson, one of the most enlightened members of the English ministry, made some advances toward Free Trade, as early as the year 1823; and even before that time, the merchants of London had petitioned Parliament in behalf of commercial freedom. Their argument was remarkably forcible and clear. They said:—

"That unfortunately, a practice, the very reverse of freedom from restraint, has been, and is, more or less adopted and acted upon by the governments of this, and almost every other country; each trying to exclude the productions of other countries, with the specious and well-meant design of encouraging its own productions, —thus inflicting upon the bulk of its citizens who are consumers the necessity of submitting to privations in the quantity and quality of commodities; and thus rendering what ought to be the source of mutual benefit and harmony among States, a constantly recurring source of jealousy and hostility. That the prevailing prejudices in favor of the protective or restrictive system, may be traced to the erroneous supposition that every importation of foreign commodities occasions a diminution or discouragement of our own productions to the same extent; whereas it may be clearly shown, that although the particular description of production which could not stand against unrestrained foreign competition would be discouraged, yet, as no importation could be continued for any length of time without a corresponding exportation, direct or indirect, there would be an encouragement for the purpose of that exportation, to some other production, to which our situation might be better suited; thus affording at least an equal, or probably a greater, and certainly a more beneficial employment to our own capital and labor."

The petition ended with an earnest protest against "every restrictive regulation of trade not essential to the revenue; against all duties merely protective; and against the excess of such duties as are partly for the purpose of revenue, and partly for that of protection." In answer to the petition, Lord Liverpool, then Prime Minister, said that "he agreed in every sentiment expressed in the petition; and that if he were forming a Commercial Code, such would be its fundamental principles." Perhaps the most insidious enemy to every reform is that valueless concession which agrees to the principle of it, and regrets that the present "is not the time;" as Mr. Eaton is reported to have said in Congress, when opposing Mr. Morrison's bill, "He hoped that the United States would be a Free Trade country— forty years from now."

It is curious that Sir Robert Walpole, as Prime Minister of England, anticipated Huskisson by more than a hundred years. At the opening of Parliament in October, 1721, which, by the way, was before Adam Smith was born, he inspired the King to say that:

"It is very obvious that nothing would more conduce to the obtaining so public a good—the extension of our commerce—than to make the export of our own manufactures and the import of the commodities used in the manufacture of them as practical and as easy as may be; by this means the balance of trade might be preserved in our favor, our commerce increased, and greater numbers of our poor employed. I must, therefore, recommend to you, gentlemen of the House of Commons, to consider how far the duties on these branches may be taken off, and replaced without any violation of public faith, or laying any new burthen upon my people. And I promise myself that by a due consideration of this matter the produce of those duties, compared with the infinite advantages that will accrue to the kingdom from their being taken off, will be found so inconsiderable as to leave little room for any class of objections."

In pursuance of this policy more than one hundred articles of British manufacture were allowed to be exported free of duty, while forty articles of raw material were allowed to be imported in the same manner. In explaining the motives that governed Walpole in this matter, the author of the " History of the Four Georges" says: " Walpole was anxious to make a full use of this indirect system of taxation. He desired to levy and collect taxes in such a manner as to avoid the losses imposed upon the revenue by smuggling, and by various forms of fraud. The principle was that the necessaries of life and the raw materials from which our manufactures were to be made should remain, as far as possible, free from taxation."

Some people entertain the delusion that, although the laws of mathematics and the physical sciences are applicable to all countries, yet that the same inflexible quality does not belong to the laws of moral science. They believe that these can be changed according to the whim of legislatures, and the exigencies of climate and geography. They think that the principles of Free Trade may be philosophical and wise in one country, and the reverse in another; that "infancy" is a good plea in behalf of Protection in a new country, but not in an old one; that agriculture ought to be protected at the expense of manufactures in England, and manufactures protected at the expense of agriculture in America. We have statesmen in Congress who believe in longitudinal Free Trade and latitudinal Protection; who think that Free Trade would be scientific and valuable between us and the nations to the north and south of us, but mischievous and unwise between us and the nations east and west. But the laws of political economy cannot be bent to suit the differences of latitude and longitude. The freedom of trade that benefits England would benefit the United States. Commercial principles cannot vary between Liverpool and New York, nor between Boston and Montreal. It is very curious that, while the citizens of London were petitioning their Parliament for commercial freedom, the citizens of Boston were asking Congress for the same right. It gives a rude shock to the vanity of an American revenue reformer of the present day to find that his arguments were anticipated by his countrymen sixty-five years ago. In 1827, when our "infant industries" were much more infantile than they are now, a committee of the citizens of Boston thus protested against the injustice of a protective tariff. They declared it false to say that "dear goods made at home are better than cheap ones made abroad; that capital and labor cannot be employed in this country without protective duties; that it is patriotic to tax the many for the benefit of the few; that it is just to aid by legislation manufactures that do not succeed without it; that we ought to sell to other nations, but never buy from them." They go on to say "these are, we have long since known, fundamental principles among the advocates of the American system. It is, however, extraordinary that these ancient and memorable maxims, sprung from the darkest ages of ignorance and barbarism, should take their last refuge here."

It is not so very extraordinary after all. Every nation must pass through commercial barbarism to commercial civilization, from Protection to Free Trade. The desire to get rich at the expense of others is well nigh universal. It is easy to persuade most people that to "protect" their own artisans from the competition of "foreign pauper labor" is an act of patriotism. This admitted, it is easily narrowed down to our own state, our own county, our own city, our own village, or even our own street. In the last century the farmers of Middlesex, the county in which London is situated, petitioned Parliament against improving the abominable roads of England. They frankly claimed that so long as the roads were bad they had a monopoly of the London markets for the sale of their vegetables, fruit and grain; that if the roads were improved, the farmers of other counties would be able to bring their produce to the London markets, which would be disastrous to the "industry" of Middlesex. This looks very foolish on the face of it, and yet in principle it is the doctrine of American Protectionists to-day.

The attempt to encourage agriculture, manufactures, shipping, experimental enterprises, special trades, "infant" industries, and so on by protective laws, was persevered in by England at a wasteful expense for centuries, and it was abandoned only when it was found out that Protection was the paralysis of industry. To suppose that the United States was born wise in these matters, would be as unreasonable as to suppose that it was born old. .It must have the same education in economics that England had. Its term of tuition will not be so long as that of England was, but the discipline and instruction must be the same. The Protective doctrine, too, has the same advantage here that it had in England. So long as it prevailed the nation grew in wealth, power and population. Not until Protection was abandoned did the people see that their progress had been made in spite of it, and that their prosperity would have been much greater, had their commerce been free. So it will be here. Under "Protection," and in spite of it, this country is growing in wealth and power. When Protection is abandoned the people will be astonished as they were in England, at the multiplication of their wealth and comforts under a Free Trade policy.

With impudent audacity the Tory journals placed all the greatness and glory of England to the account of the Protective system, but not any of the poverty or the crime. In the light of subsequent history their claim reads like a jest, and yet many of them were serious in making it. The following portentous *propter hoc* appeared in *Fraser's Magazine:* "In favor of the restrictive system it may be fairly urged, that with it, and therefore by means of it, the country rose to the pitch of prosperity and greatness at which we find it;" and *Blackwood's Magazine*, in solemn reproof of the Free Traders, declared that the Protective system "was the system under which England had become free and great and powerful." Indeed, as far back as 1825, when the ministers under the inspiration of Mr. Huskisson proposed to relax in a small degree the grip of the restrictive system, *Blackwood's* sounded the Tory tocsin, and rallied the cohorts of monopoly to the defense of privilege in the clamorous notes of mock patriotism which protectionists like to use. After deploring the moderate reduction of duties proposed by the ministry, and after boasting that never before was prosperity so abundant, *Blackwood's* said: "That man has not a drop of British blood in his bosom who can contemplate this without a throb of joy, and who can witness attempts to tamper with it, to make it a subject of experiment, to cut, twist, disjoint and disorganize it, in order to saddle it with untested theories, without dislike and apprehension." That artful appeal to national feeling has been stolen from *Blackwood's* by the American protectionists, who with equal vehemence declare that the man who would interfere with their extortion has not a drop of *American* blood in his bosom. To the very end of the struggle, and even after it, *Blackwood's* maintained that Sinbad the sailor moved about more freely and comfortably than he otherwise could because he carried on his broad shoulders the old man of the sea.

The "Protection" laws for England passed between the years 1340 and 1840 would make a more entertaining book than Mark Twain ever produced, especially if it showed the contrary efforts made to effect the same purpose. Sometimes exports of raw materials were forbidden in order that they might be abundant in the Kingdom, to the encouragement of the trades which used them, while the importation of the same raw materials was forbidden lest they might become abundant to the discouragement of the industries that produced them. In one reign, shoemakers were forbidden to exercise the trade of a tanner, "in order to promote and improve the manufacture of leather." In a subsequent reign, shoemakers were encouraged to engage in the tanning business by act of Parliament "to promote the manufacture of leather;" and again, for the very same object, shoemakers were forbidden by law to exercise the tanner's trade.

All sorts of contradictory laws were passed at various periods to "protect" the wool manufacturer and the wool-grower at the same time. For instance in the reign of Elizabeth the export of sheep was prohibited in order that wool might be plentiful in England and scarce in France. Still the weavers clamored for more protection, so that in the reign of Charles II., an act was passed requiring that every dead body should be buried in a woolen shroud. This failed, because the effect of the law was to deprive the living of woolen clothes, in order to dress the dead. Besides, the people would not die fast enough to suit the weavers, and therefore in the reign of George the First, another act was passed "for the encouragement of the woolen and silk trades." By the provisions of this law any person wearing a garment of calico was subjected to a fine of five pounds, and any person selling it was liable to a fine of twenty pounds. Still the wool-growers and weavers were not satisfied. They demanded that the cotton trade should be suppressed for their protection, and to that end a law was passed imposing heavy protective customs duties on all raw cotton imported into

England. All this was like sending fire engines to put out the Aurora Borealis, and had not the laws of social existence been stronger than acts of Parliament this legislation would have strangled, in its infancy, the cotton industry, which is to-day one of the main supports of the British empire. A board of trade was erected by King James the First, in 1622. Hume informs us that one of the reasons assigned in the commission is, "To remedy the low price of wool, which begat complaints of the decay of the woolen manufactory,"—the patent falsehood that dear wool is a good thing for the men who make cloth, and the tailors who make coats, being as ignorantly asserted then, as it is impudently asserted now.

In the year 1363, in the reign of Edward the Third, when the exportation of wool was strenuously forbidden, a law was passed which regulated the clothing of the people and prescribed what apparel might or might not be worn by them according to their respective conditions and rank in life. The pretense for this law was, that people were becoming extravagant in dress, and that luxury in this direction ought to be restrained. This law was repealed in the following year, either because it could not be executed, or because it was an injury to trade. But a hundred years later it was re-enacted, because it was discovered that the people indulged in excessive array "to the great displeasure of God, the impoverishing of England, and the enriching of strange realms." The "Protection" character of this law is easily seen in the reasons given for its enactment. The English were buying goods abroad because they could get them there cheaper and better than they could buy them at home. The Protectionists of that era, like their descendants in this, regarded all purchases made abroad as a waste of money, which went to the "enriching of strange realms." It never occurred to them that the articles they bought came to the "enrichment" of their own country. In the blind economy of the time, men could not see that riches might consist of other things than money.

The manufacture of certain commodities was restricted to certain places, to "protect" them from the competition of other places, and to encourage their industry. In the reign of Henry the Eighth, an act was passed restricting the making of cloths to Worcester, and a few other favored towns; and in the same reign the trade in worsted yarn was limited to Norwich and the county of Norfolk; and it was provided, that no person should weave or manufacture it save the artificers belonging to said city or county.

In vain and tiresome gyrations, the Protectionists of old whirled round and round trying to give special aid to some callings without injuring others. In the reign of Edward the Sixth the saddlers were protected by a monopoly of the trade in leather, and their business flourished to such an extent that all who doubted the wisdom of the law were silent and ashamed. "See what Protection has done for the saddler trade," said the advocates of the law, and the Free Traders could not answer them. After awhile it was noticed that what was a good thing for the saddlers was a bad thing for the cobblers, and they presented a petition to Parliament complaining that the monopoly had "wrought their utter impoverishment and undoing." So, therefore, in the reign of Mary, the obnoxious law was repealed, in order to "protect" the cobblers from the extortions of the saddlers.

It was also learned by costly experience that the leather monopoly enjoyed by the saddlers had not only operated as an unjust tax on the cobblers and shoemakers, and on everybody who wore shoes, but that leather had deteriorated in quality as it had increased in price. In consequence of the petition of the cobblers, the law was repealed, and in the act repealing it, Parliament acknowledged that it had learned a good lesson in political economy. After bewailing the condition of the cobblers, the act gives this additional reason for abolishing the monopoly of the saddlers, "and forasmuch also as sithence (since) the making of said estatute all kind of leather is more slenderly and deceitfully wrought and made than ever before, nevertheless as dear or dearer." This preamble will apply to every protected monopoly in the world.

It is not necessary to multiply examples. The English laws are full of vain and mischievous attempts to make rivers run up hill, to divert moral science from its principles, and make the beneficent streams of trade and manufactures flow the wrong way. They failed, as such attempts must ever fail. They gave to certain special classes an artificial prosperity, but this prosperity was abstracted from the community at large. The belief in witchcraft was accompanied by the kindred superstition that "Government" always kept on hand a large surplus of prosperity created by itself, which it could ladle out at pleasure to help destitute people, professions, and trades. It was not then known in England, as it is not yet known in America, that "Government" can create nothing; and that if it pours a cupful of prosperity upon this trade or that one, it must dip it up from the common fund of prosperity created by the labor of all the rest of the people. There is positively no bounty, help, or endowment having a money value, that government can give to one without taking it from others. When government used to sell monopolies this truth was more apparent than it is now, because the money received for the franchise was a confession that the buyer of it must get it back with profit out of the consumers whom he was allowed to overcharge for the article on which he had the monopoly. That government gives the monopoly for nothing does not change the principle, but it makes it harder to detect. It really makes no difference to the consumer whether the Pennsylvania mine owners and manufacturers pay the government for a protective tariff or get it for nothing. If there is any money value in it for them, that value must come out of the people who are compelled to buy of them whatever they have to sell.

Although the so-called Protective system prevailed in England for centuries, it must be remembered that it never had a peaceful reign. Its victims always protested against it, and it never altogether satisfied even its beneficiaries and advocates. The hundreds of laws enacting, amending, and repealing its details prove this. It is very likely, also, that while the system was necessarily perverted to the unjust privilege and profit of special classes, its authors originally designed it for the encouragement of home industry. They did not look beneath the surface of the scheme. They saw at the first glance that a certain trade was benefited when freed from foreign competition, and they thought that therefore there must be concealed within it an economic principle that required the legislature to protect every business that suffered from foreign rivalry. Then began the scramble of "interests" for special protective enactments. The archives of the British Parliament will show that there is scarcely an interest in the country that has not petitioned for a monopoly of its own trade. The Protective system which roused the fierce opposition of the English manufacturers from 1836 to 1846 was really the work of their fathers. For centuries the manufacturers of woolens, cottons, and other fabrics believed that Protection and monopoly were indispensable to their trade, and they resisted every attempt at commercial reform.

It was that historic lesson which caused the *Edinburgh Review* to say: "For centuries the government has labored to misdirect the industry of the people. It has taken upon itself the task of rendering them, or certain classes of them, rich. It has dictated to them what they shall produce and to whom they shall sell, and what they shall purchase, and to what markets they shall resort. It has considered the whole body of consumers as a prey to be sacrificed to any class or to any section of a class that chooses to ask for a monopoly. And, when one class has complained of the privileges granted to another, it has bribed it into acquiescence by allowing it to inflict a further injustice upon the public."

As the land owners of England comprised an overwhelming majority in both houses of Parliament, it was natural that they should gradually direct the protective legislation of the country so as to give them a monopoly of the home market in every article constituting the food of the people. This they did; and the vice of their system reached its climax in the Corn-

Laws of 1815. When the battle of Waterloo had brought the war of the French revolution to an end, and it became necessary to adapt the commercial system of England to an era of peace, it was agreed that inasmuch as the landlords had not the power to decree how many bushels of wheat should grow on an acre of land, they would, in retaliation for this oversight of Providence, declare and establish by law how much a bushel the consumer should pay for whatever quantity the acre might happen to yield. It was conceded that the farmers could not pay the high rents demanded by the landlords unless the minimum price of wheat was fixed at eighty shillings a quarter, and they established it at that figure. This was about two dollars and a half a bushel, American money; or, as wages was then, about three days' work of a mechanic for a bushel of wheat. The protective tariff was "so adjusted" as to insure that price. The law had been altered two or three times in the interval, but the principle of it remained from 1815 to 1846.

The law was fiercely and continously assailed, but the opposition to it was only a sentimental protest, having no practical value. The cry of hunger was unheeded by the legislature. The law was discussed by the newspapers and the magazines, but only occasionally, and rather as a question of ethics and abstract political economy, not as a "live issue," dividing parties and having any immediate bearing on the welfare of the people. After the passage of the Reform Bill in 1832, the cry grew louder, and the passionate verses of Ebenezer Elliott stirred the feelings of the people, and aroused a sentiment of indignation against the Corn-Law. Unfortunately for Elliott, he was known as the "Corn-

Law Rhymer," and the nickname, of which indeed he was proud, has led the world to believe that he was a rhymster, and nothing more. But Elliott was a true poet, and the poetic flame burned within him ardent and bright as the fire in his forge at Sheffield. Carlyle, in a review of his verses, declared that he was a real poet, and one who had something to say; a poet whose voice it would be well for the government to heed. Colonel Perronet Thompson, in his "Catechism of the Corn-Laws," also started an agitation that steadily increased in power. The scattering fire of an irregular skirmish line advancing against the Corn-Laws could be heard, from London to Liverpool, and from there to Glasgow. Nevertheless, it was not until about the year 1836 that the Free Traders made any well-organized effort against the insular and bigoted system of restriction which had burdened the industries of England for hundreds of years. Up to that time the liberal and scientific principles of Free Trade were regarded by "practical" statesmen as political abstractions, beautifully adapted to some undiscovered Utopia, which might be expected to appear about the time of the millennium. Up to that time the efforts of the Free Traders were feeble and scattered over an extensive field, fortified by the Protectionists so strongly in every direction that the reformers made but slight impression upon the works of the enemy. The wealth, profits and social force derived from hundreds of monopolies had combined and consolidated into a political power, controlling both branches of the legislature, the church, the aristocracy, and the crown. Not only that, but Protection had shielded itself with a national sentiment borrowed from a popular patriotism jealous of "foreign competition." It appeared to be invincible. In 1839 the isolated forces of Free Trade became a coherent and disciplined organization under the name of the Anti-Corn-Law League. They massed themselves for a concentrated attack upon the Corn-Laws, the key to the whole Protective System. The Corn-Laws were to Protection what the Malakoff was to Sebastopol. When that fell the city fell. The repeal of the Corn-Laws meant the doom of Protection and the triumph of Free Trade. The efforts of the League were directed to the success of a specific measure—the repeal of the duties upon corn. Under the general term "corn" in England is comprehended flour, wheat, oats, and breadstuffs, of every kind.

CHAPTER II.

THE PROTECTION TRIUMPH.

Just at the dawn of midsummer, 1837, the King died, and the Victorian era began. With the old King there went out an age of ignorance, vice, and political superstition. With the young Queen there came in a better, brighter, and a wiser day. There was vice enough left, indeed, but it was no longer respectable. The Parliament died with the King, and a new Parliament was chosen. The contest was between the Whigs on one side, and the Tories on the other. The issues were like many of the issues between the Democrats and the Republicans in our own country now—rather of the past, historical, than of the present, real. The offices, however, were at stake, and the Whigs won. They had a majority in the new Parliament of about thirty in the House of Commons. This in a membership of six hundred and fifty-eight, was barely a working majority; but by keeping close in shore, and not venturing out upon the wide ocean of statesmanship, they could get along with it comfortably well, and enjoy the power, the honors, and the emoluments of office.

The commercial policy of the country was not much of an issue in the election. The Tories were all Protectionists and so were most of the Whigs. They differed only in degree, not in principle. Thirty-eight Free Traders obtained seats in the new Parliament.

They ranged themselves with the Whigs, as did the Irish Repealers, and the Liberals of every grade. What progressive elements existed in the politics of the time, were supposed to be represented in the Whig party. The Tories, if not reactionary, were at least conservative.

The trifling difference between "the two great parties" was amusingly shown. In 1839, the ministers came within six votes of defeat on the bill, providing a new constitution for Jamaica, and as this was too narrow a margin on which to administer the government with dignity, they resigned. Sir Robert Peel, the leader of the Tory party, was sent for by the Queen to form a new administration. He had been Prime Minister in 1835, and was the most competent statesman then in Parliament. He agreed to form a government, but required that certain Whig ladies of the Queen's household should be removed from office—in other words, they should go out with the ministry that had brought them in. The Queen would not consent to this, whereupon Sir Robert gave up his task, and the Whigs resumed their places. Those drawing-room politics were now about to be rudely shaken by the new power just born into the State: the Anti-Corn-Law League. A "live issue" was about to be presented to the people, something of greater consequence than the politics of the ladies attached to the Queen's household. The question was whether or not the food and clothing of the people, and all the comforts of life, should be made scarce and dear by import duties on foreign grain, and meat, and wool, and other things, levied for the "protection" of special classes; whether or not the shackles which had fettered industry for centuries should be removed and the commerce of England made free.

It is somewhat curious that the first leader in Parliament of the commercial reformation came not from the mercantile or manufacturing classes, neither was he a "man of the people." He was of the titled aristocracy, a brother of the Earl of Clarendon. The Hon. Charles Pelham Villiers, member for Wolverhampton, a young man of 35 or so, was the head and front of the Free Trade party. He had eminent capacity for leadership, a thorough knowledge of the question, an intense conviction of the wisdom and the justice of his cause, good temper, and what Lord Beaconsfield, his most sarcastic enemy, freely accorded him, a "terse eloquence, and vivid perception." He was almost the first man of his time in Parliament who had vision bright enough to see that the feudal system of commerce was crippling the industries of Britain, and he was the only one who had faith to believe that the system could be overthrown. He was in the House of Commons six years before Cobden appeared within its walls, and eight years before John Bright obtained a seat there. Although in actual debate he was contented to fall behind those powerful tribunes, and although Cobden "fairly trampled him down," as Cobden himself rather mournfully said, yet the leadership of the party in Parliament was never taken from him. He is now, at the age of ninety, still in active political service in the House of Commons as member for Wolverhampton.

Some years after the termination of the Free Trade struggle, *Fraser's Magazine*, another opponent, not quite so fair as Lord Beaconsfield, spoke thus of Mr. Villiers:

"The advocacy of a repeal of the Corn-Laws has been the one special hobby of the Hon. C. P. Villiers—a hobby he rode around the political arena with the flourish which usually attends hobby horsemanship, until the real men and horses of the Anti-Corn-Law League came on the scene. Year after year he made his formal motion for a repeal of the corn laws, and delivered almost the same speech—at least the same arguments applied to new facts, with but little effect upon the House. Sometimes he was counted out; sometimes the matter was disposed of by a single speech from the Government, or latterly from an agricultural member; but at all times his subject was regarded as a disagreeable one, and the House was always as thin as a decent respect for the proprieties would allow. Even after the league had begun to make a figure in the House the annual motion of Mr. Villiers was still regarded as an annual bore; and when at last the out-of-doors agitation had invested the subject with a greater political interest, other and more powerful speakers commanded the attention of the House, and Mr. Villiers was, comparatively speaking, lost in the throng, although still allowed to retain his original position as the practical leader of the party."—*Fraser's Magazine, Vol. 34.*

On the 13th of December, 1838, the Manchester Chamber of Commerce resolved to petition Parliament for a repeal of the Corn-Laws, and in January, 1839, a meeting of deputies from all parts of the Kingdom was held in Manchester to consider the best means of obtaining the repeal. On the assembling of Parliament in the same year, the delegates met at Westminster and organized the Anti-Corn-Law League. Mr. Villiers was unanimously chosen leader of the cause in the House of Commons. Referring to this meeting, some years afterward, a London paper, in a brief sketch of Mr. Villiers, said, "It needed no common courage to undertake the leadership. There were but few Free Traders in the House. The ministry and the expectants of office were alike opposed to Mr. Villiers. Whatever party there might be for some change in the Corn-Laws, there was in reality no party for the total and immediate repeal. Free Traders on principle—those who would admit no compromise were few, either in the house or out-of-doors. Public opinion and a Parliamentary party had both to be made."

Several months before that memorable meeting, Mr. Villiers had begun the great Parliamentary struggle for Free Trade. On the 15th of March, 1838, he moved that the House go into committee on the Corn-Laws. Like Mr. Benton with his expunging resolution, Mr. Villiers renewed this famous motion every year until the victory was won. He began by remarking, "that it might be said that this was not a fit time to bring forward the subject, because the public mind was in a state of repose with respect to it. The purpose of the Corn-Laws was protection to the landed interests." He then showed that the House of Commons was composed of landlords, and he contended that the Corn-Laws were measures adopted by themselves in the selfish pursuit of their own profit and advantage at the expense of all the rest of the people.

In ridicule of the claim that in order to "protect" the landlords, foreign grain must be excluded from the Kingdom until the domestic article had reached a certain price, Mr. Villiers made this happy comparison, "Suppose a majority of hand-loom weavers in Parliament. Might they not be expected on this principle to prohibit power looms, or, at all events, enact that until cloth produced by hand labor reached a certain price, that produced by power should bear a fluctuating duty?" He contended that the resources of the country would be best developed "by employing the population in those pursuits for which the country afforded the greatest facilities." This really seems like an economic axiom, and yet it was then denied in England as it is now denied in America. The contrary doctrine is maintained, and we are passionately told that industries not profitable must be made profitable by taxing all the others. Mr. Villiers charged that the hostile policy of other nations was provoked by the Protective System of Great Britain. He said, "Our own prohibition system has driven Prussia and the United States to have recourse to a corresponding one, nor would they consent to take our manufactures unless we consented to receive their grain." The motion for the committee was refused by 300 to 95. To this majority the Tories furnished 226 and the Whigs 74. There were 263 members absent, and three-fourths of them might fairly be counted as against the motion.

The League, once formed, soon showed that it was in earnest, and its activity disquieted the "two great parties." Its agents were in every town. It circulated pamphlets by the million. It assumed the task of instructing the whole people in the elements of political economy. Its orators were everywhere. In every corner of the Kingdom they challenged the Protectionists to public discussion, and threw them painfully on the defensive. In the manufacturing districts its meetings numbered thousands. Those masses of people did not have political influence in proportion to their numbers, for few of them had votes. Before the League was two years old it had become a great power outside the walls of Parliament, although, inside, it had no strength, except in the character and ability of its advocates, and the irresistible logic of its argument.

The work before it was appalling. Monopoly was so strongly entrenched in England as to seem invincible. It was supreme in both houses of Parliament. The privileged orders and the "protected" classes were, of course, all defenders of it. The middle classes — the real John Bull — were very much imbued with the idea that British patriotism required them to support the policy that made them "independent of foreign countries." Worse than all, the masses of the people, the working classes, were Protectionists, as will appear a little farther on. They were everlastingly haunted by a ghost called "overproduction;" they believed that scarcity was a good thing because it created a demand for labor, and they dreaded lest they be brought into competition with the "pauper labor" of foreign countries.

The Parliamentary session of 1839 opened inauspiciously for the Free Traders. They were weak enough at best; and, as bad luck would have it, they were literally extinguished by the indiscretion of one of their own men, and this was the manner of it: The form of opening Parliament is by a speech from the throne. After that, an address to the Queen in answer to it is adopted by each house; and the speeches made in moving and seconding the address are supposed to contain the program, or "platform" of the ministers, as well as a defense of their past policy. The mover and seconder of the address are selected by the Ministers at a Cabinet council, and to be chosen for that duty is regarded as a personal and political distinction. The honor of moving the address in the House of Commons is generally conferred upon some member connected with the aristocracy or the "landed interest," and the privilege of seconding it is generally given to a member identified with what the Americans call the "business interests" of the country, somebody interested in merchandise or manufactures. In the present case the distinction of seconding the address was bestowed upon Mr. G. W. Wood, a Free Trader, and Chairman of the Manchester Chamber of Commerce.

Of course, the mover and seconder of the address are expected to polish up the politics of the ministerial side, and make them look as bright and attractive as possible. Mr. Wood, thinking it was his duty to make a good showing on such an important occasion, declared that everything was flourishing and prosperous; that trade, commerce, agriculture and manufactures were at the present moment in a most satisfactory condition, and he produced the statistics to prove it all. He said that the tranquillity of the country on the subject of the Corn-Laws was owing to a fortunate cheapness in the price of bread. Mr. Wood was flattered by generous cheering, but what confused and bewildered him was that it all came from the wrong side of the House. His encouragement came from Sir Robert Peel and the Tories, and not from his own party. His own friends were writhing in pain, because Mr. Wood, being a Free Trader, should have talked in a different way. The Tory leader could well quote the pious exclamation of Cromwell at the battle of Dunbar, "The Lord hath delivered them into our hands."

Sir Robert Peel was quick to avail himself of the advantage given him by Mr. Wood. With affected gravity he congratulated everybody on the prosperous condition of everything, and showed from the statistics of Mr. Wood the value of the "Protective System." He said: "Coming, as this speech did, not only from the seconder of the address, but from the Chairman of the Chamber of Commerce of Manchester, nothing could go further to confirm those who were favorable to the continuance of the present state of things in their opinions, and to awaken the doubts and suspicions of those who had been desirous of an alteration."

Mr. Villiers tried to counteract the mischief done by Mr. Wood, but failed. He censured Sir Robert Peel for condescending to avail himself of the miserable and fallacious reasoning of Mr. Wood. He then tried to show where the fallacies lay, but he was embarrassed by Mr. Wood's admissions, and, after stumbling over that gentleman's "facts" until he was tired and sore, he sat down. He was in the situation of the senior counsel trying to correct the mistakes of his associate brother, whose awkward ingenuity has drawn from his own witness some testimony very damaging to his own side.

Lord John Russell, the leader of the Whig party in the House of Commons, the minister who had selected Mr. Wood to second the address, probably enjoyed that gentleman's innocent blunders as much as anybody. At all events, he did nothing to help him out of his tangle. He contented himself with some vague generalities to the effect that "the time had arrived" when things must be looked into, and when it should be considered whether the present system acted beneficially or not. With this feeble flicker the debate ended. The Free Traders had lost ground.

Mr. Villiers was not disconcerted, and in a few

days he returned to the attack. His courage was proof steel, and his temper perfect. He knew that the "protection" argument was a contradiction and denial of the very mathematics of political economy. It delighted him to see his adversaries tripping one another up with contrary reasons why the Protective System ought to be maintained; to make things cheap and to make them dear, plentiful and scarce, to promote the acquisition of riches by transferring wealth out of one pocket into another, and to keep in perpetual motion that circular benevolence which robs Peter to pay Paul, and Paul to pay Timothy, and Timothy to pay Peter, and thus round and round forever. A biographer said of Mr. Villiers that he was "a political economist, not only by study, but by a natural aptness, amounting almost to instinct." On the 19th of February, 1839, he renewed the conflict by moving that certain persons be heard at the bar of the House in support of a petition complaining of the operation of the Corn-Laws.

In supporting his motion Mr. Villiers said: "In comparing ourselves with America, we find her possessed of great natural advantages; proximity to the raw material, and cheapness of power." He showed that the Protective System had made England a dear country to live in, and that its operation was to help the rival manufacturers of Germany, Switzerland and the United States. Mr. Villiers could not then anticipate that the Americans would with perverse deliberation set themselves to work to nullify their "great natural advantages;" that they would with inverted statesmanship contrive and establish a policy for the very purpose of making the United States "a dear country to live in;" and that by the ingenious folly of a high protective tariff they would shut their manufactures out of the great markets of the world.

Sir Robert Peel resisted the motion, but on this occasion he had the serious task of answering the strong arguments of a political economist and a statesman. The weak and imprudent concessions of Mr. Wood would not avail him now. He said that he could not admit that English manufactures were in an alarming state, and that "our former customers were about to drive us from the markets." "The object of the gentlemen opposite," he said, "is to increase the price of grain in foreign countries in order to check the progress of their manufactures. Not a very benevolent object, I must confess." He then said, "We use 52,000,000 quarters of grain yearly. Would it be wise that this country should be called upon to make the experiment how far in case of war and famine it might rely upon procuring the necessary amount of food from foreign countries?" It was the very irony of fate that seven years after this, when the Protective System had culminated in "famine," Sir Robert Peel himself, as Prime Minister, should be compelled to throw his country for salvation upon food "from foreign countries."

It is evidence how insignificant was the influence of the Free Traders in England at this time, that although they supported the Whig party, and the Whigs were in power, they could not obtain respectful consideration in the House of Commons. The motion of Mr. Villiers that the Manchester petitioners might be heard at the bar, was lost by 361 to 172, and Lord John Russell, and Lord Palmerston, the Whig leaders in the House, both voted in the majority, both destined to be Free Trade Prime Ministers of England.

The difficulties in the way only stimulated the industry of the League, and within two years it had become a source of alarm to the Tories, and of perplexity to the Whigs. Many of the Whig members sympathized with it in a negative sort of way and to a limited extent. They were, however, timid and irresolute. The Whigs carried on the Government in a lazy, languid manner, and were anxious to be "let alone." They thought they could live forever on the Reform Bill triumph of 1832, but the Reform Bill was only a beginning, not an end. The fierce discussion of that measure had stimulated the mental faculties of the people, and had excited within them a craving thirst for knowledge, and an appetite for debate. The *Penny Magazine* was in active circulation, lectures were popular, Mechanics' Institutes were multiplying, and, in the expressive language of Lord Brougham, the schoolmaster was abroad in the land. The Whigs were afraid to risk their small majority by the introduction of any great measures of public policy; and by reason of that very timidity, their trifling majority was gradually dwindling away. They asked permission to doze in comfort on the treasury benches, but the noise of the League disturbed their slumbers, and the Tories were watching and waiting their own opportunity which was close at hand.

Suddenly it occurred to the Whigs that in this new active world of politics, even governments must do something for a living. They saw the great moral power already in the hands of the League, and Lord John Russell thought that if he could borrow some of that, he might spiritualize the Whig party and save the administration. Accordingly, in the month of April,

1841, he gave notice that on the 31st of May he would move that the House go into committee to take into consideration the duties on the importation of foreign grain. This announcement startled the Tories, for it showed that the doctrines of the League had permeated the administration itself. They closed their ranks, and assumed the offensive. Lord Sandon, member for Liverpool, asked Lord John Russell what the Government intended to do with the Corn-Laws? He answered that they proposed to abolish the "sliding scale," and impose a moderate fixed duty of eight shillings a quarter (24 cents a bushel) upon wheat, and a proportionate duty upon other grain. The "sliding scale" was a contrivance by which the duties on foreign grain were fixed according to the prices of it in the domestic market. When the price of wheat in Mark Lane was high, the duties on imported wheat were low, and *vice versa*, the intention being to keep the price of grain always at such a height as to furnish the British farmer a fair degree of "Protection" against the "pauper labor" of the United States, the creative sunshine of the American sky, and the fertility of the American soil.

In that moderate proposition the Tories beheld a menace against the privileges which they had enjoyed for centuries. With the bravery of desperation they determined to come out of their intrenchments and attack. They would not wait until the 31st of May, but would precipitate the issue there and then. Sir Robert Peel, amid great excitement, declared that unless Lord John Russell consented to submit his motion at once he might be compelled to do so; for the House would not make itself the instrument of agitation. Mr. Labouchere, a member of the Cabinet, anticipated General Hancock by a period of thirty-nine years. He tried to allay the excitement by declaring that "the revision of the tariff is not a party question." He was laughed at for the statement as General Hancock was in the next generation.

So long as the agitation for the repeal of the Corn-Laws was confined to the Anti-Corn-Law League outside of Parliament, the public mind retained its usual tranquillity; but when an attack upon the protective tariff was made by the Government itself, the affair became serious, and all classes of society became greatly agitated and some of them alarmed. Both parties went into training at once, for the approaching contest. The League redoubled its exertions. It organized new branches of the association, and sent lecturers and pamphlets into every part of the Kingdom. On the other hand, all the protected "interests" combined for mutual defense. Meetings were convened of parties connected with the Shipping and North American "interests," of the planters, merchants, and others interested in the West India Colonies, of the representatives of East India property, of the societies for the abolition of slavery, and all the threatened monopolies consolidated for "Protection."

It was unlucky for the Government that it was on the defensive from the start; and shortly on the run. Like Louis Napoleon in 1870, it declared war, and instead of invading the enemy's territories, took up a defensive line of battle, was beaten, routed, and destroyed. The opposition in Parliament at once advanced, and their first attack was made in the House of Lords. On the 3d of May, the Duke of Buckingham presented 120 petitions against the repeal of the Corn-Laws, and he improved the occasion to attack Lord Melbourne for his inconsistency in consenting to alter the Corn-Laws after the strong language he had formerly used against any such "revolutionary" project. Revolutionary, besides being a fine oratorical word, is full of mysterious portent wherewith to "fright the souls of fearful adversaries," and monopoly in danger always uses it; as the protected interests in England used it in those days, and as the privileged orders use it in America now. The Duke of Richmond had a large pecuniary interest in dear bread, and in his opinion any attempt to make flour cheap was "revolutionary." And like our American dukes, the beneficiaries of the Protection policy, the Duke of Buckingham thought that a man with a cheap dinner inside of him must be a "cheap man."

It so happened that Lord Melbourne was at this time Prime Minister of England, and he presented an exceedingly big target for the shafts of the Duke of Buckingham, because, only the year before, he had said contemptuously, that the repeal of the Corn-Laws was "the most insane project that ever entered a man's head." And he also said that "it would be as easy to repeal the monarchy." Lord Melbourne made a rather lame apology for his present position, but maintained that he had never committed himself to the opinion that the Corn-Laws were perfect, and should never be amended. This was true; but the strong language used by the Prime Minister in sustaining the Corn-Laws warranted the Duke in believing that they were not to be amended by Lord Melbourne's administration.

The Earl of Ripon then asked Lord Melbourne

whether the proposed alteration of the Corn-Laws was to be on the principle of taxation for revenue, or for protection? He said, "The principle of 'Protection' rests on humane and consistent grounds, but by abandoning this, and taking up the principle of taxing corn for revenue, you would do that which had never been attempted in any country of the world, and which would be the most impolitic, unjustifiable, and cruel act ever imposed upon a reluctant Parliament." The "cruelty" of giving the people abundant food was maintained by the Protectionists until that "humane" system actually culminated in famine. When Lord Ripon said that it was "cruel" to tax corn for revenue, he meant public revenue. To tax it for private revenue was "humane," and Lord Ripon's doctrine is as vigorously maintained by the American Protectionists in 1892, as it was by Lord Ripon in 1841. The American formula is this: "A tariff for protection with incidental revenue." This is a reversal of the elementary principle of liberty, that the necessity of revenue for the public service is the only excuse that Government has for taxing the people at all. Lord Melbourne, in answering the Earl of Ripon, said that the alteration of the Corn-Laws would be unquestionably upon the principles of "Protection."

The Earl of Winchelsea, a weak-minded old gentleman, said "that it is a universal axiom that no country should be left dependent on others for the necessary articles of subsistence." He consoled the House with the assurance that "the people are too reflecting to be deceived with the promise of cheap bread. They know," said the noble Earl, "that cheap bread means low wages." The report of the debate is authority for the statement that this nonsense was received with "loud cheering." It would be incredible in this enlightened day, did we not know that the same argument is greeted with "loud cheering" in the halls of the American Congress.

The attack in the House of Commons was made on the 8th of May, when Mr. Baring, Chancellor of the Exchequer, presented his annual budget. The discussion of the budget resolved itself into a debate on the corn and sugar duties. There was a deficiency in the revenue, and Mr. Baring proposed to make it up by a reduction of the duties on sugar. This may seem to the American economist a strange way of increasing the revenue, but the plan of Mr. Baring was undoubtedly sound. The duty on sugar was a "Protective" duty for the benefit of the planters of the British West Indies. To the extent of that protection it discouraged importation, and, while the revenue suffered, the people received no benefit. They paid the tax, but it went into the pockets of the planters, and not into the treasury. The following figures make the matter clearer than a long sermon could. In 1841, under a high tariff, the ration of sugar to each inhabitant of Great Britain was fifteen pounds; in 1891, under a low tariff, the ration was more than seventy pounds, or nearly five times as much. The low duties increased importation and revenue at the same time. Mr. Baring proposed to avail himself of this principle, and supply the deficiency of the revenue by reducing the duties on sugar. The Protectionists all rallied to their colors to resist this encroachment on the "humane" system of taxing the food of the people for the benefit of the landlords and the sugar planters.

The challenge to the Government came in the shape

of the following motion offered by Lord Sandon, "That, considering the sacrifices made by the country for the abolition of slavery, this House cannot consent to a reduction of the sugar duties." It is important to observe that the opposition to cheap sugar was placed by the Protectionists on high moral and humanitarian ground, the discouragement of slave labor. The opposition to cheap sugar in the United States is placed on the same ground. In 1881 an old slaveholder, sitting in the American Congress as a member from the State of Louisiana, made a heart-breaking appeal to the House not to reduce the tariff on sugar, because, if they did, it would encourage the wicked sugar of Cuba and Brazil, the product of the unpaid toil of the slave. The very same appeal was made in the British Parliament in 1841, by the old slaveholders there, who had made their wealth out of their West India plantations, and who had strenuously resisted the Act of Emancipation passed in 1832.

That affectation of sympathy for free labor actually melted the hearts of some of the genuine abolitionists, and Mr. O'Connell, who was a partisan of the government and a Free Trader, gave notice of a motion to the effect "that any diminution of the duty on foreign sugar should be strictly limited to that which was the product of free labor." So ingeniously did the Tories manage to mix up philanthropy and protection, slavery and sugar, that some of the veteran abolitionists, unable to separate them, actually voted against the Government. Within a month from that time Mr. O'Connell, who was an extreme abolitionist, saw through the deception, and said: "The country is in distress, yet the Tories refuse cheap bread. They also refuse cheap sugar, having now found out that they are enemies of slavery, though, like the citizen in Molière, who had all his life unconsciously been speaking prose, they had never before suspected themselves of such a tendency."

Lord John Russell uncovered this impudent pretension and made fun of it. He said: "If the House is resolved against taking slave-grown sugar, what do you say to the admission of other articles of slave-labor? Slave-grown coffee, for instance. Did the man who was horrified at drinking a cup of slave-grown coffee redeem the potation and relieve his conscience by putting in a lump of free-labor sugar?" He was sarcastic and severe upon the Tories for having opposed emancipation, although they now pretended to be shocked at using slave-grown sugar.

Lord Stanley and Sir Robert Peel were the principal speakers on the Tory side. Lord Stanley opposed the reduction of the sugar duties upon "Protection" grounds, and said that, if it was necessary to foster a manufacture in its infancy by protection, it was especially necessary in the present case of the sugar trade. He also opposed it on anti-slavery grounds, and he denounced the scheme as "the last effort of expiring desperation on the part of a falling Government." It should be stated here that Lord Stanley himself did vote for emancipation; but when he did so he was a Whig.

The plan proposed by Mr. Baring fixed the duty on foreign sugar at 36 shillings, and on Colonial sugar at 24 shillings per hundred weight, and, although he explained that the proposed alteration would still leave a protection of 50 per cent on Colonial sugar, the Tories were not satisfied. The planters were not willing to share with the Government in the proceeds of sugar taxation; they wanted it all. In presenting his plan, Mr. Baring asked the House to look at the present prospect of public affairs. There was the German League extending its influence and increasing its protective duties; there was the American tariff. It would be in vain to press upon those nations a liberal line of policy if this country were to keep up prohibition under the name of protection. If there was any intention to admit the produce of foreign countries, the House would see that they ought not to delay until they lost the markets of the world.

Sir Robert Peel opposed the reduction of the sugar duties for the reasons given by Lord Stanley. He said: "If I had been in office I should have taken the same course that I did take; and if I should be in office, I never contemplate changing it." Then addressing Lord John Russell personally, he said: "I don't propose to follow your example, to resist the proposition now under discussion this year, and come down the next with a motion for its adoption." He was deceived by his own self-confidence. There is a warning in the Bible: "Let him that thinketh he standeth take heed lest he fall," and the value of it was exemplified in the fate of Sir Robert Peel. The next year he was Prime Minister, and he did "come down to the House," and do the very thing that in taunting boast he told Lord John Russell he would not do.

The debate lasted from the 7th to the 18th of May, and upward of eighty members addressed the House. When it ended the Tories had the best of it. Lord Sandon's resolution prevailed; and the Government was beaten by the unexpected majority of 317 to 281. The cheers of the Protectionists rang out peal after peal like the laughter of a chime of bells; they reverberated through the great hall of William Rufus; they burst into Palace Yard and chased each other among the Gothic arches of the old Abbey across the way, where Pitt and Fox lay sleeping side by side.

To the amazement of the country the ministers did not resign, but on the next evening Mr. Baring with exasperating hardihood, coolly announced that on Monday night he should move the annual Sugar Duties. Lord Darlington in a great rage, and amid loud cries of "order" demanded to know when Lord John Russell intended to bring on the question of the Corn-Laws. His Lordship quietly answered: "On Friday, the 4th of June." Before that day sentence of dismissal was pronounced by the House of Commons against him and his Government, and he never got a chance to introduce his plans. Before he again became minister the League had overthrown the "sliding scale" and the "eight shillings tariff," too.

Sir Robert Peel determined not to allow the ministers any time to recover from their defeat. At the earliest moment possible under the rules, he gave notice that on the ensuing Thursday (the 27th of May) he should move the following resolution: "That Her Majesty's ministers do not sufficiently possess the confidence of the House of Commons, to enable them to carry through the House, measures which they deem of essential importance to the public welfare; and that their continuance in office under such circumstances is at variance with the spirit of the Constitution." After four nights' debate his resolution was carried by a majority of one vote; the numbers were 312 to 311. From this blow the Whig party never recovered. The ministers were stunned and bewildered by it, although they had provoked it by refusing to resign after their defeat on Lord Sandon's amendment. Their continuance in office was a challenge to Peel, daring him to propose a "want of confidence" resolution. It appeared to many persons almost impossible that within ten years of the Reform Bill the Tories should once more be in the ascendancy. Thinking that perhaps the country was on their side, although the House of Commons was against them, the ministers refused to resign, but dissolved the Parliament. They appealed from the verdict of the House of Commons to the tribunal of the people at the polls, and there also the judgment was against them.

CHAPTER III.

A TORY MINISTRY.

In the midst of scarcity and business depression the general election of 1841 was held. Although only a few Free Traders were elected, the inspiration of the whole contest came from the Anti-Corn-Law League. By the moral strength of its ideas it crowded nearly all of the other issues out of the way, and forced a discussion of the Free Trade question at every polling place in the Kingdom, where there was any contest at all. The Whigs appeared before the country in a defensive and apologetic attitude. Having no beneficent measures of public policy to their credit in the late Parliament, they offered the country a large assortment of future statesmanship at a heavy discount for another term of power. Unfortunately, the constituencies had not much confidence in their promises or in their ability to perform them. They had done enough to alarm every "protected" interest, and they had not done enough to win the Free Traders, nor even the moderate reformers, who, while opposed to Free Trade, desired a reduction and revision of the tariff. There was a feeling abroad that the proposal of the ministers to reduce the duties on corn and sugar was a measure of expediency, with no strong convictions behind it; a mere infusion of political starch to stiffen a limp administration.

The friends of the Government, however, used the proposal as a campaign battle-cry. They declared that the defeat of the ministry on the "Want of Confidence" resolution was due to their advanced and liberal policy in attempting to remove some oppressive disabilities from trade; and that they had been borne down by a combination of class interests, united for the preservation of a hundred monopolies. This claim, to a certain extent, was true, and it gave something of moral character to their cause, but it availed nothing. The election resulted in a surprising victory for the Tories. They had a majority in the House of Commons of nearly a hundred over all opposing elements combined, and on a square issue with the Free Traders they could command a majority of more than three hundred and fifty votes. Among the astonishing results of this election was the defeat of Lord Morpeth and Lord Milton for the West Riding of Yorkshire; and Lord Howick was overthrown in the contest for Northumberland. Westminster performed the supposed impossible feat of electing a Tory over Sir De Lacey Evans; Mr. O'Connell was defeated for Dublin, and even Lord John Russell himself had a very narrow escape in his contest for the City of London. In the late Parliament the City of London was represented by four Whigs; to the new Parliament it elected two Tories and two Whigs, and a Tory was at the head of the poll. Lord John Russell, notwithstanding his talents and his position in the Government, and with all the vast influence of the Bedford family to help him, came within eight of a defeat in a poll of over twelve thousand votes. The Protectionist victory was complete; yet this was the Parliament that was destined within five years to overthrow the Protective System, and establish Free Trade in England as firmly as the British Islands are anchored in the sea.

In the new Parliament was a new man, a calico printer from the North, a moral and mental force so great that he was afterward regarded by many Englishmen as the most important personage that had been seen in the House of Commons since Oliver Cromwell had a seat there. His name was Richard Cobden and he might very truthfully be called an Oliver Cromwell, without a sword. This man had already become the electric principle of the Anti-Corn-Law League. He was a leader without selfishness or any personal ambition for place or power; a guide easy to follow. He was a statesman by weight of knowledge and the power of molding it into politics. He was an orator of such convincing powers that he converted more men to his views by simply talking to them than any other man of his time, or perhaps of any time; not only Manchester operatives, but even farmers, who had been persuaded that Free Trade would ruin them. Lord Beaconsfield spoke of the "persuasive" oratory of Cobden, but "convincing" is the proper adjective. Cobden spoke straight at the intellect. Without any special advantages of personal grace, although he had the grace of a natural and easy manner, and although careless of the arts of rhetoric, there was an earnest truthfulness about him that made a great impression. He was fluent enough, without redundancy, and his language was of the best and easiest English. His voice was pleasant and clear, though not loud. He had a great fund of industrial information, much of which he had picked up in the United States and on the continent of Europe. He always had the facts at hand to verify his assertions, no matter how extravagant they appeared to be. He grouped them together with great skill, and molded them into irresistible arguments. He fastened responsibility upon his adversaries with scornful and indignant emphasis. In playful fancy, and in the art of making lessons easy by familiar illustrations drawn from every day life, he resembled Abraham Lincoln—or perhaps it would be more correct to say that Lincoln resembled him. He resembled him in the abundance of his humor and the quaint sharpness of his satire. Both of them had the art of condensing the rays of an argument to a focus and burning a moral into the consciences of men. Above all things, there was a candor and sincerity about Cobden, as about Lincoln, that went far toward persuading men that he was right. A deep love of humanity pervaded all he wrote and all he said. His life was pure, his character without reproach. With the factory dust upon him, he faced the patrician landlords on the Tory benches with a courage as high as that of the purest Norman of them all. He was as effective inside the House of Commons as out of it, and he converted Sir Robert Peel, the leader of the Protectionist party, to a belief not only in the expediency of Free Trade, but in the wisdom and the justice of it. In fact, it boded ill to the Tories when they saw that their chief permitted his face to show how he was hurt by the shafts of Cobden, and it boded still further mischief to them when they noticed how he sat intently listening to every word that fell from his enemy. We know now that Peel at last came completely under the fascination of Cobden's intellect, and permitted that intellect to dominate his own.

Before Cobden had been in parliament a year, his hypnotic influence over Sir Robert Peel had attracted attention. Curious contemporaneous evidence of this may be found in the *Illustrated London News* for July 6, 1842. In a sketch of Cobden, after speaking disdainfully of him, and with an affectation of contempt for his views, as we now speak of a crank, that paper said, "Mr. Cobden sits for the Borough of Stockport, and as a debater occupies a very creditable position in the House. He is a close reasoner, very seldom going beside the question, or losing sight of the main points of his own or his opponent's argument. He has sufficient power of declamation to impart energy to his manner, but he is never led away by it, or falls into that style which invariably meets with the greatest contempt from the House, that of the loud-tongued empty ranter. He is always well prepared to support his statements, and generally has with him a formidable array of documents. It is a creditable tribute to his abilities that he generally commands the attention of the House; and if he has failed to convince the Premier of the expediency of the policy laid down by the Anti-Corn-Law League, *it is not because the Right Hon. Baronet has failed to listen to him.*" The point and pith of all that are in the last words, which I have put in italics. These admit that Cobden, even thus early in his parliamentary career, had compelled the attention of the Prime Minister; and this of itself was an achievement full of important consequences to England.

The ministerial defeats in the counties were not unexpected, but the Tory gains in the towns and cities were a great surprise. They proved that the cry of "cheap bread" had been successfully met by the counter cry of "low wages." The benighted superstition that cheap bread and sugar and clothes made low wages, was entertained not only by the landed aristocracy and the opulent planter, who had a selfish object in proclaiming it, but by the hungry workingmen themselves, whose interests were all in the opposite direction. Worse than that, men claiming to be statesmen conceded the truth of it as an economic law, even when advocating a reduction of the import duties on grain. Many men who considered themselves rather liberal "tariff reformers" could not free themselves entirely from the delusion until a radical experimental test compelled them to abandon it. It is a "theory" now in England resting on forty-six years of "practical" trial, that increased abundance increases wages, while scarcity lowers it. It is now proved that if the goods needed by the laborer are made scarce, he must work longer for the same pay. If they be made more plentiful, he can supply his needs by less labor.

Notwithstanding the adverse verdict of the people at the polls, the Whigs declined to surrender office until the meeting of the new Parliament. If they must go out, they would insist on being dismissed in a technically constitutional way; and by a formal vote of the House of Commons they were dismissed accordingly. When Parliament met, the Tories offered in both Houses an amendment to the address in answer to the speech from the throne, and the debate upon it was very much like a repetition of that on the "want of confidence" resolution in May. Earl Spencer, in the House of Lords, moved the address in a good speech advocating a removal of the oppressive restrictions on the importation of corn. The address was seconded by the Marquis of Clanricarde, who, while defending the government program, was weak enough to admit that "if corn became cheaper, wages would undoubtedly fall, but," he said, "if the workman for a certain sum was able to obtain a larger supply of food and clothing than he could before, then his condition would undoubtedly be bettered." And Lord Bruce, who seconded the amendment to the address in the House of Commons, declared, "That for his own part he would consent to no plan of Free Trade, because it would throw vast numbers of his fellow-subjects out of employ." The above two specimens will show how far Whig and Tory statesmen in England had progressed in the study of political economy in the year 1841. They stood then, just where Democratic and Republican statesmen in America stand now, victims of the same sophistries and the same delusions. Of course there was a man in the House of Commons ready to lay the whole blame for everything on "machinery." Mr. Baillie thought that the distress of the people was all owing to the invention of machinery, and except for that, everybody would be prosperous and happy.

In this debate the Duke of Wellington, in the House of Lords, foreboded the ruin of agriculture. He "earnestly recommended their Lordships not to lend themselves to the destruction of our native cultivation. Its encouragement was of the utmost and deepest importance to all classes. He earnestly begged of them not to consent to any measure which would injure the cultivation of their own soil." While the Duke of Wellington was talking so feebly in the House of Lords, Mr. O'Connell was talking thus wisely in the House of Commons. He said, "The present law is doubly iniquitous, as it raises prices and at the same time diminishes the vent for manufactures. He was weary of experiments on the poor. He heard of a man who complained that nothing could fatten his horse, although he had tried tobacco, and twenty other things. A friend asked him did you ever try oats? He wished the legislature would try the people with bread. He would only agree to Lord John Russell's plan as an installment of justice, until he could get rid of Protection altogether." The Protective System of the United States performs the same double iniquity here that the English system did there fifty years ago. It raises prices, and at the same time diminishes the vent for manufactures.

It was in the course of this debate that Mr. Cobden spoke for the first time in Parliament. He exposed the sufferings of the people to the gaze of the Senate, and charged against the Protective System the prostration of English industry. He lifted the question clear out of the realm of office-hunting intrigue, far above the wretched expedients of factionism and party. He placed it on the high plane of moral science, and gave notice to both Whigs and Tories that the question of the Corn-Laws must be met, and that a guilty responsibility should be laid on those who taxed the food of the people. He condensed the whole argument of the debate into a couple of sentences that fell upon Peel like the flash of light that smote Paul on the way to Damascus. One was this: Mr. Cobden contended that the protective duty upon foreign grain was an unequal tax upon the subsistence of honest, struggling working people, and that it pressed upon them in an infinitely heavier proportion than upon the rich, for, said he, "the family of a man worth £20,000 a year, scarcely consumes more bread than the family of the laborer."

The injustice of the tax had never before been shown so plainly in the House of Commons. The comparison, although stated in few words, revealed at a glance how impossible it was for the poor man to evade the tax, for he must have bread for his family, while the family of the rich man could easily escape the tax by living on daintier food. Peel was a man of very large private fortune, and such illustrations disturbed him, for his sensibilities were kindly, and his instincts just. The other sentence was the startling proposition that the man who is not allowed to spend his wages to the best advantage is not free. Mr. Cobden said, "If it is criminal to steal a man and make him work for nothing, it was equally criminal to steal from a free man the fair reward of his labor." He disposed of the "cheap bread and low wages" doctrine by showing that the increase of trade which must follow from a repeal of the Corn-Laws would increase the demand for labor, and with that increased demand would come an increase of wages. There were some who sneered at this unpleasant person, but it is certain that the country gentlemen would have spent a more agreeable Christmas if he had not spoken at all.

When the debate ended, a division was had and there appeared to be, for the address 269, for the amendment 360, majority against the Government 91. Then the Whigs resigned. They had been constitutionally turned out as they had resolved to be. Sir Robert Peel came into power with an obedient and well-disciplined majority behind him, sufficient to carry every measure proposed by ministers. He formed a strong Cabinet, including among its members Lord Stanley, Sir James Graham, and the Duke of Wellington, while in subordinate positions of importance were such men as Mr. Sidney Herbert, Lord Lincoln, and Mr. Gladstone.

In spite of all attemps to draw him out during the first session of the new parliament, Sir Robert Peel refused to disclose the policy of his Government. He demanded time in which to form his plans. This was bitterly condemned by the Whigs, who insisted that he should propose his measures at once. October came, and still his plans were wrapped in mystery. Subsequent events convince us that he did not know them himself. Parliament adjourned until February, and he took the intervening months to consider what was best to do. His compact majority of ninety-one rendered him quite independent of all minor factions within the party like those that had embarrassed the Whigs. Since the days of William Pitt, no Prime Minister had rested so absolutely secure in the support of such a well-organized and coherent party.

Peel soon found that a statesman in power is a different personage from a politician on the opposition benches. In the latter case he has a jaunty time of it. Without any responsibility or care, he can criticise the other side, and show his opponents what they ought to do, but a Prime Minister of England carries on his own shoulders the welfare of a people, and the burthen is heavy to a man ambitious of lasting fame, and who really wishes to do right. That Peel desired the welfare of his country is not to be denied, and when he began to reflect on the tremendous responsibility that had fallen upon him, he saw that the tariff and the Corn-Laws as they existed then, could not wisely or justly be maintained. He saw that some change must be made. Then he realized how weak and vain is the boasting of the strongest man. In the debate on the "want of confidence" resolution in May he had proudly inquired, "Who in this House has more steadily stood forward in defense of the existing Corn-Laws than I have done?" And during the late canvass, he had said to the electors of Tamworth, "Who pay the highest rates? Who pay the church rates? Who pay the poor rates? Who pay the tithes? I say perhaps not altogether, but chiefly the landed occupiers of this country. If corn be the product of their land, and subject to these burdens, it surely would not be just to the land of this country which bears them all to admit it at a low rate of duty. I have come to the conclusion that the existing system should not be altered, and that our aim ought to be to render ourselves independent of foreign supply;" the ready jargon which Protectionists have used in all countries, and in every age. His boastings and his promises could not endure the strain of his new responsibility. His conscience told him that he must either give up office or amend the law. He resolved to amend the law.

During the recess the League was hard at work. The Free Trade agitation was extended to Ireland and Scotland. Newspapers were started, and vast numbers of pamphlets were distributed in every direction. Heaps of information concerning every trade and occupation in the Kingdom were piled up for use in the next Parliament. Meanwhile, there was great anxiety throughout the country as to the intentions of the Government. Cabinet meetings were held, but not a word of their debates leaked out. The two or three speeches made by Cobden at the short session had sunk deep into the mind of Peel. The proof of it is clear. During the canvass in the summer he had proclaimed that " the existing system should not be altered," in the winter he had changed his mind. In that interval he had heard Cobden.

A trifling incident which came to light a little while before the opening of Parliament alarmed the landlords, and convinced the country that the League was actually making discord in the Tory cabinet itself. It was this: The Toryest Tory in all England was the Duke of Buckingham, and he was in the Cabinet. With the blood of Henry Plantagenet in his veins, and the lordship of thousands of broad acres in his possession, he was a feudal specimen of that haughty Norman aristocracy which for nearly eight hundred years had held the Saxon in a state of serfdom, and his lands by right of conquest. He stood in the House of Lords like a decayed old castle, with the ivy and the moss all over him. So long as he was in the cabinet, modern civilization must be shut out of its councils; and no such vulgar theme as " economics " be debated at its meetings. So long as he continued in the Cabinet monopoly might sleep in peace; the baronial system would stand firm, grim, and defiant as the Tower of London. One morning it was whispered at the Carlton Club that the Duke of Buckingham had resigned, and the whisper was correct. Then the people knew that some changes in the Corn-Laws had been determined on. Stimulated by the news the League worked harder than before.

CHAPTER IV.

THE TARIFF OF 1842.

The year 1842 opened gloomily. There was much distress in the country, and a revenue deficit of twelve million dollars. When Parliament met in February, there was great anxiety to know what the Government intended to do. To the consternation of the monopolists, Sir Robert Peel announced that it was his intention to meet the deficit by the imposition of an income tax; and that although he should maintain the "sliding scale," the duties on corn and provisions would be reduced. He also said that it was the intention of the Government to revise the tariff, so as to deprive it of its prohibitory features, and to lower the duties on about seven hundred and fifty articles. This from a Protectionist Tory ministry was a great advance, and it showed that numerically weak as were the Free Traders in the House of Commons, the ideas of the League had actually affected the policy of the Government.

The natural result of half-way measures followed. The Government was assailed by both sides; by the Protectionists for yielding anything, and by the Free Traders for not yielding more. Cobden was unsparing and fierce in his denunciations; immense meetings were held in the North, and in all the manufacturing country, at which resolutions were passed savagely condemning the ministry. At some of these meetings

Sir Robert Peel was burned in effigy, a barbarous insult which deeply wounded him, and of which he rightfully complained. Cobden and the leaders of the League were not responsible for those excesses any further than all popular leaders are responsible for the mad acts of their disciples when they rush past them and get out of their control. The Chartist agitation had produced a great deal of seditious talk, and some rioting. Ireland was discontented and miserable. In Peel's own language it was the "chief difficulty" of his Government. Altogether there was immense responsibility upon the ministers, and the business of the country required for its safe management the highest qualities of statesmanship.

The debate of 1842 is a great event in the political history of England. For the first time in Parliament the revenue and economic system of the country was subjected to the test of scientific analysis, by minds trained not only in the schools, but in trade, commerce, manufactures, agriculture, and in all the practical industries by which men earn their own living. In this debate the men whose living was earned by others were at a humiliating disadvantage. Norman nobles, whose fathers had fought at Hastings, and Agincourt, and Cressy, were laughed at for their ignorance by smoky people from Lancashire and Derby. Heretofore, debates of this character were the mere competition of class interests seeking to obtain the advantage of one another in the "Protective" legislation of the country. Now, the whole theory and practice of class legislation were placed on trial, with the entire people of England as an interested audience. That the true principles of political economy had been proclaimed in Parliament hundreds of times before the debate of 1842, is true, but they were given and accepted as abstractions only; and as they were conceded to have no practical bearing, they fell like good seed upon stony ground. They failed to obtain the notice of the people. It was not so now. The League had taken care to wake up the people, and compel them to listen to the debate.

In February, 1842, Parliament was opened by the Queen in person. She was then in the pride and bloom of young motherhood, looking radiant and joyful, for her married life was happy. Additional grandeur was given to the occasion by the attendance of the King of Prussia, who had come over to attend the christening of the infant Prince of Wales. Immense crowds lined the route of the procession, and they generously cheered the Queen. A cloud of anxiety passed over her face as she heard mingled with the acclamations of the people the ominous cries of "Cheap Bread," "Free Trade," "No Corn-Laws." The first official knowledge obtained by the people that any change in the Corn-Laws had been resolved on by the Government, was given in the following paragraph in the speech from the throne: "I recommend also to your consideration the state of the laws which affect the importation of corn." It was less than a year since Lord John Russell had said those very words to the House of Commons; and for saying them the Whig ministry was overthrown in Parliament, and the Whig party defeated at the polls. The advance made in those few months measured the power of the League.

On the 9th of February, Sir Robert Peel moved that the House go into Committee of the whole to consider the duties on corn. He introduced his programme in a very ingenious and comprehensive speech; a speech that showed he was complete master of the subject, and familiar with all the details of England's commercial and industrial condition. He admitted the distress of the people, but he didn't believe that the Corn-Laws were responsible for it. He found reasons for it in all the corners of the earth, from China to America. He was weak enough to attribute some of it to the displacement of hand-labor by steam power, to over-investment of borrowed capital, and to alarms of war; to everything, in fact, but the Corn-Laws. Still, he proposed some amendment to those laws. He thought that the "sliding scale" could be so amended that the price of wheat would not vary much from somewhere between fifty-four and fifty-eight shillings a quarter (about a dollar and seventy-five cents a bushel), and he contended that the people should rely upon home production for their food and should be willing to pay an extra price for it, in order to be "independent of foreign countries." He said, "I certainly do consider that it is for the interest of all that we should pay occasionally a small additional sum upon our own domestic produce, in order that we might thereby establish a security, and insurance against those calamities that would ensue if we became altogether or in great part dependent upon foreign countries for our supply."

In the course of his argument Sir Robert said: "A comparison is made between the dearness of food in England and its cheapness in other countries; but that led to a fallacious conclusion. The true question is, not what is the price of bread? but what command the laboring classes have over bread; and what command they have over the enjoyments of life?" There was much truth in this, but it was presented in such a way as to evade the conditions of Cobden's axiom that high prices resulting from prosperity might be permanent, because founded on public riches, whereas high prices resulting from scarcity must ever be precarious, because the resultant poverty rendered customers powerless to buy, thus dragging prices down, sometimes to the actual loss of the producers. A restricted market lowered wages by lessening the demand for goods, and low wages restricted the command of the workingman over bread. Sir Robert Peel saw this afterward, and acknowledged it; but he did not see it then, and some American economists do not see it yet. They still persist in raising prices by making scarcity, and they dread "a flood of cheap goods" as a calamity to be provided against by law. In the language of Mr. O'Connell, they persist by a restrictive policy in closing the "vent for manufactures;" gradually proverty steals over large numbers of the people, and at last there is a glut in the market, because customers are no longer able to buy. Up goes the cry of "overproduction" and a "flood of cheap goods" is poured out of our own factories at the absolute loss of the men who have produced them. So precarious is American business under this bad system that a horde of people have grown up who actually make their living by speculating on its uncertainties, and the "operations" of our domestic trade have largely degenerated into gambling.

Another parallel between the argument of Sir Robert Peel then, and that of the American Protectionists now, is the boast that whatever comforts the people enjoy over those of other nations is due to the Protective System. He said that the people of England each consumed fifty pounds of meat annually, sugar seventeen pounds per head, wheat sixteen bushels each; and he easily showed that no other people on the Continent of Europe consumed so much of those articles. Hence the protective system increased the comforts of the people of England. It was difficult to answer this argument, because it was supported by tangible evidence, the meat and sugar and corn. As there was no Free Trade experience to contradict it, the refutation of it could be nothing better than a speculation and a hope. It was easy enough for the Free Traders to assert that under their system those comforts would be multiplied, but they had no proof of it, for their system had never been tried. They have the proof of it now. In 1842 Sir Robert Peel boasted that under the beneficent operation of the protective system the English people were able to enjoy in one year the luxury of seventeen pounds of sugar each. In 1881, after thirty-five years' experiment of the Free Trade policy, the consumption of sugar in England amounted to fifty-eight pounds each for every man, woman and child in the Kingdom. Before 1890, the ration of sugar was over 70 pounds per head. Other comforts were multiplied in the same proportion. The bountiful resources of the United States, which are able to defy the ill treatment of the protective system, are called up as witnesses by the American Protectionists in favor of that mischievous policy which is crippling them to the full extent of its power, as the same policy crippled for centuries the magnificent resources of Great Britain. A free trade policy would increase the comforts and prosperity of the people here as it did in England.

Although he was then making concessions to the

contrary principle, Sir Robert Peel maintained as the American economists do now that the "protection" of one class of the people at the expense of another is to the benefit of both. He said, "It is my firm belief that the total repeal of the Corn-Laws would aggravate the manufacturing distress, the prosperity of the two classes, agriculturists and manufacturers being identical." He maintained that the artificial prosperity conferred upon the agriculturists by the protective duties which excluded foreign grain, although apparently at first taken from the manufacturers, came back to them again in the creation of a "home market" for their goods, which the farmers were thus enabled to buy. So the protective stimulus given to manufacturers performed a return miracle in creating a "home market" for grain. This doctrine is vigorously asserted in the United States to-day. A similar juggle is performed by Bulwer in one of his novels. A great landlord is making a speech to his tenantry, and boasting of the generous manner in which he spends the rents which he takes from them every quarter-day. He builds here and he improves there; he gives them employment at this place, and their sons good wages over yonder; he buys this of them, and that; he entertains great company up at the hall, and scatters money about like a king. He concludes by saying, "So you see that what I take from you with one hand I bestow upon you again with the other." Those dull farmers can not see the fallacy in this boasting; they can not see that all this liberal squandering comes out of their own hard labor, so they give the enterprising landlord three rousing cheers and go home. In this fashion a thousand industries in the United States engage in the "Protection" pastime of merry-go-round, protecting everybody at everybody's expense, always getting back to the place whence they started, with much loss from friction and wasted power. Every man in the game thinks that he has made something off the rest, and all are cheated by the statesmen who pretend that nobody has lost anything, because each has given back to his neighbor with one hand that which he took from him with the other. No account is taken here of the unfortunates who are not allowed to have any part in the play, except the victim part, the unfortunate consumers who are not allowed the legal privilege of picking any body's pocket.

According to the etiquette of Parliament, the duty of answering the Prime Minister fell upon the leader of the opposition, and Lord John Russell rose to perform that duty. He had very little to say. A Protectionist himself, he did not know how much of the ministerial plan he might venture to criticise, and no doubt he felt himself that night entirely overmatched by Peel. He stammered a few sentences in condemnation of the "sliding scale," and sat down. But there was a man there who was not afraid even of the accomplished minister. That man was Cobden. He denounced the plan of the Government as quite insufficient and unsatisfactory, because it did not reach down and remove the real causes of the people's poverty. That kind of argument, though severe, could be endured; but when the orator out of his abundant knowledge showed that the Prime Minister was in error as to his facts, and in that way toppled over the stately framework of his reasoning, the House of Commons recognized at once that the "smoky country" had sent a man to Parliament, who was so thoroughly informed as to the agricultural, the manufacturing, and the commercial condition of England, that not even Peel, the greatest debater there, could safely make a statement on insufficient evidence, or even venture an opinion on any doubtful testimony. Here was a man whose facts fell upon his hearers with the force of the blows delivered by the steam hammer. The oratory of the colleges retreated from a contest with the untutored eloquence of this new member who actually earned his own living. Sir Robert Peel, grand, impassive, cold, lost his ancient self-command under the oratory of Cobden, and allowed his face to betray the emotions that stirred his conscience and his intellect. Among other things Mr. Cobden said, "The present proposal is an insult to the sufferings of the people, but I have not expected anything better. I do not expect to gather grapes of thorns, or figs of thistles. This policy toward the people of England will end at no remote period in the utter destruction of every interest in the country."

Sir Robert Peel pleaded the Statute of Limitations in behalf of the Protective System, just as the American Protectionists do to-day. A long possession of unjust privileges had ripened into a good title. Replying to Mr. Roebuck who had called upon the Government to establish their policy on broad and enlightened principles the Prime Minister said, "It's easy enough to say apply great principles, but I find that mighty interests have grown up under this present law, and in full dependence on its faith. If you disregard those pecuniary and social interests which have grown up under that protection which has long been continued by law, then a sense of injustice will be aroused that will redound against your scheme of improvement, however conformable it may be to rigid principles." Even in this very debate, Mr. Labouchere, a member of the late Whig ministry, in moving a reduction of the duties on sugar, admitted "the injustice of withdrawing a protection under which great interests had grown up, but he would substitute protection for prohibition." The injustice of doing justice is an apology for political wrong quite as popular in the United States in 1892, as it was in England in 1842. The tax imposed upon the English people was either just or unjust; if unjust, there could be no wrong in removing it.

During the debate Lord John Russell introduced a resolution condemning the "sliding scale." This he offered as an amendment to Peel's motion to go into committee. In support of the amendment Lord Palmerston said, "Why should the agriculturists be secured against the contingencies of the seasons, when such insurance is not attempted in any other trade?" And referring to the benefits of Free Trade, he said, "It is that man may be dependent upon man. It is that the exchange of commodities may be accompanied by the diffusion of knowledge—by the interchange of mutual benefits engendering mutual kind feelings—multiplying and confirming friendly relations. It is that commerce may freely go forth leading civilization with one hand and peace with the other, to render mankind happier, wiser, and better. Sir, this is the dispensation of Providence, this is the decree of that power which created and disposed the universe. But in the face of it, with arrogant presumptuous folly the dealers in restrictive duties fly, fettering the inborn energies of man, and setting up their miserable legislation instead of the great standing laws of nature." This was the lofty eloquence of a politician out of office. For many years Lord Palmerston had been a Cabinet Minister, and had never once attempted to apply those beautiful principles. As a matter of fact he had voted four years before against allowing the Manchester petitioners to be heard at the bar of the House. And what is still more remarkable, he was not ready to reduce those lofty sentiments to practice even at the very moment he was uttering them. He was a lenient and gentle "Tariff Reformer" radical in talk, but conservative in deed, a life-long accomplice in the furtive work of the Protective System, and a Protectionist in theory and action still. His liberal sentiments were nothing more than the prismatic air bubbles which formed the Whig strategy of the time. It also appears in the report of the debate in the *Annual Register* for 1842, that Lord Palmerston said that "for four centuries the proprietors of the soil had been legislating so as to raise the value of their properties * * * * He had not read any writer on ethics who justified a modification of wrong." I am of opinion that there is a mistake in the report, and that the words last quoted were said, not by Lord Palmerston, but by Mr. Villiers.

With the exception of his affected superstitious dread of "steam power" which was unworthy of him, it was noticed that Peel in his great speech had been careful not to insult the intelligence of his hearers by asserting the false and flippant maxims which formed then, as now, the stock in trade of the Protectionist party. He scorned to use the customary cant that high prices made high wages and therefore were a benefit to the workingmen. He knew that his speech was going down to posterity and he preferred that it should not be disfigured by such fallacies. As *The Edinburgh Review* said at the time, he left the utterance of these absurdities to his subordinates. With what inward pity he must have heard Sir Edward Knatchbull, a member of his own Cabinet, declare amidst uproarious ridicule, that "The duty on corn should be calculated in such a manner as to return to the landed interest full security for their property, and for the station in the country which they had hitherto held." No matter how biting the hunger of the industrious poor might be, the price of bread must be kept so high that the idle, fox-hunting, horse-racing aristocracy might still riot in profligate extravagance, becoming to their "station in the country."

The progress of this instructive debate proved how true it is that "fools rush in where angels fear to tread." "Peert and chipper" young statesmen on the Tory side hurled right in the face of Cobden, Protectionist maxims that Peel would have been afraid to utter. One of the Prime Minister's young statesmen was the Marquis of Granby, a coming duke, who knew as much about political economy as the wooden effigy of his ancestor, the historic "Markis o' Granby," which swung from the sign post of the hospitable tavern at Dorking, once kept by Mr. Tony Weller. The Marquis told the House of Commons that "the experience of all Europe shows that the certain consequence of making food cheap is to lower wages." Sir Francis Burdett, the father of Lady Burdett Coutts, a man who for forty years had been a radical reformer and a revolutionist, who had once been committed to the Tower by the House of Commons, and who had joined the Tories in his old age, declared that "to the laboring classes, the price of corn did not signify one straw." Lord Mahon and Mr. Stuart Wortley talked in the same strain, and even Mr. Gladstone fluently prattled about "the fallacy of cheap bread." No wonder that Mr. Cobden taunted the Tory members and laughed at their incapacity, declaring that no such ignorance could be found among any equal number of workingmen in the North of England. Notwithstanding all this, the winding up of the debate showed a very comfortable majority for the Tories of 123. The numbers were: For going into committee, 349; for Lord John Russell's amendment, 226.

That patrician legislators should talk economic nonsense was natural enough, because they had been taught it by the "thunderers" of the press and by the great magazines. They were apt scholars, for it is easy to convince men on the side of their own interests. Why should the Marquis of Granby be laughed at, and the *Quarterly Review* escape ridicule? That profound philosopher that ought to have known better, and probably did know better, had lately said with axiomatic solemnity, that "The new measure may fail to fulfill even as to the foreign supply, the promises of its promoters; but if it should really cheapen bread, cheap bread must inevitably produce low wages."

CHAPTER V.

THE HORIZONTAL PLAN.

Sir Robert Peel soon found that this friendly difference between the Tories and the Whigs, as to which kind of Tax-torment was the easier to bear, a fixed duty or a sliding scale, while it might be of grave importance as an office-holding question between rival bands of Protectionists, was of trifling consequence to the small but resolute fragment which had resolved that the torment should altogether cease. He found that he must now discuss the question with men of far greater debating power than the Whig party possessed, and that he must discuss it as a principle; not an abstract principle either, but as a practical principle, bearing immediately and directly upon the welfare of all the men in England who lived by useful industry. Lord Beaconsfield, in his life of Lord George Bentinck, truthfully describes the formidable enemy that now confronted Peel, where he says, "Inferior in numbers, but superior in influence from their powers of debate, and their external organization were the members of the confederation known as the Anti-Corn-Law League."

Peel had barely time to congratulate himself on his victory over Lord John Russell, when on the 18th of February he was called to a more serious conflict. On that evening Mr. Villiers moved his resolution that duties on grain should altogether cease. The House of Commons looked upon this as the Quixotic chivalry of a man who could not see that the question had been settled the other night in the defeat of Lord John Russell's amendment. But the question presented by Mr. Villiers was far broader than that presented by Lord John Russell, and it was not at all settled by Peel's recent victory over the Whigs. Like the slavery question in our own country, it was destined never to be settled until it was settled right.

The resolution was debated for five nights, and much of the argument was a repetition of what had been said before. The most effective speech was made by Cobden. He completely overthrew the " cheap bread and low wages " fallacy by an object lesson that every man could read, the actual price of bread and the state of wages then existing in the country. He contended that it was a complete delusion to suppose that the price of food regulated the price of wages. The last three years had fully demonstrated the folly of this principle. Bread had not been so high for twenty years, while wages had suffered a greater decline than in any three years before. He also contended that the price of labor was cheaper in England than on the continent because of its superior quality. The English workman produced three times as much for a dollar as the continental workman did for half a dollar; which is about the ratio of excess expected of the American workman to-day. With earnest emphasis he said, "Are you prepared to carry out even-handed justice to the people? If not, your law will not stand, nay, your House itself, if based upon injustice will not stand."

It is not surprising that ordinary men should waver on great questions like this, when the powerful mind of Macaulay was swayed by Cobden to the side of Free

Trade, and by Peel to the side of Protection. He saw on the side of justice a great principle that ought to be established, but a " great interest had grown up," and on the side of charity he saw injury to the protected classes, and this persuaded him that the principle ought not to be established—now. He said that he wished a total repeal of duties, but objected to immediate withdrawal of Protection. He would therefore decline to vote. Peel taunted him with timidity, and called upon him to vote on one side or the other, but he adhered to his resolution, and did not vote. It should be said for Macaulay that he was always a Free Trader; but as a member of the late Whig ministry he was implicated in the "eight shillings a quarter" compromise, and he may have thought himself in honor bound to stand by Lord John Russell and the Whig platform. On the frivolous question as to the amount of duties, and how they should be levied, the Whigs and Tories voted against each other; but when the principle of Protection was at stake, they voted on the same side. Eighty-nine members followed Mr. Villiers into the lobby, and three hundred and ninety-two followed Peel, a majority for the Government of 303 in a vote of 489 members, leaving 175 who did not vote at all; and most of those might as well be added to the Government majority.

In the month of May there was a long debate on the New Tariff. This debate is a curiosity now. With that speculative wonder which moves us as we roam through the great national museums of Europe and gaze on the mummies of old Egypt, we wander through the mazes of this debate and look upon the mummified theories of "Protection." It is hard to realize that only one generation ago English statesmen actually believed that by making everything scarce and dear the general prosperity was increased. It would be even laughable if the mischievous delusion had not emigrated to America and taken possession of our statesmen here, to the serious injury of the country. The old superstition, now obsolete in England, still flourishes in the United States. As Mr. Thorold Rogers remarks in "Six Centuries of Work and Wages," page 555: "In the United States the process is being exhibited on the most gigantic scale. The freest people in the world, where administrations and parliaments have been able to study and avoid the errors and crimes which older Governments have committed against labor, have submitted to a tariff which clips the wages of the working man to the extent of 50 per cent, under the pretense of supplying him with a variety of employment .... The motive of the impost is, of course, to increase the profits of capital; and this has hitherto been the result, to the impoverishment and dependence of labor—a consequence as certain though not so manifest." It is often said that our much vaunted American system of Protection is an emigrant from England, but that is a mild and gentle way to describe it. Literally it is a convict expelled from England by sentence of transportation for life.

Sir Robert Peel introduced his New Tariff with many apologies to the Protectionists, and assurances that it would not hurt them very much. Like a mother giving medicine to her children, he told them it was good for them, and that if the taste was slightly unpleasant at first, they would be all the better for it in the end. When the portly gentlemen of the "landed interest" complained that fat cattle and lean were to be admitted at the same figures, instead of being taxed according to their weight, the bland Sir Robert told them it was all the better for them, because, said he, English graziers can import lean cattle at a low rate of duty, and fatten them for market; and, as to fat cattle, they wouldn't be imported anyhow. They couldn't stand a sea voyage. "No fat ox," he said, "could stand a trip across the Bay of Biscay," and, as for France, why, no cattle would come from there, because France herself was importing cattle. He showed that none would come from Belgium, Holland, Germany, or the Prussian League; and then, with grim flattery, he told them that English beef was so much better than any other kind of beef that it would always bring a higher price in the market. With one side of his mouth he was telling hungry people that he was about to cheapen beef by letting foreign cattle in, and with the other he was quieting the Protectionists with a lot of blarney, and the assurance that, although he was about to open the gates, the lean cattle wouldn't come in, and the fat cattle couldn't.

Sir Robert Peel made his reductions of the tariff on the "horizontal" plan, the only scientific way in which they could be made at all. The exceptions were in the case of some raw materials of manufactures, and these he put on the free list. This plan was imitated by Mr. Morrison in the American Congress a few years ago, and was made the theme of much sardonic ridicule by the Protectionists throughout the country. In defence of the "horizontal" plan Sir Robert Peel said: "The Government has made its reduction on a great variety of articles, so as to give to almost every one of those classes which might suffer from some one or more of the reductions a compensation upon others." This reason was wise in the experiment, and vindicated by the result. When Mr. Morrison offered the same reasons for a like policy he was laughed at; but they will yet be justified here as they have been justified in England.

In removing the protective duty from raw materials, Sir Robert said that he did so to protect the mechanic and the manufacturer. Referring to the protective duty on timber, he said that it had greatly discouraged the industry of cabinet-makers, and all workers in wood. He spoke the same way about the high protective duties on foreign ores. He reduced the duties on whale oils, he said, because they were cheaper in the United States than in England, and by reason of that cheapness the United States was successfully competing with England in foreign markets, "in all manufactures extensively consuming this article." He reminded the House of Mr. Deacon Hume's dictum that "this country having plenty of untaxed iron, and untaxed coal, wanted only plenty of untaxed wood to give employment to her industries." The very echo of those words so applicable to our country, rung through the American Congress in 1890, only to be ridiculed and condemned. The cast-off rags of "Protection" which Sir Robert Peel threw away in 1842, and 1846, are proudly worn by our statesmen in Washington to-day. In the course of his remarks Sir Robert referred to the tenacity with which men clung to their own special privileges while generally sacrificing those of their neighbors to the common good. In the new tariff the duty on herrings was reduced fifty per cent, and he read a letter to the House which he had received from a man who was engaged in the business of curing herrings. He said, "I am a Free Trader in every other respect, but with regard to herrings I caution you against the general ruin which you are about to inflict on those engaged in that branch of trade."

When Sir Robert sat down Mr. Joseph Hume congratulated the ministers on their conversion to the principles of Free Trade. . This pleasantry was resented by Mr. Gladstone, who declared that no conversion had taken place, and that their opinions remained unchanged. As a discrimination was made in the new tariff in favor of the British colonies, a great deal of alarm was manifested, lest the Americans should smuggle their bacon into England by way of Canada, and thus obtain the benefit of the colonial tariff; but this was quieted by Mr. Gladstone who "did not think the proposed duty could facilitate fraud by the importation of American produce through the colonies." This alarm about American bacon was not because the revenue might be defrauded by it, but was entirely a Protectionist fear that its introduction might make meat a little cheaper to the hungry people of England.

Notwithstanding the plausible persuasions of Sir Robert Peel, the Protectionist country gentlemen were not at all satisfied that lean cattle would not come in, and fat cattle too. Mr. Miles, member for Somerset, actually took issue with his chief and moved an amendment to the effect that imported cattle should be taxed by weight. The amendment amounted to nothing, for Sir Robert had his party too well in hand, and they feared to break away from him. At the same time the reformation they were called on to support, mild as it was, put them into such an irritable mood that when

Mr. Villiers attempted to speak to the amendment, they greeted him with impatient marks of displeasure, and much interruption. Mr. Hume received no better treatment.

Lord John Russell ridiculed the contrary arguments of Sir Robert Peel and Mr. Miles; one pretending that cattle wouldn't come in, and the other contending that they would, and not only that, but that their coming would be disastrous by lowering the price of beef. He thought the argument of Mr. Miles against the bill was very strongly in its favor, while those of Mr. Gladstone and Sir Robert Peel in its favor were very much against it. He said, "If the alarm of Mr. Miles is well founded that the measure will give us better beef at a cheaper rate, let us by all means adopt the proposition. What are we here for? Is it to prevent the people from having cheap food?"

Even potatoes had been shut out of the country by high protective duties. The New Tariff admitted them on payment of two pence per hundred weight from foreign countries, and one penny per hundred weight from British Colonies. It was contended that twelve pence per hundred weight was little enough protection for the English potato grower, and that it was the highest patriotism to keep old England independent of foreign potatoes. Mr. Palmer gravely said that this was a question of very considerable importance to the agricultural interests of the country, because it "resolved itself into the consideration whether we should or should not be dependent on foreign supplies." Mr. Stuart Wortley, who had defeated Lord Morpeth at the general election, expressed much nervousness on the potato question, because "he had been given to understand that potatoes might be imported from France and Holland at a very low rate." Mr. Gladstone pacified those timid persons with some soothing syrup to the effect that it was not likely that many potatoes would come in even if the tariff should be taken from them altogether.

It is not easy to reconcile with principles of exact political good faith the conduct of Peel and Gladstone on this occasion. While they acted like statesmen they talked like ambidextrous politicians. Their bill reducing the tariff on beef, bacon and potatoes was intended, on the face of it at least, to encourage the importation of those articles for the benefit of the English people; and yet those ministers appeared happy to say that their bill would fail of its pretended purpose. Following the lead of Peel, who had apologized for the cattle schedule, Mr. Gladstone, in effect, said: True, we are inviting bacon and potatoes into the country, for we want to increase the food ration of the people; but I am happy to say they won't come, so don't be alarmed. In saying that, if he believed it, he showed himself deficient in that prescience which is one essential quality of a statesman. The bacon and potatoes did accept the invitation, and they came over in shiploads, so that whereas in 1842 the importation of these articles was merely nominal, in 1888 the quantity of potatoes imported was 150,000 tons, and of bacon and hams it was 200,000 tons. The value of this great importation may be imagined when we remember how much hunger would have been suffered had the importation been prohibited by law. It also created a corresponding demand for labor, because it was nearly all paid for by manufactured goods exported in exchange.

Every monopoly declared against the new tariff. The

6

mine owners of Cornwall protested against a reduction of the duties on metal ores, and the members from that county gave warning that if the deep mines of Cornwall were once abandoned they would never be worked again. Some other people vehemently resolved against a reduction of the duty on iron, because it was necessary that British iron should be protected against the "pauper" iron of Germany. A few persons owned a stone quarry on the Isle of Portland They protested against a reduction of the tariff on building stone, and declared that such reduction would be the ruin of their "industry." Even the wretched Irish peasant claimed protection for his pig, and Mr. Smith O'Brien actually moved to increase the duty on swine from five shillings a head all round to four shillings a hundred weight. Every "interest" predicted ruin to the country if its particular monopoly should be disturbed. In this way nearly everything from steam engines to apples, and from fat cattle to lobsters, had to fight for a reduction of taxation, and Sir Robert Peel was solemnly warned a hundred times to be careful, or he would afflict the land with cheapness and abundance.

Like the selfish conflict of "interests" which rages at Washington, when the Tariff is in jeopardy, was the struggle at Westminster in 1842. It was thus described in *Fraser's Magazine*: "Nothing is more amusing than to read the petitions of every trade against either the increase or the decrease of the present duties. Every trade seems thoroughly resolved to shift the burden from its own shoulders, and put it on its neighbor's, and leaving it to get quit of it as it best can. Such is the morality of the present religious age—We have 160 firms in the city petitioning against a reduction of the duty on coffee, and suggesting a scale of their own. Above half the mining interests of the country have adopted a series of resolutions, condemning the measures proposed by ministers with respect to copper, tin, and the ores, and preparations in these metals, and declaring with the usual exaggerations that such alteration would be the total destruction of the property invested in mines, not forgetting the injuries sustained by the parties supplying the timber, iron, ropes, and tallow candles. The glove trade is also up in arms, as well as the boot and shoe makers: and to quiet the alarm of those persons it is proposed by a revised tariff to increase the duties about one-third. The cork cutters however have not been so fortunate; for instead of being prohibitory, as heretofore, the duty is to be reduced one shilling or two a hundred weight; by which it is gravely pretended by persons having authority, and engaged in the trade, that 30,000 men will be thrown out of employment; a greater number in all probability than are employed in the trade in Europe. But the most extravagant part of the tariff, is a reduction of the timber duties by which 600,000 pounds of revenue is given up, apparently for no purpose whatever."

Among the curiosities of this debate was the statement of Sir Robert Peel, that he could not conceive any possibility of "danger" from the importation of cattle from the banks of the Mississippi river. This was in answer to Major Vivian who wanted the duty on Canada cattle to be equal to that on cattle from other countries, because if it was not, he feared that cattle from the Western States would invade England by the way of Canada. That a Prime Minister of England should speak of the prospect of cheap cattle as "dangerous," proves that English statesmen in 1842, were as unenlightened as to the principles of political economy, and the true ingredients of wealth, as our American statesmen are in 1892. Yet all through this debate Peel and Gladstone were soothing and wheedling a lot of parliamentary dunces with predictions that although they were reducing the import duties on several hundred articles, yet, for all that, there was not much "danger" that they would take advantage of it; that in fact, there was no danger that the country would be "flooded with cheap goods." They knew that water seeks its level by a law of physics, but they did not know that human products seek their level, too, by force of an economic law equally inexorable. It was certain that cattle being abundant in the Mississippi Valley and scarce in England, they would emigrate from one country to the other unless prevented by natural or artificial obstacles; and now Mr. Gladstone rejoices that more than 300,000 head of livecattle enter Great Britain annually, a very large number of them from the Mississippi Valley; to say nothing of dead meat in even greater quantities. After a weary journey of several weeks, through the committee of the whole, the New Tariff bill passed the House of Commons, and went up to the Lords.

When the bill went up to the Lords it had to run the gauntlet of the same opposition it had met in the House of Commons. Lord Stanhope used an argument which has a familiar sound to us here in America. The reduction of duties, he said, would cause great distress among the industrial classes who would be unfairly put in competition with the "foreigner." Free Trade, he said, could not be introduced into England on account of the habits and prejudices of the people, but this bill would go far to introduce that system. Then he uttered the solemn prediction that "the measure would tend to the utter destruction of the country." The Duke of Richmond opposed the bill because it brought the English producer into competition with the "pauper" labor of foreign countries. And Lord Melbourne said that the difficulty and distress now experienced were inseparable from, and belonging to a state of manufacturing prosperity, and were the consequence of the great amount of capital invested in manufactures in Great Britain. The man who said that had lately held the great office of Prime Minister of England, which proves how little statesmanship is necessary to govern a people. Sullenly and grudgingly the Lords allowed the bill to pass.

The House of Lords, being composed almost exclusively of great land owners and monopolists, it is not surprising that the principles of Free Trade were looked upon in that House as very plebeian and low, as revolutionary in fact, and destructive of that hoary feudal system which the aristocracy of England has projected, with much of its injustice, into the nineteenth century. The noble peers regarded pheasants and peasants as alike made for their exclusive use and pleasure; and, being rather dull by reason of indolence and self-indulgence, they were easily thrown into panic whenever they thought their privileges were threatened. They regarded the Anti-Corn-Law League as a monster more dangerous than the steam engine or the electric telegraph, or even an untaxed newspaper. On the 21st of July, 1842, a member of the House of Commons, having proposed that Parliament reassemble in October to relieve the poor by releasing bonded grain, the Secretary of State for the Home Department answered with patrician disdain, "You know that we shall then be pheasant shooting." On the 19th of April, 1842, Lord Brougham moved the House of Peers that no tax should be levied upon corn, either for protection or for revenue. It is not surprising that this motion was lost by 89 to 6. The wonder is where the six came from.

On the 8th of July, the state of the country being under discussion, Mr. Cobden censured Sir Robert Peel for affecting to believe that the prevailing distress was due to the introduction of machinery. He said machinery does not throw people out of work if its perfection and introduction to practical use are gradual. He called upon Sir Robert Peel not to treat the subject with quibbles about machinery, nor as a mere Manchester question, but to look at it in connection with the whole condition of the country—and it must be done this session.

Sir Robert made his escape on this occasion with great ingenuity and skill. Mr. Cobden was member for Stockport; and Sir Robert cited practical authorities from Stockport itself, showing by the evidence of one of the relieving officers of the Stockport Union that some of the distress prevailing there was to be dated from the introduction of improved machinery into the mills, whereby a large number of hands was rendered unnecessary. This, however, was only the statement and opinion of one of the relieving officers of the Stockport Union, and it was not at all conclusive, yet it was legitimate evidence which Sir Robert Peel had a right to use as argument.

The same class of topics being under debate in the House of Lords, Lord Brougham labored to disprove what he considered one of the grossest fallacies that had ever been asserted, that the increase of machinery was the cause of the distress. He said, also, that if the House did away with protective duties it would be impossible for other countries to maintain them, and therein he made a serious mistake. The United States, Germany, Canada, Australia and other countries have not relaxed restrictive duties in accordance with Lord Brougham's prophecy. On the contrary, they have made them more onerous than ever. Not until they have all passed through the same costly experience that England underwent will they relax that unwise constriction which is strangling their industries and destroying their markets, as it strangled the industries and destroyed the markets of Great Britain.

In August, Parliament adjourned, and people had leisure time to foot up the accounts of the session, and strike a balance of party gains and losses. There was a difference of opinion as to the amount of profit and loss, but all agreed that the gains must be placed to the credit of the Free Traders, and that the losses were all on the side of the Protectionists. The material gain to the Free Traders made by the reduction of duties in the new tariff was trifling compared to the moral victory they had won in compelling the ministry to concede the principle of Free Trade. It was noticed that in debate the ministers had been careful not to defend Protection on its merits. They apologized for it and pleaded for it. They said that great interests had grown up around it; that society had shaped itself to it, and that it could not be suddenly and violently overthrown without carrying in its fall the ruin of the protected classes and shaking violently the business of the country; but they did not attempt to defend it as a correct principle of political economy.

Armed with this concession the League renewed its assault upon monopoly, and during the recess it was busy educating the people and creating a public opinion that should be more potent in the next session than it had ever been before. Great meetings were held in all parts of the country, and Free Trade resolutions were adopted at all of them. On the 22d of November, at the Town hall, Manchester, a very large meeting was held, composed of merchants, spinners, manufacturers, machine-makers, and other capitalists, and employers, to consider the steps to be adopted in consequence of the ruinous effect produced on trade by the operation of the Corn-Laws, and the restrictive commercial policy. This meeting was called by the League, and it was resolved to raise $250,000 for the work; $20,000 of it was put into the hat there and then. This was considered a great collection for one meeting, and yet before the work was ended $300,000 was contributed at one meeting in that very same town to the funds of the League.

CHAPTER VI.

HARD TIMES.

The Protective System had reduced the working classes of England to a pitiful state of poverty, and many of them to a condition of debasement so squalid that men born within the last fifty years, not having seen it, can hardly believe it possible. In utter desperation the Chartists broke into rioting and tumult at Manchester, Preston, Blackburn, and nearly all the manufacturing towns. Great loss of life and property resulted from these riots. The police force was not strong enough to subdue the rioters, and they were finally suppressed by the military power. The condition of England excited great anxiety and alarm. The influence of the League was thrown in favor of moral force agitation alone, but the Chartists contended that no reform was possible except through the agency of a violent revolution. The counsel of the League proved itself to be the wiser in the end.

It was about this time that John Bright began to be recognized as a power in the State. Although not yet in Parliament, his influence outside of it was almost as great as Cobden's inside. A massive Englishman was John Bright; a stalwart man, strong of body and brain, one of the few great orators of modern England. His eloquence was pure, sparkling, strong. His invective burned like fire, and he was the most combative Quaker that ever spoke in Parliament. He was more fluent and stately than Cobden, though no man could be more convincing. His voice was melodious, his magnetism great, and thousands of men crowded and jostled one another to get near him. They saw in him one of the great apostles of plenty and international peace, a man whose politics were prompted and controlled by a moral guide that kept him always in the road that leads to justice and to liberty. He subdued the mad passions of the hungry multitude, and he created within the people a moral wisdom and a patient energy that gained the victory at last. Second to Cobden, and to Cobden alone, was John Bright in the great work of lifting the incubus of the protective tariff from the industries of Great Britain. He rendered great service between the close of the session of 1841 and the opening of the session of 1843. Considering the place he occupies in the political history of England how puerile appears the ponderous humor of *Blackwood's Magazine*, seeking to diminish him and snuff him out by referring to him as "a man by the name of Bright."

During the fall and winter of 1842, notwithstanding the evidence of the riots, and the figures of the Poor Law Guardians, there were newspapers, magazines, and even statesmen, who insisted that the reports of public distress had been exaggerated by the emissaries of the League; this for the sake of political capital, and to create a popular alarm that should operate on the Government, and by a sort of moral duress compel the ministers to make some concessions to a mischievous policy. *Blackwood's* declared in mockery of the people's hunger, that "For any real mischief which they can work, the present Corn-Laws are as quiescent as the laws of gravitation;" and the effort to relieve the people by the importation of grain was described as "the wicked Corn-Law agitation." In one article by Christopher North himself, and to which he attached his name, the Free Traders were described as "the mischievous vermin of the Anti-Corn-Law League." Cobden, Bright, Villiers, and the other leaders of the movement he stigmatized as "ignorant and vulgar babblers," and he denounced "the systematic and mercenary wickedness of their intentions."

Equally venomous, although not so influential, nor of such high literary and political rank as *Blackwood's*, was *Fraser's Magazine*, and with brazen effrontery it also insisted that the public distress was purely imaginary and that it existed only in the mendacious croakings of the League. It said, "The Anti-Corn-Law League, as dishonest a combination as ever existed, purposely close their eyes to the truth, in order to be able the more confidently to propagate an atrocious falsehood. They continue daily and hourly repeating that the people are woefully distressed, and that the sole cause for this distress is to be found in the Corn-Laws. They are perpetually reminded that the Corn-Laws have existed in their present shape for fourteen years, and that the country has been in a state of great prosperity even so late as 1836, but it is useless to adduce facts to such men. They resolutely refuse to look at them, but keep up their cuckoo cry 'The Corn-Laws are starving the people.'"

In spite of all efforts to conceal the sufferings of the people and to underrate the extent of them, the aspect of public affairs at the opening of the year 1843 was of a dark and threatening character. The public mind was feverish with anxiety and alarm. The revenue figures appeared as witnesses, and they could neither be impeached nor browbeaten out of court. They showed a serious falling off in the receipts from those articles, the use of which gives evidence of prosperity. Parliament met on the 2d of February, 1843, and then the ministers themselves were compelled to give official recognition to the public distress in the speech from the throne. It contained these words:

"Her Majesty regrets the diminished receipts from some of the ordinary sources of revenue.

"Her Majesty fears that it must be in part attributed to the reduced consumption of many articles, caused by that depression of the manufacturing industry of the country, which has so long prevailed, and which Her Majesty has so deeply lamented."

This was not the seditious talk of the League; it was the official testimony of the Prime Minister and his cabinet, but it offered nothing in mitigation of the public distress, except the sympathy and sorrow of the Queen.

The Earl of Powis who was appointed by Sir Robert Peel to move in the House of Lords the address in answer to the speech from the throne, stepped very tenderly over that part of it which referred to the public distress. He said his piece very much like a school-boy skipping the hard words in a reading lesson. He lightly remarked, "We cannot conceal from ourselves the conviction that great masses of the population of this country in the course of the last year have been unable to avail themselves to the same extent as formerly, of those enjoyments which they usually possess." He did not like to use so unpleasant a word as "starvation" in such lordly company, neither did the Earl of

Eglinton who seconded the address. He trusted that the worst was over. He had that hopeful philosophy which believes that things will all come out right, and that most likely something will turn up. He hoped that "by the revival of trade and commerce the sufferings of the people would be alleviated." There was a dull inconsistency in this hope, because the Earl of Eglinton and his party were at that very moment bent on preserving a protective tariff for the very purpose of restricting "trade" and preventing "commerce." In the House of Commons the mover and seconder of the address talked very much as their colleagues did in the House of Lords. The criticisms of the opposition were feeble and rather apologetic, as if the Whigs felt themselves to some extent guilty of the surrounding misery. Lord John Russell, however, made an irresistible point against Peel when he twitted him with having reduced his supporters to this difficulty, "that they were obliged to vindicate the tariff on principles of Free Trade, and the Corn-Laws on principles of Protection."

A clamorous Yorkshireman, Mr. Ferrand, member for Knaresborough, declared that there would be no protection for the poor unless machinery was taxed sufficiently to restrain its use and activity within such bounds as would prevent its competition with hand-labor. This comical statesmanship excited the laughter of all parties, and yet it was in logical harmony with the Protective System. Importation produced abundance, which it was the intent and purpose of protective taxation to restrain. Machinery created abundance, and why should not that also be restricted by the device of taxation? Besides, had not Sir Robert Peel himself, in his debate with Cobden in July, ascribed the distress of the country, in part, to the competition of machinery with hand-labor? And had he not proved it, too, by the official statements of the guardians of the poor in Mr. Cobden's own borough of Stockport? Why, then, should the statesmanship of Mr. Ferrand be laughed at, and that of Sir Robert Peel admired?

On the 18th of February, 1843, Lord Howick moved that the House resolve itself into committee of the whole to consider the distress of the country; and thereupon arose a very instructive debate. Lord Howick maintained that the protective tariff had crippled the agricultural, mining, manufacturing, and shipping interests of the country; and he argued that the Corn-Laws ought to be repealed. He said that the distress was largely caused by laws which went directly to the restriction of importation. This restriction was not an incident arising from taxation for revenue purposes, but it was intentionally created in order to check importation from foreign countries. He insisted that increased importation would stimulate and encourage domestic industry instead of aiding to depress it. This assertion was rather a speculation in England at the time Lord Howick made it, but experience has proved the truth of it as firmly as any proposition in Euclid is established by demonstration. "If you tell me," said Lord Howick, "that my argument is only a theory, what is yours? Your whole system of restriction is built on a theory which cannot be defended now, a theory which took its rise in the notion that gold and silver constituted wealth—that all that a nation gained by trade went to increase the amount of its gold and silver, and that to increase its exports and to decrease its imports, in order to leave a favorable balance of trade, was a wise policy."

We can hardly conceive that the present great leader of the Liberal party, was that night the Tory champion, whose duty it became to answer Lord Howick. Mr. Gladstone admitted the distress of the country, although he thought Lord Howick had exaggerated it. He conceded much of the argument of his adversary, but resisted the motion on the ground of expediency. It was not the time to repeal the Corn-Law. The measures of last session had not had a fair trial. They ought to see what other nations would do to reciprocate a reduction of duties. England could not be expected to open her ports while she had hostile foreign tariffs to contend against, and so on. Never once did he contend that the Protective System was good, either in morals or as a scheme of social science. His plea was an excuse for Protection, not a justification of it, except, perhaps, where he sought to make a distinction between protection to agriculture, and protection to other interests. No commercial law, he said, could be permanent, but that of protection to agriculture was so, and he was not prepared to abandon it so long as protection was given to any other interest. He further said that Lord Howick might have spared himself the trouble of advancing abstract principles when the real question was one of time and degree. He wound up with the usual flippant formula that the motion was fraught with disaster to every interest in the country. It is still the religious belief of every Protectionist that if you assail his monopoly you threaten disaster to every interest in the country.

Fifty years afterward we hear the echo of Mr. Gladstone's speech ringing through the halls of Congress. "This is not the time: give the McKinley bill a fair trial." And the patent-air brake "Reciprocity" which Mr. Gladstone used in 1842 to stop the train laden with food and freedom, is now in active operation at Washington. "Let us wait and see what other nations are going to do to *reciprocate* a reduction of duties."

Not by way of reproach, but purely for instruction, I place on record here what Mr. Gladstone thought of the Free Trade system after it had been in operation for nearly thirty years. Speaking to the electors of Mid Lothian in the month of November, 1885, he said: "I do not deny that there is distress, but it is greatly less than it was before the Free Trade reformation. When that reform began trade increased to a degree unexampled in the history of the world. Periods of distress have been due to special causes which have been beyond human agency to deal with. Such times of hardship have become almost, if not absolutely unknown, owing to the blessed effects of Free Trade. The country has made a great step forward and will not go back." Then pointing to the mountains in the distance, he said: "You might as well try to uproot the Pentlands from their base and fling them into the sea." This contrast is not presented here to show Mr. Gladstone inconsistent, but the reverse. A man is really inconsistent when he clings to error after he has found it out. Mr. Gladstone was converted to the Free Trade faith by argument in 1846. He merely testified in 1885 that he was confirmed by the experimental practice of the system for nearly thirty years in England.

The Protectionist principle, that the end of all true political economy is to promote scarcity, found out spoken champions in this debate. Mr. Ferrand contended that the distress of the country was all owing to machinery, and that, if machinery could be done away with, the conveniences of life would become scarcer, and this would create a demand for labor, the people would all get employment at good wages, and prosperity would come. He therefore moved the following amendment to the motion of Lord Howick, "and also to inquire into the effects of machinery upon the moral and physical condition of the working classes." He advocated returning "to the principles of our forefathers," as opposed to Free Trade, which new-fangled heresy was destroying the interests of the working-classes. Mr. Ferrand was not alone in his opinions, for Mr. Liddell thought that Lord Howick's plan of opening up new markets would do no good, because such was "the tremendous power of machinery in England that they would soon be overstocked as well as the old." Mr. Ward apologized for machinery on the curious ground that it was necessary in order for the English to compete with the cheaper labor and more fertile soil of other countries. He thought that the Americans had made a mistake in their high protective tariff of 1842, but contended that the English had provoked it by fixing such a high duty on American grain. The most bewildering doctrine that this remarkable debate produced came from Mr. Muntz, member for the important town of Birmingham, who contended that the present condition of things was unnatural, and that "we must either repeal the Corn-Laws or *lower the price of silver.*" No wonder the common people had such crude notions about political economy, when the statesmen of the country showed such prejudice and such a lack of information as they did in this debate.

Mr. Disraeli took part in the debate. He was then an ambitious young man, conscious that he had some talent which ought to bring reward in the political market, where talent was in demand. He was literally a parliamentary adventurer "seeking his fortune." He had started in politics a violent Radical, but soon discovered that the Radicals were burdened with an "overproduction" of talent, while it was rather scarce in the Tory market, where it brought a much higher price than the Radicals were able to pay. He therefore joined the Tory party which, to say the least of it, was always generous in the appreciation of talent. He had made some crochet novels which had given him a footing in the literary guild, and he was flattered when people pointed him out at Lady Blessington's, and said, "That's young Disraeli, the man who wrote Vivian Grey;" but he shrewdly saw that this perfume was fleeting and unsubstantial, and that if he was ever to win advancement and make some gold and velvet he must do so in the House of Commons. He failed at first, not because there was not merit in what he said, but because it was all covered over, like his waistcoat, with cheap jewelry and tinsel. That sort of thing may do very well for some places, but the House of Commons "won't have it, you know," and he was chaffed and ridiculed. He diligently sought Peel's patronage by rather obsequious flattery and tenders of loyal service, but Peel, to the day of his death, could never see anything in him, and contemptuously refused to employ him. He regarded him as an Asiatic exotic that could never be developed into an English statesman. This was bad for Peel, because Disraeli afterward took revenge in a shower of poisoned arrows that gave pain to that minister in the hour of his fall. Besides, Peel's judgment of him was erroneous; because, although to the last there was much of the gaudy and theatrical about Disraeli, there were beneath all that frippery the solid qualities of statemanship; nor was it of the Asiatic kind; but of that practical, fighting, acquiring, conquering, Rule Britannia sort, peculiarly English. Peel never dreamed that this young politician, whose services he would not have at any price, was destined to be an Earl, a Knight of the Garter, and Prime Minister of England.

Mr. Disraeli opposed the motion on "reciprocity" grounds. He contended that much of the distress was to be attributed to the fact that treaties of commerce had not been carried out with France, Brazil and other countries, which countries were consequently closed against the manufactures of England. He improved the occasion to offer himself unconditionally to the Tory aristocracy. He had the daring to declare that "he thought the present Corn-Law not injurious to commerce, while it maintained as it ought to do the preponderating influence of the landed interest." He then went off into rhetorical hysterics about the "Doge of Venice, who when looking out on the Lagunes, covered with the ships engaged in the trade of the Levant, said that, 'notwithstanding all he saw, Venice, without its *terra firma*, would be like an eagle with one wing.' So should he say of England, and he should not therefore consent to destroy the preponderating influence of the landed proprietary of the country." All that eastern embroidery went for nothing. The "landed proprietary" knew little and cared less about the Doge of Venice and his Lagunes, but Mr. Disraeli's bid for employment was taken into consideration, and in due time it was accepted; but not by Peel.

Mr. Villiers made an argument so strong in common sense and so sarcastic in its application that it created much nervousness and irritation on the Tory benches. He said that Mr. Gladstone had vindicated the restrictive principle of the Corn-Laws, because it had always been the rule in legislation to treat corn in a peculiar way. "Of course, that has been the rule," said Mr. Villiers, "and why? Because the legislation of the country has always been under the control of the landed aristocracy." Legislators who had great interests of their own to serve would always be found passing laws to protect and advance those interests. Mr. Villiers said: "There have been twenty-five Corn-Laws since 1765. Yes, and in five hundred years there have been forty." He then threw ridicule upon the whole Protective System by a couple of illustrations drawn from the records of Parliament. Less than a century ago, he said, a petition was presented by one county against another; the former had always grown beans, and wished to retain the monopoly. It wanted "Protection" against the competition of the neighbor county, which had lately set itself up as a rival in the bean-raising industry. The other illustration was the petition of the county of Middlesex against the making of good roads, because thereby the farmers of that county would lose the monopoly of the London Market. Mr. Villiers contended that the argument to preclude one county from competing with another was precisely the same as the argument to preclude one country from competition with another, and that the principle and the result were alike in both cases. The answer to this was the statement of Lord Sandon that the ancient policy must be continued in order to protect the "home market," as if that were not the very criminal then on trial; as if the experiment of centuries had not shown that the restrictive system had crippled and weakened, not only the foreign market, but the home market also.

Mr. Cobden, with his usual earnestness, went straight and fearless right to the merits of the question, as affecting, not only the manufacturers, but all the people in the land. "My chief objection to the motion," he said, "is that it does not include agricultural as well as manufacturing distress." This point, however, should have been made, not against Lord Howick's motion, but against that paragraph in the royal speech on which the motion was founded. In the speech from the throne the ministers had been careful to say nothing about *agricultural* distress. To have done so would have been to condemn the Corn-Laws. They were maintained as a special "Protection" to the agricultural classes, and an admission that they had failed would have embarrassed the ministers in the subsequent debates. Cobden would not allow them to evade the question in that way, and, to the serious annoyance of the "landed proprietary," he dragged the agricultural laborer into the debate. He showed the wretchedness of his condition, and contended that even the tenant farmers themselves were suffering loss and privation by reason of the Corn-Laws. All this was very irritating to the "landed proprietary," because they knew that it was true; but it was endurable, and even pleasant, in comparison with what followed.

Mr. Cobden in a few fierce thrusts that could not be parried, gave a mortal wound to the false pretense of the landlord classes that they constituted the "landed interest" of the country. He showed that on the contrary they were its blight and plague. For centuries the landlords had masqueraded as "agriculturists," the "landed interest," the great "stock-breeders," the "model farmers," and the like, when, in fact, with a few exceptions, they were simply a tax upon the landed industry of the country. The delusion was kept up at cattle shows and fairs, where Dukes and Earls in farmer looking broad-brimmed hats and top boots would walk about chewing straw, and discussing sheep and turnips with the yeomanry. As a rule the English landlord had no higher claims than a cut-worm to be called an agriculturist. Cobden tore away the mask and revealed the hypocrisy of the claim. He declared that the landlord had no right to class himself with the farmers of the land. He might live all his days in Paris or in London. "The landlord," said Cobden, "is no more an agriculturist than a ship-owner is a sailor." Then turning to Peel, he said, "You have reduced the tariff on 700 articles, but you have omitted the two that can give material relief to the people, corn and sugar."

The conclusion of this speech, though vigorous, proved very unfortunate. Mr. Cobden declared that he held the Prime Minister "individually responsible" for the distress of the country, and this expression, which he had used several times lately in the north, he repeated with strong emphasis. Sir Robert Peel rose in a state of nervous excitement, quite unusual with him, and resented this personal attack. His private secretary, Mr. Drummond, had been assassinated a few days before, in mistake for him, and the tragedy had shocked him greatly. It had also alarmed his family, and perhaps it had alarmed Peel himself, although an English statesman is not likely to be driven from his course by threats or personal fears. He referred to several attacks of this kind which the honorable member had lately made upon him elsewhere. He accused Mr. Cobden, of pointing him out for assassination, and the sympathy of the House was with Peel. In vain Mr. Cobden tried to explain that a wrong interpretation had been put upon his words, and that he only alluded to the right honorable baronet in his official capacity as the head of the Government. The House refused to hear him. Peel has been accused and with some reason, of playing a melodramatic part on that occasion; and while his admirers deny it, there is little doubt that in his worried and nervous condition he seized rather eagerly upon Cobden's words, and used them to create a diversion from the main question, and also as a ground for sympathy.

This incident was an unhappy one, for it placed those important men in the attitude of personal enemies for three years, a position which caused Cobden to be unjust to Peel on more than one occasion. In contrast it must be said that the treatment of Cobden by Peel was magnanimous. The suspicion of a motive so abhorrent to his gentle nature wounded Cobden so keenly that it seemed almost impossible to forgive the man, who, even in the excitement of a great debate could impute it to him. Three years afterward Peel publicly acknowledged in his place in Parliament that in this personal conflict he himself was in the wrong; as he undoubtedly was; although the phrase "individually responsible" was language of which he might rightfully complain. It was the opinion of many persons that although the Free Traders had the best of the argument, this advantage was thrown away by Cobden's indiscreet attack upon the Prime Minister. It is not likely that it affected any votes either one way or the other. The division showed a majority for the Minister of 115. The numbers were, for Lord Howick's motion, 191; against the motion, 306.

CHAPTER VII.

AMERICAN WHEAT AND THE DRAIN OF GOLD.

It had long been the claim of the "landed proprietary" that the Protective System was only a just compensation in return for the "peculiar burdens" thrown upon land by the poor rates, the highway rates, the church rates, and many other taxes that fell exclusively upon the land. A great many people knew that this claim was largely fictitious, but as the "great parties" were both interested in advancing it, there was no serious contradiction of it so long as the "burning issues of the hour" consisted chiefly in a fight for the offices between the Whigs and the Tories. But a new element was now in Parliament caring for neither Whigs nor Tories, and it proposed to test this claim. On the 14th of March Mr. Ward, member for Sheffield, moved for a special committee to inquire "whether there are any peculiar burdens specially affecting the landed interest of this country, or any peculiar exemption enjoyed by that interest." Should the committee be granted Mr. Ward agreed to show, not only that the claim was unfounded, but also that the power of the landlords had been systematically employed to relieve themselves from taxation, and that a combination existed among them dangerous to the other interests of the country.

Instead of granting the committee, or answering Mr. Ward, the Protectionists attacked the Anti-Corn-

Law League; and Mr. Bankes moved as an amendment to Mr. Ward's motion, "that the attention of the House should be directed to certain associations dangerous to the public peace, and inconsistent with the spirit of the constitution." Mr. Cochrane in seconding the amendment thought that the House was indebted to Mr. Bankes for directing its attention to the dangerous and treasonable proceedings of the League. He charged the League with sending emissaries and spies into the country to disturb the peace and comfort of the peasantry; which is curiously like the accusations that used to be charged in this country against the Abolitionists.

Sir Robert Peel opposed the motion, and insisted that the "peculiar burdens" on the land were great. He promised that at some future time returns of these burdens should be laid before Parliament. As the nervous system of the "landed proprietary" was just then in a fevered condition, resulting from anxiety as to Peel's intentions, a soothing influence was felt when the Prime Minister declared that if he were convinced that it was for the interest of the country at large that the Corn-Laws should be altered, he would not for one moment hesitate to alter them; but he was not so convinced. There was great cheering when he said that as the continuance of doubt as to the intentions of the Government must have a tendency to unsettle business, he felt bound to say that it was his intention to maintain the present law.

Whenever the owners of an unjust privilege conferred by law, behold their title challenged, they immediately appeal to the timidity of commerce for protection, and more clamorous than a Chinese gong, they declare that business is in danger. So the proprietors of that scheme of larceny called the Protective System whenever it is assailed, either in detail or in mass, horizontally or perpendicularly, try to fright the markets by declaring that all assaults upon their exclusive privileges "have a tendency to unsettle business." As it was with Peel and Gladstone fifty years ago, so it is with Blaine and McKinley now. The "tendency to unsettle business" plea, no longer available in England, having been imported free of duty into the United States, performs the office of a scarecrow here.

When the cheering caused by Peel's announcement had subsided, Mr. Blackstone congratulated the House and the country on the declaration just made by the Prime Minister. It would give universal satisfaction, and put an end to the hopes that existed in some quarters of being able to tamper with the law. He trusted, also, that the threat of importing American grain at a nominal duty through Canada would not again be heard of. The promise of an angry nation to fire shot and shell into the ports of its rival may fairly be described as a "threat," but only the perverted and inverted logic of a Protectionist could make a "threat" out of the promise of one great nation to fire sacks of grain among the hungry people of another. "I was ruined," said the little cobbler in the Fleet prison, to Sam Weller, "by having money left me." So, in the jargon of monopoly, England was "threatened" with ruin by the cheap grain of America, and to-day America is threatened with ruin by a "flood of cheap goods from England." Our statesmen tell us that we need an armor-plated navy, and guns that can shoot like earthquakes, for England, our enemy, has a great artillery loaded to the muzzle, ready to fire into us blankets, and clothes, and rails, and wire, and a hundred other bombshells of equal mischief. Another foe wants to fire sugar at us, and another leather, and another wool. Let us cover the seas with war ships and defy their "threats." Let us make the great ocean a lake of burning fluid if necessary to "protect" our people from the missiles of enlightenment and peace. Mr. Ward's motion was defeated without an effort by a majority of ninety-nine.

In May, 1843, Mr. Villiers brought forward his annual motion to go into committee of the whole "to consider the import duties on foreign grain, with a view to their immediate and total abolition." The debate on this motion was, if possible, more remarkable in its display of statesmanlike ignorance than the other, but, unlike the other, it was not all on the side of the Protectionists. Even Mr. Villiers himself showed a forgetfulness of his geography when he said, "The use of wheaten bread is denied to ten millions of people in the British islands, while a plague had arisen in Louisiana because the produce was left to rot upon the ground for want of a market." He evidently had a confused idea of where Louisiana was, or what was the nature of her products. A plague produced by wheat rotting on the ground was a new phenomenon in Louisiana. Perhaps Mr. Villiers referred to the vast territory formerly known as Louisiana, and if he spoke prophetically he was not so very far wrong. Probably his remark was merely an exaggerated word painting of the folly of one people "protecting" themselves from sharing in the superabundant wealth of another. He worried the House with some uncomfortable facts. He asserted that ten millions of the British people could not afford to indulge in the luxury of wheaten bread; that a large portion of the Irish lived on potatoes, and that the inhabitants of Scotland lived on oatmeal. He also showed that in England great numbers of the working classes were limited to a supply not exceeding fourteen ounces a day, and many had not half that quantity.

Once more it became the duty of Mr. Gladstone to answer the Free Traders, and he contented himself with leaving them unanswered. In fact, there was but one way to answer Mr. Villiers, and that was by contradicting him, and showing that his statements were erroneous. This Mr. Gladstone did not dare to do, for he knew that the figures were correct. He did not deny either the facts or the conclusions. He admitted the distress of the people, but contended that they were better off than they were two hundred years ago, which was an unsubstantial sort of comfort, and hardly satisfactory. He met the motion by an emphatic negative, and declared that the Government would not consent to any further modification of the Protective System. He said that last year the House had rejected the motion by 393 to 90, but if the motion was unreasonable twelve months ago it was doubly so now. He then condescended to use the false pretense that is so glibly maintained in the United States to-day, namely, that a Tariff for the Protection of certain trades is in the nature of a "contract" between the Government and the protected interests. This doctrine would perpetuate extortion by converting a law for raising revenue to support the Government into a contract with certain parties that it should remain upon the statute books for the purpose of raising revenue for them. He maintained that the tariff of last year was a "contract" with the protected classes that could not be violated. History repeats itself, and we are told in America, in the year 1892, that the clumsy juggle known as the Tariff of 1890 is a contract with private interests that shall not be further disturbed. "What the country needs," exclaimed Peel and Gladstone, "is rest from tariff agitation." "What the country needs," remark the millocrats and tariff statesmen of America, "is rest from tariff agitation."

Mr. Gladstone was not yet free from the ancient superstition about the "drain of gold" and its debilitating effect upon any country that suffers from it. He still believed as the Blaines and the McKinleys yet believe that wealth consists in gold and silver, but not in corn and cotton and wool. He thought that a gold sovereign was riches that ought not to be allowed to go out of the country, and that a sack of corn or a hide of leather was poverty that ought not to be allowed to come in. He still thought that it was the duty of Government to make the stream of commerce and trade run up hill and not down, and that it should waste its energies forever in watching the "balance of trade" and guarding against the exportation of silver and gold. Wiser it was to drain the lives of the people by hunger than to drain gold from the country by purchasing flour in New York. With the air of a minister announcing the loss of a battle, Mr. Gladstone sorrowfully informed the House of Commons that already since the beginning of the year, three million pounds had been sent to America in payment for the products of that country, and there was a gloomy prospect of still further disaster impending over the nation because "wheat was so cheap in the Mississippi valley, that if a protective tax upon its importation should be abolished vast quantities of it would be poured upon England." Even a heart of pig-iron might be softened into compassionate putty at the prospect of such calamitous abundance. As the measures of last year had not yet had a "fair trial," Mr. Gladstone concluded that the Government would be unworthy of the confidence of the country should it agree to the motion of Mr. Villiers.

Mr. Roebuck supported the motion, but scolded the League. He ridiculed Gladstone's alarm about the "drain of gold," which he called an idle and groundless fear. He also said that in 1815, the landlords consulted their own interests by keeping up high prices and high rents by means of a law prohibiting the importation of foreign corn. This was the reason for establishing the monopoly, and it was hypocrisy to deny it. Lord Howick also supported the motion, although he declared himself in favor of a small fixed duty as a compromise between conflicting parties. At the same time he was emphatic in declaring his belief that "Protection" of every kind was a robbery of the community. Lord Howick was a Whig. His father, Earl Grey, was the Prime Minister who had carried the Reform Bill in 1832. As a Whig, and a Ministerial colleague, Lord Howick was implicated with Lord John Russell in the plan of a "fixed duty," and therefore had to pay a small tribute of devotion to it, and, besides, compromise was a Whig trait, courteous and quiet. Although Lord Howick believed that Protection of every kind was robbery, he was willing to compromise on the basis of petit larceny, and therefore he was in favor of a "small fixed duty" on grain. Certainly petit larceny is preferable to grand larceny, but why compromise with larceny at all?

With a frank, blundering honesty that amused everybody, Sir Edward Knatchbull described some of the "peculiar burdens" laid upon the land. Among these he placed the duty of "making provisions for younger children," and so long as that duty remained, of course "Free Trade was quite impracticable." The elder children of the landed aristocracy being provided for by the law of primogeniture, their younger children should be taken care of by that furtive system of taxation known as "Protection to home industry." It never occurred to Sir Edward Knatchbull that it was the duty of land-owners to support their own younger children as other people had to do; nor did he conceive it possible that society in England could ever degenerate so low as to require those younger children to earn their own living. The mediæval sentiment that a gentleman must not work, nor engage in trade, nor in manufacturing, still prevailed in Britain. He might belong to the "professions," but not to the trades. A millionaire tradesman was not eligible to membership in any club in London, while his brother, a penniless lawyer, would be welcome at them all. Sir Edward Knatchbull was not an ignorant old fox-hunter, like many of his order. He ranked as a statesman, and was in fact a cabinet minister at this time. Lord John Russell made great sport of Sir Edward Knatchbull's admission of the Tory object of tariff taxation. At the same time he declared himself a Protectionist, and in favor of a fixed duty. He must therefore oppose the motion. Although the claim of Sir Edward Knatchbull appears very stupid now, it was consistent with English custom and with English law. The feudal theory that the children of the nobility must not work for a living at any useful thing, had become a hereditary dogma among the Knatchbulls and their order. The right of landowners and their children to live on other people had been the law so long that it had ripened into a "contract" between the Government and the Aristocracy; in which contract, the protective system was merely one of the stipulations.

The debate in Congress on the Morrison bill of 1884 is nearly a transcript of the debate in the House of Commons on Mr. Villiers' motion offered in 1843, proving that principles vary not with latitude, and that the selfish instincts are the same in every land. Commerce demanded freedom for the same reasons in both debates, and monopoly defended itself on the same arguments. Those who have read the debate of 1884 will see the parallel. In the House of Commons Mr. Ewart exposed the fallacy that high prices made high wages. He maintained that, by extended commerce, consumption was increased, and this expanded business and wages too. Other members took the opposite ground, and maintained that the English farmer and mechanic and laborer were entitled to a protection at least equal to the difference in the rate of wages between England and the nations of the continent. Mr. Scrope admitted that all indirect taxes on consumption gave incidental protection, but that, considering the greatness of the public debt and the enormous expenses of the Government, we could not repeal those taxes, and, therefore, Free Trade was impracticable. He thought, however, that the tariff should gradually be adapted to the principle of "revenue only." Col. Wood asserted that the Corn-Laws were mutually beneficial to manufacturer and agriculturist, and he claimed that the protectionists were actuated by no other motives than the good of the whole community. Sir Howard Douglass considered a repeal of the Corn-Laws fatal to the best interests of the Empire, commercial, manufacturing and agricultural. Compelling the people to buy of one another by the scheme of protective taxation was the highest wisdom, because it gave us the "home market." With clap-trap ostentation worthy of our Congress he exclaimed, "England is the best customer of England," and he said that by giving direct protection to one industry you indirectly give protection to some other. Sir Howard Douglass traveled in a circle, like the lost man on a prairie, a mode of progression very popular just now with Protectionists in the American Congress, and in every other Congress, too, for that matter. He was well-answered by Mr. Muntz, who supported the motion for the very reason that the Corn-laws and the tariff had been so arranged that they protected some classes and not others. He declared that labor was not protected at all. If there was to be any protection, he said, the poor should have the benefit of it; but he contended that the leaning of Protection was always in favor of the rich. He seemed to labor under a dreamy delusion that the protective system might be arranged, "according to the principles of Christianity," in favor of the poor and against the rich, a miracle, it is needless to say, that never has been and never will be achieved. Mr. Muntz declared that the protected classes received so many millions more for what they sold than they would get if the people were allowed to buy in a free market, and he admitted the claim of Mr. Gladstone that this prevented a "drain of gold;" he admitted that this money was not lost to the country, but remained in it. "But," said Mr. Muntz, "I'll tell you where the money does go, although it stays in the country. It goes out of the pockets of industry into the pockets of idleness." He thought, however, like some of our American statesmen, that it was useless to reform the Tariff until the "currency" was properly arranged. Mr. Milner Gibson contended, in opposition to Sir Howard Douglass, that it was certain the protective system injured commerce and manufactures, while it was not at all certain that it benefited agriculture. Mr. Gibson afterward became one of the leaders of the Free Trade revolution, and his words in this debate had peculiar weight, because he did not belong to the "Manchester class." He was not in trade, but was himself a country gentleman and a land-owner.

In this debate the childish policy of "Retaliation" appeared in the House of Commons, pleading for a stay of execution on behalf of the protective system; and the long-eared wisdom of biting off your nose to spite your face was maintained by some undeveloped statesmen who knew no better, and by some intelligent statesmen, like Mr. Gladstone, who did know better. It was contended that if foreign countries would not open their ports to British manufactures, England should close her ports against their wheat and bacon. That the English people were suffering for want of food made no difference. They should maintain "Reciprocity," even at the price of starvation. Fifty years afterward the American Congress, "cribbed, cabined and confined" by the narrow genius of the protective system, gravely adopted the principle of "Retaliation" as the economic law of the United States, thereby reducing the Great Republic to the moral dimensions of the insular Kingdom of Lilliput.

The "Reciprocity" theory did good service to the ministers in this debate. Whether or not they believed in it themselves is doubtful; perhaps some of them did. It is quite evident that a large majority of the House of Commons had not yet learned that it is wise to buy in the cheapest market, even if you cannot sell in the dearest, and so they kept ringing the changes on "Reciprocity." Mr. Christopher maintained that to adopt Free Trade without any guarantee of "Reciprocity" from foreign countries would be useless to the manufacturers, and ruinous to the agriculturists.

One ardent member, Mr. Thornley, had become so zealously interested in the "Reciprocity" plan, that he just stepped over to America to consult the President of the United States about it. It is a mortifying fact that the President filled him full of deceptive promises, and then sent him home again. Mr. Thornley told the House that if the English would adopt Free Trade, the Americans would immediately do the same; that Mr. Tyler told him so. Mr. Tyler also told him that the only obstacle to an extended commerce between the two countries was the English Corn-Law. All that was necessary to establish "Reciprocity" was for the English to begin.

Mr. Cobden said, "The law inflicts scarcity upon the people or it does nothing; and the condition of the agricultural laborer is the severest condemnation of the law." He turned Sir Edward Knatchbull's unlucky argument against him, and all the landlord class. He said, "If the object of the law is to make provision for the younger sons of the aristocracy, and effect marriage settlements for their daughters, what benefit does the farmer derive from that?" He said that the only way to raise the price of corn was by making it scarce, and that this was the object of the law. He declared that no party had the right to make the food of the people scarce. To ordinary minds these propositions appear to be self-evident, and yet there was a great party in England that denied them and maintained that the food of the people ought to be made scarce in order to protect the farmer against the cheaper labor, the richer soil, and the finer climate of other lands. Unhappily, this party controlled the House of Commons, as the division showed, for the Free Traders were beaten by the crushing majority of 381 to 125.

In the month of June the subject came up again in a discussion as to the relative merits of Tweedledum and Tweedledee. Lord John Russell moved to go into committee to take into consideration the laws relating to the importation of foreign grain. As he was at that time a Protectionist himself, and differed with Peel only in preferring a "fixed duty" to the "sliding scale," his motion had no practical value whatever, except to keep debate alive, and on that ground Mr. Villiers declared that he should support it. It gave an opportunity for a repetition of the old arguments against the Corn-Laws, and Mr. Gladstone answered them again as before. That the Whig doctrine of Protection differed little from the Tory doctrine was curiously shown by the speech of Lord John Russell. He exhibited the same dread of abundance that Mr. Gladstone had shown a few weeks before. Under the working of the sliding scale, he said, that just prior to the harvest, when the farmer was in anticipation of a good price for his produce, "the deluge of foreign corn was poured in," and he found himself disappointed. "The blame of these inundations of corn was attributable to reckless speculators, but speculators, he trusted, there would always be; and if they were sometimes reckless it was the law that made them so." Let not the American reformers be discouraged at the inverted political economy of their own statesmen. Let them reflect that Lord John Russell when he talked in that benighted way was a mature statesman fifty-one years old, the leader of a great party, and a future Prime Minister of England. Yet he had an economic use for speculators in grain; he spoke of a "deluge of corn" as if it were some new flood threatening England as a punishment for sin; and he arraigned the guilty delinquent upon whose shoulders rested the "blame" of inundating the country with food. Truthfully did Mr. Gladstone in replying to him, say, "There appears to be little difference between the noble Lord and myself as to the Protection to be extended to existing interests." Certainly; he was right; there was no difference except the difference between Tweedledum and Tweedledee.

This debate served the useful purpose of drawing from the Government the positive avowal that no change in the Corn-Laws would be permitted. Mr. Gladstone declared that the measures of last year were a virtual contract between the Government and the agricultural interest, and that it would be dishonorable to disturb it. This loving debate between the Whigs and Tories as to whether a fixed duty or a sliding scale was most effective in protecting the aristocracy, was rudely broken into by blunt old Hume, who declared that all "Protection" was spoliation and injustice, and ought to be abolished. Sir Robert Peel insisted that the measure of last year was a "compromise" between all the interests concerned, and which was assented to by the agriculturists on the faith of its being adhered to, therefore it was his determination to maintain the law of last session. Notwithstanding this "determination," there was a fidgety unrest among the "interests" for fear that the ministers would be again driven from their policy by the Anti-Corn-Law League. The motion was defeated by a majority of ninety-nine. Lord John Russell's motion had the support of Mr. Villiers and the Free Traders, although the motion of Mr. Villiers did not have the support of Lord John Russell and the Whigs, for the political party reason that the Whigs were "Tariff Reformers" only, and they were anxious to convince the country that they were innocent of the Free Trade heresy.

CHAPTER VIII.

OVERPRODUCTION.

Thus far we have chiefly spoken of the Free Trade struggle as it was fought in Parliament up to the summer of 1843. Outside, the contest was sharper still, and far more vigorous. The work of the reformers was harder too. A whole people had to be aroused, instructed, convinced. An irresistible public opinion must be created without which all efforts in Parliament would be in vain. The upper classes of the English people were protectionists from real interest, the lower classes from supposed interest and prejudice. The middle classes were divided on the question, but among them lay the strength of the Free Traders.

It is not surprising that the English lower classes were protectionists. All their prejudices were in favor of restricting competition. The Englishman was exclusive, partly by nature, and partly because of geographical conditions. His island being cut off by the sea from the continent of Europe, he became a sea-girt sort of personage himself. He was boastful and patriotically vain. He undervalued foreigners, never admitting that any change of latitude or longitude could make a foreigner of him. The extravagance of the comic opera was genuine poetry to the Briton. He seriously believed that really it was "greatly to his credit" that he was an Englishman; and he thought it highly meritorious that "in spite of all temptations to belong to other nations, he remained an Englishman." His combative temperament urged him sometimes beyond the bounds of international politeness to bid a fighting "defiance to the world." He christened his war ships "Bulldog," "Vixen," "Spitfire," "Destruction," "Devastation," "Terrible," "Vengeance," "Conqueror," and similar pet names. His great chest would pant like a blacksmith's bellows as he sung in the ears of all mankind his impolite refrain, "Britannia rules the waves." He thought that the people of other nations had very little to eat; that the Frenchman lived on frogs, the Italian on macaroni, and the German on an inferior quality of cabbage. He was a natural protectionist. To appeal on behalf of the protective policy to this baseless pride was the ignominious device of the Tories, and they scared the working-men away from the League by a ghost made out of a hollow pumpkin, which they called "Foreign pauper labor." I quote from *Blackwood's Magazine:* "The freedom of which the advocates of 'Free Trade' are most fond, is that which enables the moneyed capitalist to encourage the highest competition between the poor workmen. Competition between manufacturer and manufacturer at home will not content him; he has discovered that there are a number of poor wretches on the continent who have been inured to labor for a little black bread and a little water daily. He pants, therefore, to run those poor wretches against the English beef-fed and beer-drinking weaver, confident that he shall soon be able to reduce the price of manufacturing labor in England to the price of labor in France."

That "beef-fed and beer-drinking weaver" was a myth, as any man will testify who remembers the English weaver as he actually was before the Free Trade era, gaunt, sullen, anxious, and literally without hope in the world. And yet so strong was the English pride within him that although he was famishing for bread he was flattered and soothed by demagogues when they described him to his face as a fat, rosy, "beef-fed and beer-drinking" citizen. He knew the compliment was false, and yet he flaunted it above him like a flag, and swaggered about under it as if it were actually true.

The lower classes of the English people were much like the lower classes of some other people, insanely jealous of those whom they regarded as lower yet than themselves. In America it may be the negro, or the Chinaman; in England it was the frog-eating Frenchman, the frugal Dutchman—who was too mean to squander all his wages—or the barbarian Russian who lived on tallow, and whose clothes cost him nothing, the skin of an ox furnishing a complete outfit for a year. Any demagogue could easily arouse the enthusiasm of the working classes by denouncing Free Traders as an unpatriotic set who were seeking to subject the noble British workman to a ruinous competition with the "black bread and a little water" peasants of the continent. It was a part of the stock business of Tory statesmen at every hustings in the Kingdom to glorify the wisdom of that policy which was to make England "independent of foreigners," especially in the matter of meat and flour. Even enlightened statesmen like Peel and Gladstone did not disdain to use this narrow argument in the House of Commons itself.

In addition to their insular prejudices the English working classes believed in the blessings of scarcity, and the miseries of abundance. They lived constantly in fear of an impossible dragon called "overproduction." They regarded machinery as their chief enemy because it saved labor, and filled shops and warehouses with goods. It was the grimy coal-fed monster, breathing smoke and flame whose offspring was "overproduction." They opposed railroads because of their labor-saving tendency, and many of them could tell the exact number of men thrown "out of work," between London and Bristol, by the Great Western Railway alone. There were so many stage coachmen and guards, so many wagoners whose busy teams moved the merchandise of the country, so many inns where the stages stopped for dinner, and to change horses, involving the employment of so many hostlers, cooks, waiters, and other people. Then look at the blacksmiths, whose business it was to shoe the stage horses, and the wagon horses; look at the harness-makers, whose business it was to make the harness for them. Think of the ruin of the inn-keepers themselves, to say nothing of the loss to the farmers and stock-raisers, who would no longer have a market for coach horses, or wagon horses, or for the oats to feed them. It was useless to point out the army of men that the railroads would throw "into work," the comforts and conveniences they would multiply to all the people. These advantages were too abstract and remote. The injuries were direct, near, and palpable.

In the political economy of the English artisan, all destruction of property was a blessing, because, to replace the property gave employment to workingmen. The burning down of a block of buildings was a providential gift, because the houses had to be rebuilt, thereby giving employment to bricklayers and carpenters. About this time a remarkable hailstorm visited London.

Every exposed pane of glass was broken by the hailstones. This was regarded as a merciful dispensation, because it made a scarcity of glass in London. It was merely a sum in simple addition to show the value of the storm. It was evident that the glass-makers and the glaziers would make a good thing out of it, and the money they earned would be spent for the comforts and necessaries of life. The tailor and the shoemaker would get some of it, and the butcher, the baker, and the candlestick-maker. It was useless to explain that this money was drawn from other employments of industry, and that to the full value of the glass destroyed it was a total loss to the community. This, too, was abstract; it was like complex fractions to scholars who were not yet out of long division.

All public improvements that lessened wear and tear were bitterly opposed by those primitive economists. The wooden pavement was a dangerous innovation, because, if it should be generally used in a great city like London, it was easy to see that the wear and tear of horse-shoes and wagon-wheels would be greatly lessened, and blacksmiths would be thrown "out of work." A street sweeping machine, invented about this time, had to be protected by the police, as a mob of scavengers were determined to prevent its use. It was claimed that the machine could do the work of twenty men. The scavengers, of course, made their living by dirt; the more dirt, the more work for them. Here was a machine that caused an "overproduction" of cleanliness, and, true to their protectionist ideas, they proceeded to destroy it.

There is nothing surprising in all this. An ignorant people only reason from first appearances to the immediate and visible result. To the unthinking workingmen of England, the first effect of a labor-saving machine was to throw somebody "out of work"; the first effect of the hailstorm was to throw somebody "into work"; therefore they looked upon the machine as an enemy, upon the storm as a friend. In like manner, the first effect of a cargo of merchandise imported from a foreign country was to make abundance apparently and to lessen the demand for labor in that class of goods, although creating a greater demand for labor in the production of other things to pay for them; therefore they were in favor of promoting scarcity by a high protective tariff that should compel those foreign goods to stay across the sea.

It was not to be expected that the workingmen would voluntarily explore the depths of political science, and thus obtain a knowledge of the true principles of social and political economy. As reasonably might they have been expected to saw wood for pleasure. Their minds became tired when not aided by visible object lessons, and the men who could appeal to their mutual experiences had a great advantage over the abstract reasoner, no matter how well-built his logical structure was. Often, in the coffee-houses, the club-rooms and other places where workingmen used to meet and discuss the problems of the English political and social system, the Protectionist champion, confused and overwhelmed by the reasoning of his Free Trade antagonist, would extricate himself by an ingenious recourse to the "overproduction" hobgoblin. "What caused the distress," he would shout, "in the hard winter of 1835?" "Overproduction." "What shut down the Birmingham forges in 1836?" "Overproduction." "What stopped the wheels in Lancashire and Yorkshire in 1837?" "Overproduction." "What sent the shoemakers of Northampton on the tramp in 1838?" "Overproduction ;" and so on, to the end of the chapter. It was certain that among the audience were some of the fancied victims of overproduction, and all the rest were sympathizers. It was of no use to explain to them that what they called "overproduction" was nothing but the blessing of plenty, which, if not hindered by protective legislation, would soon diffuse itself throughout all the land, sharing its benefits among all the people, acting and re-acting upon every member of the community. Nor could they see that overproduction was a misleading name for under-consumption resulting from poverty and the inability to buy. To comprehend all this required a mental effort, and that was labor. They were not ready to think, just then, and the discomfited Free Trader would take his seat, leaving the victory to his adversary. The workingmen of England had literally to be educated in sounder principles, to be taught like children, from the alphabet of politics upward until they were forced to throw aside their prejudices to make room for the knowledge that was crowding itself upon them. "If you bring the truth home to a man," said Cobden, "he must embrace it." To bring the truth home to the people of England became the duty of the League. Let us see how well the work was done.

"What is 'over' in our production?" inquired the *Westminister Review*. "Do they mean that we have produced more than other nations want, or more than they are able to pay for? They could not mean this for it would be a palpable falsehood, or do they mean— they must if they mean anything—more than our legislators, will allow us to exchange with those who do want it? Does this charge mean that even our own countrymen are all filled and comfortably clothed? Or does it mean that we have produced not more than our people want but more than they are able to buy? Does it not mean that our aristocracy have so impoverished the laboring classes by injustice and oppression that they have no longer the means of purchasing sufficient supplies for the necessaries of life? And they then turn round upon the manufacturers and reproach them with having produced the necessaries of life in too great abundance. The fact is simply this, that almost any amount of production may be made excessive by laws which forbid the purchase of the articles produced; and that almost any amount may be made insufficient, by the restraint of that perfect liberty of commerce which permits to every nation its full capacity of interchange."

The working people of England were divided into two classes, the city operatives and the rural population. They differed from each other in dress, in dialect, in manners, and in personal appearance. The city workman was quick of movement and of great mental activity, the farm laborer was heavy, dull, and slow. He aspired to nothing higher than eating, drinking, and rest. Although the Corn-Laws were made for the "Protection" of agricultural industry, the tiller of the soil was overworked and underpaid. His life was passed in abject poverty. He had no more hope than the team he drove. He was still in fact—though not in law—a serf; and he went with the land. Whoever bought that, bought him. In 1843 the traveler in the West Riding of Yorkshire, meeting a rustic with a drove of hogs in front of him, looked for the brass collar about his neck, expecting to read upon it the old familiar legend preserved by Scott: "Gurth, the son of Beowolf, is the born thrall of Cedric of Rotherwood." The brass collar was not there, but the swineherd was as much a "thrall" as was his ancestor in the days of Wilfred of Ivanhoe. Less than sixty miles from London, and within hearing of the college bells of Cambridge, the roughshod clown thrashed his master's grain with a flail, as his forefathers did in the days of Alfred the Great. He knew no more than they, and his dialect was very much like theirs. Of the politics of England he knew about as much as he did of the politics of Japan. Although great in numbers the agricultural laborers contributed literally nothing to that public opinion which is so important an element in the Government of England. When the Free Trade missionaries went amongst them they were mobbed and pelted out of the villages by the "yeomanry" and the agents of the landlords. They were treated very much as Abolition lecturers would be treated by the Carolina planters in the days before the war.

It was different with the working people in the towns. They were restless, ambitious, and discontented. They mingled much together, and they discussed political and social problems. They formed clubs, benefit societies, and trades unions. They attended political meetings and debating clubs; they read a great deal, and they could furnish more stump orators to the hundred men than even we can furnish in America. There was always a speaker on hand, and an audience. It is a prevalent opinion that the "stump orator" is peculiarly an American production, but this is a mistake. He abounds in England, and there his talk flows on for ever. It is not confined as in America to the election season; it flourishes at all seasons. It is perennial in England, and always fresh and blooming. One reason for this is that the drinking places in England are also places of resort. They are not "saloons" as in America, merely drinking places, and nothing more. They are what their name expresses, "public houses." They have rooms apart from the bar, and in those rooms men sit down and drink their beer. There they smoke their pipes and talk. Besides the "tap-room" and the "parlor," which are promiscuous and belong to everybody, there are rooms up-stairs for society meetings, clubs, and exclusive gatherings. Here business, debate, and conviviality mingle together. The orator fires away while the audience drink their beer and smoke. If the English public houses have rendered any compensation for the mischief they have made, it must be in furnishing those rooms for association, and for the discussion of public questions. They have been the nurseries of the stump orators of England. For the reason above given it was necessarily in the towns that the principal work of the League was done.

At first the League met with opposition even in the towns; and its meetings were often interrupted by hostile mobs,.and sometimes broken up. The Chartists insisted that a radical reform of the Government itself should be attempted before economic changes. When universal suffrage and a free ballot were obtained, then would be time enough to repeal the Corn-Laws; and they demanded that the League should unite with them. Besides, the jealousy of foreign competition was not easily removed; "foreign pauper labor" was still a phrase to conjure with; and there was a prevalent suspicion that the object of the League was to lower the wages of the workingmen. In 1843 *The Quarterly Review* made the accusation in these words: "The first great object of the League was and is the lowering of wages." This view of it had prevailed from the very first organization of the League, and often in the Free Trade meetings the Chartists were able to defeat the Free Trade resolutions and carry resolutions of their own. In 1839 there was a great Anti-Corn-Law meeting at Rochdale, at which Mr. Bright offered a Free Trade resolution, and supported it with one of his most convincing speeches; but Mr. James Taylor, a Chartist, proposed an amendment to the effect that before agitating for a repeal of the Corn-Laws the people should obtain possession of their political rights. The amendment was adopted. In Smith's Life of John Bright, the biographer in relating this incident, remarks: "The amendment was carried, the Chartists at that moment having the ear of the working classes in the chief towns of Lancashire and Yorkshire." In the position they took on that question the Chartists were not wise. The result has demonstrated that a hungry people, while politically they may be more dangerous, are morally not half so strong as the same people when well fed. The improved condition of the workingmen of England under a Free Trade policy has strengthened their moral influence so greatly that now the Charter is almost won. Henry Vincent, one of the founders of the Chartist party and its greatest orator, on the occasion of his last visit to America, said to the writer of this book, "We shall soon have the suffrage in England, where any man who is fit to use it can reach forth his hand and take it."

One paragraph as to the Chartists for the information of the American reader. The Chartists were a democratic, and to some extent, a revolutionary body, seeking a radical change in the political constitution of England. Their demands were embodied in a document called the Charter containing the following six points, 1. Universal Suffrage; 2. Vote by Ballot; 3. Annual Parliaments; 4. Equal Electoral Districts; 5. No Property Qualification for Members of Parliament, and 6. Payment of Members. Of these it will be seen that only the first and second are important principles, the others relating merely to matters of detail and expediency. The second and fifth have been obtained, and the suffrage has been so greatly extended by progressive laws that now the English ballot is where Mr. Vincent said it would be, within the reach of nearly every man with enterprise enough to lift his hand and take it. In the years of the Free Trade struggle the Chartists included within their ranks two-thirds of all the workingmen of England and Scotland, outside the farm laborers. They had no strength in Ireland because Mr. O'Connell, who was then the paramount leader of the Irish people, kept them from joining the party. Although he was one of the original committee of ten that framed the Charter, he had become alarmed at the revolutionary character of the Chartists, and had abandoned them. It will readily be seen that the opposition of so large a body as the Chartist party was a serious obstacle in the way of the League. It may be acknowledged here also, that some of the leaders of the Chartist party were jealous of the leaders of the League. The Annual Register for 1839, speaking of the Chartists and their opposition to the repeal of the Corn-Laws, says, "in their opinion any relaxation of the duties upon the importation of corn would, by lowering the rate of wages turn to the profit of the employer alone."

CHAPTER IX.

WAGES.

The "low wages" delusion was kept alive by all the Tory journals, and by all the opponents of revenue reform. Here is a specimen argument taken from *The Quarterly Review* for December, 1842: "But even if Mr. Cobden could persuade us that his zeal was not strongly imbued with political ambition, can he deny—though he seems inclined to conceal it—that he and his associates were first prompted and are still stimulated in their warfare against the Corn-Laws by a more ignoble interest—mere mercantile gain—*the profit of the mills?* This it is that supplies the source and feeds the current of this agitation. This is the secret head of this muddy and inundating Nile. The leaders of the League, not satisfied with the great and sometimes enormous fortunes that have been realized under the present system of food and wages, are endeavoring by the undue influences of confederation, intimidation, and deception—to reduce wages still lower—to the great injury of the working classes, the ruin of the agricultural interest, and to no immediate profit but their own." Then, in order to make its criticism of the League still more impressive, it condensed the whole argument into a mathematical formula, thus: "The pretense that those mill-owners are endeavoring to lower the price of bread *for the sake of the workmen* is so absurd that we really know not how to expose it more forcibly than by four words, *cheap bread=low wages.*" *The Review* ended a very bitter article against the League by insinuating that it was a disloyal and illegal confederacy. It said, "We pronounce the existence of such associations disgraceful to our national character, and wholly incompatible either with the internal peace and commercial prosperity of the country —or in the highest meaning of the words, the SAFETY OF THE STATE."

That article in the *Quarterly* was written by the Right Hon. John Wilson Croker, a face-to-the-rear placeman, who had been in office from a boy, a relic of that old King George Toryism in Church and State which relentlessly "put down" reforms of every kind, especially reforms which promised more comfort and higher dignity to the people. In the politics of his youth and the meridian of his manhood, every advance toward freedom was a menace to the State, and now in his old age he showed the spirit of persecution without the power to persecute, by theatrically warning the Government that the League ought to be put down for the "safety of the State." *Fraser's Magazine* saw nothing "petty or mean" in raising the value of land by increasing the price of bread, and said: "In truth there is nothing of petty expediency or mean contrivance in the principle on which our Corn-Laws rest. Nothing can be broader, more solid, or more permanent than the principle that it is the first and paramount duty to protect the agriculturist of the country from the competition of those who in Poland or Prussia can by paying lower rents and lower wages greatly undersell our farmers. We neither wish to reduce the landed property of England to one-half its present value, nor our laborers to one-half their present wages. We deny that low prices are necessarily a benefit to the country."

While some of the Protection journals confined their opposition to angry denunciations of the League, others did that and more. They tried not only to arouse the prejudices and inflame the passions, but to convince the reason also. Of this class was *Blackwood's Magazine*, perhaps the ablest advocate and defender of the Corn-Laws in all Great Britain. To be sure there was much sophistry in its argument, and no doubt it said a great deal that it did not believe; but after all it *was* argument, most of it plausible, and most of it very hard to answer, because at that time experience had not shown the mistakes in it. In November, 1838, *Blackwood's* reasoned thus: "Is it then really certain that an unrestricted importation of foreign grain would in the long run lower the money price of provisions to the British laborers? . . . . It might at first . . . . We have little doubt that the result in the end would be that the price of subsistence would be raised to the British consumer. The first effect would be to cheapen. That would throw the land out of cultivation. Home production would be small, and then of course the price of the foreign product would be increased."

The above argument is worth study, because although falsified by actual experiment in England, it is just as good as new in America. It was as confidently proclaimed in Congress in 1892 as it was by *Blackwood's* in 1838. All that the American reader has to do with these quotations is to change the word "grain" into "iron," "wool," "crockery" or whatever it is, and the

Tory arguments of fifty years ago are immediately reproduced in the "Protection" reasoning of 1892 in the United States. Any person can recognize them instantly who reads the debates in Congress, or the editorials in our Protectionist newspapers. The writer of the article from which the above quotation is taken, ingeniously hand-cuffs wages and rent together, and pretends that they must rise and fall together, thus falsely pretending that the workingman is beneficially interested in dear land and high rent, when the very opposite of the doctrine is true. He then says, "There would be no increase of supply, but we should get from foreign countries instead of raising it in England. That's all." The echo of this exploded argument is repeatedly heard in the United States, although the sound of it has long been dead in England. Instead of saying fields will be thrown out of cultivation we say furnaces will be "blown out," mills will be "stopped," and then the "foreigner" having destroyed our home production will raise his prices, so that by lowering the tariff we make only temporary cheapness, to be followed in the end by higher prices, which we pay to the "foreigner" instead of to our own people. The most subtle analysis could not convince the English of the fallacy of this argument. They would not be convinced except by practical demonstration; they laugh at it now.

Mere speculative guesses were propounded by the Protectionists as though they were axioms that could not be disputed. For instance *Blackwood's*, in that same article, "The fundamental error of the opponents of the Corn-Laws on this point is that they suppose two things that can never co-exist, viz., permanently reduced prices, and a permanently overflowing supply." This dogmatic mode of expression silenced many disputants by the sheer impudence of it. Forty-six years' experience has proven that permanent cheapness, and permanent supply can and do co-exist. That prices vary is true, for they are affected by a hundred accidents, but the cheapness of bread and meat in England has been permanent ever since the repeal of the Corn-Laws, and the supply has been abundant and permanent. Besides, the ability to buy is an important ingredient of cheapness, and to increase this ability was one of the avowed objects of the Free Traders. Mr. Cobden repeatedly said that the mere nominal price of an article was a secondary consideration if the consumers of it were prosperous and had plenty of money to pay for it. It is undisputed that the ration of food enjoyed by the workingman of England is twice as large as it was fifty years ago. How does he get it? He buys it. What with? His wages. And this is a demonstration that the abolition of the protective system was followed by higher wages, because the increased consumption shows increased ability to buy.

Following the same train of reasoning the writer in *Blackwood's* goes on to say, "The impetus given to foreign agriculture would immediately and considerably lower the price of foreign grain, while the same causes would in the same proportions lower that of British. The foreign grower would beat down the British and get a monopoly of the British market into his hands." Let the reader substitute "American" for "British" in the above extract, and "manufactures" for "agriculture," and he will at once recognize a prominent figure in the tariff debate of 1892. The discarded English rags are patched and renovated, and soaped and brushed until they look like new, and our statesmen wear them with benighted vanity and pride. Having thrown all the land of England out of cultivation, and thus terrified the farmers, the writer proceeds to scare the workingmen in towns by the spectre of "low wages." He says: "Could the manufacturing operatives or any class of laborers keep their money wages up to their present level if a permanent reduction in the price of the necessaries of life had taken place? Nothing is clearer than that they could not. The money rate of wages wholly independent of the price of provisions from year to year is entirely regulated by it, other things being equal from ten years to ten years. If by the free importation of foreign grain the money price of it is reduced one-half, the ultimate result will be that wages will fall one-half also."

It was not known in England at that time, although some people suspected it, that the actual reverse of this was the true doctrine of wages, and that in proportion to the cheapness of food, clothing, rent, furniture and essential comforts was the independence of the laboring man; and in proportion to that independence was his command over the hours of labor and the rate of wages. It was prophesied that in a condition of physical comfort he could work less hours, and thus diminish competition in the labor market, and increase the rate of wages. In England a man might as well dispute the laws of Kepler now as this law, that in proportion to the dearness of home necessaries to the laborer, so is the hardness of his labor, and the length of his working day.

The infallible authority among Protectionists is Adam Smith, whenever they find a paragraph written by him which seems to lean toward their side. Pleased as a miner who has found a big nugget, this writer in *Blackwood's* said, "Mr. Smith has long ago stated that the most profitable trade in every State is that which is carried on between the town and the country, and that the home market for our manufactures is worth all foreign markets put together." This doctrine has many qualifications. Often a country excels in manufactures which the native people do not use, or use to a limited extent, and then the rule fails. The people in a cold climate may excel greatly in the manufacture of an article which is used only in a hot climate, or like the watchmakers of Switzerland, they may excel in the manufacture of a luxury far in excess of the needs or means of their own people, and there also the rule fails. Again, the very condition of the doctrine is the prosperity of the home customer, and when that fails, the rule ceases. Under the strain of this test the doctrine broke down altogether in 1843. In that year the price of grain went so low as to greatly embarrass the farming community, and the reason was that their town customers had become too poor to buy bread enough to eat.

Two years after this, in June, 1840, *Blackwood's* again referred to the Corn-Laws, and condemned the effort to abolish them. With a supercilious air of patronage to the workingmen, it affected to regard the most tremendous question that had appeared in English politics since the revolution of 1688, as a merely sentimental difference between the Whigs and the Tories, or as the clamor of a set of demagogues to serve their personal ambition. It pretended that the mighty matter of a people's food was a trifling affair in which the workingmen and their families had little or no concern. It said: "With regard to the working classes we humbly conceive that their interest in this matter is of the slenderest possible description. The additional cheapness of food which is promised them, would probably never be realized, and at any rate seems a boon of the most insignificant magnitude. If accompanied with a corresponding or more than a corresponding decrease of wages, which it infallibly would be, its advantage would entirely be destroyed. But the cry of cheap bread has long ceased to operate as a charm. The workingmen are too well informed to believe now that cheap bread is necessarily a boon to them . . . . Corn, we are told, is the standard of wages. If so, it is impossible that wages should not fall in amount in at least the same proportion as bread . . . . Cheap bread and cheap sugar mean, we believe, nothing less than lower wages, less prosperity, and increased competition of manual labor."

The artful manner in which the folly and ignorance of the workingmen are complimented as wisdom and information, is worthy of all praise; especially as it came from a journal which defended the disfranchisement of workingmen on the ground that they were too ignorant to vote. It would do credit to a first-class demagogue here. So also there was a creditable display of cunning in the smooth encouragement given to the mischievous error about the law of wages which was misleading the workingmen of England at that time. They believed that wages was a certain allowance given by employers at their own will, and that they established it on the quantity of food, clothing, and other comforts absolutely necessary to enable the artizan to live and work; much as the Southern planter established the rations for his slaves. They believed that the employers were constantly watching to see how little the workingmen could subsist on, and that whenever they found they could do without something formerly enjoyed, wages would be lowered, because no longer necessary to buy that comfort, whatever it was. To this mistake was largely due the improvidence of the workingmen. They thought that economy was a vice and a meanness that a workingman ought not to be guilty of, because it threatened the wages of his brother craftsmen. The theory was that when the masters found that the men could live on less, they would reduce their wages to the new standard of subsistence. The temperance movement in England was resisted by the workingmen on that principle. The brewers and publicans employed good talkers among the workingmen to proclaim that doctrine on the stump. They declared that the temperance movement was a scheme of the masters to lower wages, that for centuries the absolute necessity of beer to strengthen the workingman had been considered in establishing the rate of wages, and that if it should be demonstrated that he could do without beer, that element in his wages would be taken away. With loud scorn they would inquire, "Wot's a man without his beer?" and the answer would be a round of applause. For years a teetotaler was regarded as a spiritless fellow willing to put wages in jeopardy. Those ignorant people were the men that *Blackwood's* was wheedling and flattering as "too well informed" to believe that cheap bread was a desirable thing. A touch of sadness falls upon us at the bare suspicion that the crafty article above quoted was perhaps written by the great Kit North himself.

But the "low wages" delusion was not confined to the workingmen; many of the statesmen of the country entertained it, as the debates in Parliament will show. Sir Robert Peel himself, in his memoirs, confesses that for a long time he was misled by it, as he was by other assumptions of the protection pleaders. He says: "I had adopted, at the early period of my public life, without, I fear, much serious reflection, the opinion generally pervading at that time among men of all parties as to the justice and necessity of protection to domestic agriculture; they were the opinions of Sir H. Parnell, Mr. Ricardo, Lord John Russell and Lord Melbourne, as well as the Duke of Wellington, Mr. Canning and Mr. Huskisson." Neither was it proclaimed by the Protectionists alone; many of the Free Trade party conceded the principle that cheap food lowered wages, but not so much, they said, as to counterbalance the advantages of the cheapness. As far back as 1834 *The Edinburgh Review*, a Free Trade advocate, in an article on the poems of Ebenezer Elliott, just then published, which poems were chiefly devoted to a passionate condemnation of the Corn-Laws, said: "Mr. Ebenezer Elliott admits that, as a class, the peasant is at present much worse off than the mechanic.  The peasant would be worse off still, were a repeal of the Corn-Laws, by lessening a demand for his labor, to lower his wages or throw him out of employment. To whatever other objections the Corn-Laws may be exposed, our temporary facilities for the production of manufactures have been so vast that it may be doubted whether our manufacturing population has hitherto lost anything in real wages; or in employment from the addition made by the Corn-Laws to the price of bread."

Afterward, *The Edinburgh Review* changed its opinion, and admitted that wages rose as prices fell; and in eloquent criticism, which is as valuable in America to-day as it was in England then, denounced "That barbarous commercial code which every day tends more and more to diminish our enjoyments, to misdirect our industry, to render our trade hazardous, as well as unproductive, and to divide society into hostile sections. . . . In time we shall feel the wickedness of exposing millions to privation in order to supply affluence to thousands, and, in time, the small class that governs us will discover that the permanence of its rule depends on its escaping the charge of selfish legislation."

There was but one way to reach the minds of workingmen saturated with hereditary prejudices, jealous of all foreign rivalry, suspicious of the "masters" and densely ignorant of the laws of work and wages, of markets and of prices. That way was taken by the League. It was hard work to teach the abstract principles of political economy, or to show the ultimate advantages of Free Trade. The surest way to reach the multitude was by the concrete argument of a big loaf of bread for a small sum of money. A big loaf was an object lesson they could easily understand, and when throughly learned it made even abstract lessons easy. It was easily shown that the laws for the "protection of native industry" actually excluded from England shiploads of cheap flour and meal and meat that wanted to come in; that thereby scarcity was created by force of law, and the obvious and intended effect of the scarcity was to increase the price of bread. In the Free Trade processions big loaves of bread, called Free Trade loaves, and small ones, called Protection loaves, were carried on poles and exhibited at the meetings. It was thought even by the Free Traders that the discrepancy in the size of the loaves was a little exaggerated, but this was considered pardonable at the time. The result of the Free Trade policy has proved, however, that, considering the improved power of buying bread now possessed by the workingman, the discrepancy was not exaggerated at all. The big loaf argument at last took fast hold of the workingmen in the towns, and, although they still clung to their sentimental politics, and demanded radical measures of parliamentary reform, a majority of them became disciples and adherents of the League. There was clap-trap in this mode of argument, no doubt of it, but it was mathematical clap-trap, for the Free Traders proved by arithmetic how much the tariff increased the price of a barrel of flour; then it was easy to show by the rule of three what the size of a sixpenny loaf would be if the tax were taken from the flour of which it was made. The counter argument of "low wages" was weakened when Cobden showed that in the experience of the men he was talking to, wages did not rise with the rise in the price of bread. The Protectionists tried to explain this by saying that the law did not adjust itself to sudden changes like those from year to year, but that "from ten years to ten years" it did. This was not convincing, and the argument lost ground.

The Free Traders acted wisely in the very beginning of the struggle by refusing to entangle themselves by any alliance with either of the "two great parties" inside Parliament, or with the third great party, the unrepresented Chartists outside. They kept in view the one great object, the repeal of the Corn-Laws, and directed all of their energies to that. Between 1839 and 1844, the League had distributed nine million tracts among the people, and had furnished a Free Trade library to nearly every voter in the kingdom. This was Cobden's way of "bringing the truth home to a man." It cost a great deal of money, but the League had plenty. Cobden, Bright, and many orators of lesser note were continually engaged in addressing public meetings, and every part of England was canvassed; not the manufacturing towns alone, but also the rural districts. In 1842, Mr. Cobden and Mr. Bright held meetings in many parts of Scotland, and they had little trouble in convincing the people of that country that the protective system was injurious to every business and to every industry there. Mr. Bright confessed that the people of Scotland understood political economy much better than the people of England, and because of their superior intelligence and information a large proportion of them were Free Traders.

The business depression and the poverty of the people, were, of course, potent arguments in the speeches of the leaders of the League. During the winter of 1842-43 the League and its literature were everywhere, and men who could not read were compelled to listen. Great meetings were held, and all the people in the towns were excited to a discussion of the great question. The *Annual Register* for 1843, referring to the agitation, said: "Amidst the general stagnation and distress that prevailed, the Anti-Corn-

10

Law League forced themselves upon the public ear, and they failed not to avail themselves freely of the themes of depression and distress as irresistible arguments against the continuance of that system of protection which they defied the Government with all its parliamentary majority to maintain." The excitement of the previous year, instead of being quieted by the amended tariff of 1842, and the modification of the sliding scale, had been increased, if possible, by those measures. The League took advantage of every vacancy that occurred in the House of Commons to arouse the public interest by putting up Free Trade candidates, and although they were generally beaten at the polls, because the majority of the citizens were disfranchised, they made it uncomfortably plain that popular opinion was in their favor although the voting majorities were generally against them. In the spring of 1843, a vacancy having occurred for Durham, Mr. Bright offered himself as a candidate, and although the show of hands was largely in his favor, he was defeated by Lord Dungannon, the protectionist candidate, by a majority of 102 in a poll of 912 votes. In July, Lord Dungannon having been unseated for bribery, Mr. Bright offered himself again, and this time he was elected over Mr. Purvis, the protectionist candidate, by 488 against 410. This, although a small matter in itself, was ominous of future disaster to the protectionist cause. The landlords became alarmed and began to distrust the Tory Government itself, for some of the ministers had made use of reasons and dropped expressions in debate and elsewhere, which although purely abstract, and having no relation to any practical and immediate measures, were, after all, unorthodox.

The consequence was that they took up a weak defensive position, and gave the Free Traders all the advantage of a very enthusiastic attack.

By the autumn of 1843, the Free Trade agitation had reached immense proportions, and the Protectionists had almost ceased to contend against it in argument. Timid people now pretended to feel alarmed at its dimensions. They believed in the principle, but thought the League was carrying things too far. It was shaking society too much. The League was coarsely assailed by *The Times* and the Reviews, and some of the Tory papers called upon the Government to suppress it as a seditious and treasonable conspiracy. Lord Brougham, in the House of Lords, and Mr. Roebuck, in the House of Commons, both Free Traders, assailed the League with vehement anger. Its answer to all this denunciation was redoubled activity. Meetings were held in the agricultural districts right among the farmers, and Free Trade resolutions carried. At Bedford, Mr. Cobden maintained a six hours' debate with the farmers of that county, and at the end of it a Free Trade resolution was carried by more than two to one. This was the most disheartening fact of all. The Tory papers bitterly denounced their own men, because they had not the courage to meet Cobden and Bright in argument, and when they did meet them, confessed themselves defeated by Free Trade fallacies that might easily be answered.

London was roused at last. The great halls were found quite insufficient for the Free Trade meetings. They would not hold a quarter of the multitudes that flocked to hear the Free Trade orators, so Drury Lane Theatre was engaged for the purpose. Petitions to

Parliament asking for Free Trade were displayed at the street corners, and signed by thousands of people. To emphasize the struggle a vacancy in Parliament for the city of London occurred in the fall of 1843. After a severe contest, Mr. Pattison, the Free Trade candidate, was elected over the Tory candidate, Mr. Baring, a nephew of Lord Ashburton, and a man of great wealth and personal popularity. This was an omen of further disaster to the protectionists, and although the physical force of their majority in the House of Commons still remained intact, its moral vigor was visibly crumbling under the pressure of the League.

Early in the contest the opponents of the Corn-Laws discovered that a mere struggle to obtain for the manufacturing "interest" an advantage over the agricultural "interest" in the protective legislation of the country would have no moral strength whatever. They saw that in a competition to readjust the tariff on a basis more favorable for themselves, and less favorable for landlords, their own arguments would be turned against them. The manufacturers soon discovered that their demand upon the agriculturists to surrender the privilege of extorting taxes from the people must be accompanied by an offer to surrender their own power to do the same thing. Although some consented to this plan with reluctance, and maintained that the manufacturing interest should be "protected" in order to "diversify industry," and create a "home market" for the farmers, it was agreed that the only just and scientific reform was to equalize the privileges of all classes by a horizontal sweep-away of the whole protective system, and that all duties on imports must be assessed and collected on the basis of "a tariff for revenue only."

In accordance with that principle, the manufacturers of Manchester, Leeds, Liverpool, Sheffield, Derby, Wolverhampton, Birmingham and Glasgow, at their convention held on the 5th of July, 1839, declared "that this meeting, while it demands as an act of justice the total and immediate repeal of all laws imposing duties upon, and restricting the importation of corn and other articles of subsistence, is prepared to resign all claims to protection on home manufactures, and to carry out to their fullest extent, both as affects agriculture and manufactures, the true and peaceful principles of Free Trade, by removing all existing obstacles to the unrestricted interchange of industry and capital among nations."

CHAPTER X.

RECIPROCITY.

The year 1844 opened brightly for Sir Robert Peel and his Government. There had been a fair harvest, food was more abundant, trade and manufactures were reviving, the revenue receipts exceeded the estimates, and there was a hopeful feeling throughout the country. The improved appearance of public affairs, it was thought by many, had weakened the League. This may be doubted, but it had surely strengthened the ministry and enabled Sir Robert Peel to speak in an emphatic tone when he proclaimed the intention of the Government to maintain the "settlement" of 1842, and that no further alterations in the Corn-Laws would be made. The strength of the Government may have held men back from joining the League or actively assisting it, because of the belief that the work was hopeless; but, although the Free Trade agitation in Parliament may have been less vigorous than in the preceding year, the strength of it outside had not abated. On the 21st of February an immense Free Trade meeting was held at Covent Garden Theatre, at which Mr. O'Connell made the principal speech. The theatre was packed in every part, and thousands of people were crowded outside, unable to gain admission. Other meetings in different parts of the country were equally crowded and enthusiastic. Still, for all that, the ministers were not afraid to meet Parliament.

They knew that their majority in the House of Commons was yet solid and invincible; the Chancellor of the Exchequer could show a good budget, and they believed that the conservative sentiment outside was quite strong enough to take care of the League. On the 1st day of February, 1844, the Queen opened Parliament in person, and the speech from the throne contained this paragraph : "I congratulate you on the improved condition of several branches of the trade and manufactures of the country. I trust that the increased demand for labor has relieved, in a corresponding degree, many classes of my faithful subjects from sufferings and privations, which, at former periods, I have had occasion to deplore."

As Sir Robert Peel walked down to the House of Commons to meet Parliament at the opening of the session of 1844, it was noticed that his eye was clear and bright, his step elastic, his bearing proud. The wearied look which he wore at the previous session was gone. His private letters written at this time show a revival of courage and a readiness, almost an eagerness, for debate. He was not afraid of the Free Traders now. He was fortified with a weapon of defense against them, which, curiously enough, they themselves had furnished him. The country was comparatively prosperous, as he had proclaimed in the speech from the throne. Less than two years had gone since he had yielded a slight experimental modification of the tariff, and the success of it had been greater than even the "theorists" had prophesied. The reduction of import duties had been followed by an increased revenue from imports. The modification of the Corn-Laws, slight as it was, and a good harvest, had made bread cheaper, and to the utter confounding of the Protectionists, cheaper bread had been accompanied by higher wages. A small abatement of the protective system had been followed by increased manufacturing activity, capital had come forth from its hiding places, and was invested in farming, in trade, and in manufactures; labor was in demand, and the Prime Minister might properly have said, "If last year I was individually responsible for the distress of the country, I am personally entitled this year to credit for its prosperity."

The term prosperity here must be understood in a comparative sense only. There was poverty yet in the land, and hunger more than enough, but compared with the previous year the improvement was very great. Strangely enough, the success of the slight advance made by Peel toward Free Trade in the tariff of 1842, instead of stimulating him to proceed farther in the same direction made him hesitate, and finally halt, when to halt was to retreat. Help us to let well enough alone, was now the appeal of the minister to the House of Commons and the country. All the assaults of Cobden were parried by Peel with the Free Trade weapon he had borrowed from the League in 1842. By means of this, he said, I have improved the condition of the country; let us be content.

The country recognized that the "better times" were due to the labors of the League, but was not generous enough to say so. The action of the high-toned liberal papers was shuffling, compromising, and insincere. One of them, of great respectability and immense circulation, speaking joyfully of the Queen's speech and its congratulations to the country, said, "We express no opinion upon the effect of the speech upon the present Corn-Law agitation—the League does not want more vigorous opponents or more vigorous support than are engaged for or against it at the present crisis." As if every cause does not want all the support it can get. Its excuse for not supporting the League was that the League was strong enough already, and for not opposing it, that the enemies of the League were strong enough too. The truth, however, was that the liberal press was Protectionist in feeling, and afraid of change. The very paper from which the above extract is taken, in its first article for New Year's, 1844, in a rather passionate appeal to the Government concerning public affairs, and calling for all sorts of legislation in other directions, spoke thus timidly on the main question of the day, "Preserve the balance of power by sacrificing neither the commercialist nor the agriculturist to the cry of party;" which was easily translated to mean this, "As to the tariff and Corn-Laws, do nothing."

As water seeks its level, so does bread, if not hindered by artificial obstacles. No sooner did Sir Robert Peel lift the legislative barriers a couple of inches, than provisions from the United States and Canada began to flow through the opening into England, as appears by this interesting item which I quote from the *Illustrated London News* of January 20, 1844. "Some fresh importations of American and Colonial provisions advertised for sale on Thursday have excited considerable interest in the city. Samples were on view during the previous day at the office of the brokers, and were inspected by several members of Parliament and gentlemen from the Board of Trade, Victualling department of the Navy etc, etc. In the American beef, pork, and cheese, there is an obvious improvement both in the selection of qualities, and the care manifested in curing. Not only are they well adapted for ship's stores, but they are well calculated to afford a wholesome and nutritious aliment to numbers of our working classes, who have seldom the felicity of tasting animal food of any description." Like the Chairman of the Board of Guardians pronouncing on the quality of pauper soup, did the *Illustrated London News* in its lordly way patronize American beef and pork and cheese as rather vulgar invaders that might be tolerated for sailors and serfs, but not to be put in comparison for a moment with the beef and pork and cheese of England. Yet those provisions from the fertile and vigorous Western world were literally contributions from a son to his venerable mother, and without them Old England could not have lived in physical and moral health these fifty years gone by. And what a contradiction to the theoretical "beef-fed, and beer-drinking weaver," was the confession that "numbers of our working classes have seldom the felicity of tasting animal food of any description." In that last sentence the *Illustrated London News* unwittingly condemned the Corn-Laws.

Without stopping to consider any further who should have the credit of it, one thing is certain, the improved condition of the country gave the ministers a firmer grip on the Government, and when Mr. Hume and Lord John Russell, on the first day of the session, both complained that no reference to the Corn-Laws was made in the Queen's speech, Sir Robert Peel, feeling the full strength of his position, gave positive notice that no alteration would be made in the Corn-Laws.

Old Hume, however, nothing daunted, moved as an amendment to the address in answer to the royal speech, "that the provision laws should be considered and dealt with." He was overwhelmed by a majority of no less than 186 votes, the exact figures being: For the amendment 49, against it 235. Here again the Whigs and Tories voted "solid" for Protection.

As this book is written for American readers, and, as many of them are not acquainted with the somewhat intricate constitution of the English Parliament, a few words may not be out of place to explain why so many Lords have seats in the House of Commons. Briefly, then, all peers of the realm are lords, but all lords are not peers of the realm. All sons of Dukes and Marquises are "Lords" by courtesy, and the eldest sons of Dukes, Marquises and Earls are allowed by courtesy to bear the second titles of their fathers. Thus, the Marquis of Lorne bears the second title of his father, the Duke of Argyle, but he is only a commoner for all that, and in his commission as Governor-General of Canada he is described as John Campbell, Esquire, commonly called the Marquis of Lorne. Lord Randolph Churchill is only an esquire, although, being the youngest son of a Duke, he bears the title of Lord by courtesy. Therefore the Lords so frequently mentioned in the proceedings of the House of Commons are generally the younger sons of Dukes and Marquises or the eldest sons of Earls. Irish peers, also, not being peers of England, or of Great Britain, are eligible to seats in the House of Commons. Thus Lord Palmerston sat in that House until the day of his death, for he never was a peer of England, but of Ireland only. Some readers may be puzzled to understand how it happens that, in the beginning of this history, Lord Stanley takes part in the debates in the House of Commons, and toward the latter part of it appears in the House of Lords. The explanation is this: Lord Stanley was the eldest son of an Earl, and sat in the House of Commons, bearing, by courtesy, the second title of his father. During Peel's administration it was felt that the Tories needed a little more debating power in the House of Lords, and Lord Stanley was created a peer in his own right. It will thus be understood that where "Lords" are mentioned in the proceedings of the House of Commons, they are Lords by courtesy only, or peers of Ireland.

The first assault upon the tariff in the session of 1844 was an innocent question put by Mr. Pattison, the recently elected member for the city of London. Mr. Pattison inquired whether or not the sugar duties would be altered this session. Sir Robert Peel replied, "That is a question which I should have expected would have been asked by the youngest member of this house—for certainly nothing but the circumstance of a member being the youngest among us could justify such a question." As Mr. Pattison was a very great personage indeed, an elderly gentleman, member for the city of London, Governor of the Bank of England, and a member of Parliament years ago, the House enjoyed Peel's banter very much, for Mr. Pattison, having just been elected to fill a vacancy, was in fact the youngest member of the House. As Peel was a very serious man, who seldom "chaffed" anybody, the incident served to show that he was in high spirits because of the better appearance of public affairs, and the success of the measures he had adopted and passed in 1842. But the sugar question was up again in a few days in such a shape that it could not be jested out of court, but must be seriously discussed on its merits. It may be a matter of surprise that, as there was no sugar grown in England, the English Parliament should so persistently exclude foreign sugar from England by a high protective tariff; but the explanation is that the great sugar plantations of Jamaica and the other British West Indies were mostly owned by Englishmen, and the high tariff was defended on the ground that it was our duty "to protect the industry of our own colonies." To accomplish this patriotic object, and to insure dear sugar to the English people, all foreign sugar was excluded from British ports by a protective tariff amounting to 300 per cent *ad valorem*.

On the 6th of March Mr. Labouchere brought up the sugar question in a discussion of the commercial relations existing between Great Britain and Brazil. Mr. Labouchere had been a member of the Whig ministry; he was well provided with facts, and he made an argument that greatly embarrassed the Government. The debate is worth study, because of the striking parallel it shows between the commerce of England and Brazil in 1844 and that of the United States and Brazil in 1892. Mr. Labouchere showed the folly of the doctrine that exports make nations rich and imports make them poor. The highest duty levied on English goods by the customs laws of Brazil was 15 per cent *ad valorem*, while the useful products of Brazil were excluded from English ports by a protective tariff amounting to prohibition. The result of this nonsense was that an English vessel having carried a cargo of English goods to Brazil, and then exchanged them there for sugar, could not bring that sugar to England, but must take it to some third country and sell it there, returning home in ballast. The wisdom of sending ships out laden and bringing them back empty was as vehemently defended in the British Parliament in 1844 as it was in the American Parliament in 1892. Now, all the ports of Britain offer welcome to the wealth of Brazil. Her trade with Brazil is very great, while ours has become so contemptible that when our ambassador started for that country he was compelled to go to England in order to engage a passage to Rio Janeiro.

Mr. Gladstone finding himself quite unable to answer Mr. Labouchere with any statesmanlike or economic reasons, fell back to philanthropic and humanitarian ground. He declared that the effect of lowering the duty on Brazilian sugar would be to encourage the continuation of slavery in Brazil, and whatever the commercial advantage might be, they must not overlook the considerations of humanity. This was cant, so transparent that it imposed not on anybody, and Mr. Gladstone's embarrassed manner showed that it had not imposed on him. He easily defeated Mr. Labouchere by a majority of seventy-three.

Early in the session Mr. Cobden gave notice of a motion for a special committee to inquire into the effects of import duties in their bearing upon tenant farmers and farm laborers. This was carrying the war into Africa; it was part of the aggressive policy of the League. The majority in Parliament had been contending that those duties were imposed for the "protection" of those very classes whose condition Mr. Cobden proposed to inquire into. They dared not grant the motion, for they well knew that Cobden would bring a hatful of facts to demonstrate that every year the tenant farmer was sinking deeper into debt, and that the farm laborer was tottering on the very verge of starvation. "I only seek for inquiry," said Mr. Cobden, "and I want both sides to be heard." "Nothing would suit me better than for Lord Spencer and Lord Ducie to be examined on the one side, and the Duke of Richmond and the Duke of Buckingham on the other." He then went on to show that every prediction about corn had formerly been uttered about wool, "but," he inquired, "is there any lack of mutton? Are all the sheep-dogs dead, and all the shepherds in the poorhouse? So far from it that when wool was at the highest price the largest quantity had been imported; when at the lowest price the smallest quantity." This apparent paradox he explained by showing that ability to buy is an important agent in fixing prices. He condensed his explanation into the following sentence, "A high price from prosperity may be permanent, a high price from scarcity must always be precarious." This was new learning to the House of Commons, and many of the members were startled by the doctrine. Peel himself became very thoughtful under the lesson, and acknowledged afterward that the argument was new to him, and that it made a great impression upon him. Gladstone, too, looked very serious, for he was to answer Cobden. Then the orator turned upon the landlords with one of those fact-and-figure accusations that always made them tremble. He went right into the sanctuary of their order and smote the idol rent. "I can prove," he said, "that out of fifty-two shillings a quarter paid for wheat in the Lothians, twenty-six shillings goes to the landlord; and so it is likewise throughout England, half of what is eaten goes to the landlord." He concluded by pouring scornful satire upon the "home market" superstition. "You starve the agriculturists," he said, "and then offer them to us as a valuable class of home customers."

This speech is a conspicuous milestone on the Free Trade road. It had a great effect, and many protectionists were unsettled by it. *The Times*, then strong Tory and Protectionist, a scornful critic and hater of Cobden, confessed its power, and said that Mr. Cobden had stated his case "with great temper and moderation." It then lectured its own party with some asperity, and regretted that the Conservatives by their own neglect should have allowed the question of the condition of the agricultural class to fall into Mr. Cobden's hands at all. Mr. Gladstone, in reply, declared that it was a "very able speech," and he complimented Mr. Cobden on the deep impression it had evidently made upon the House. At the same time he questioned the correctness of Mr. Cobden's calculations, and also the inferences he drew from them. He opposed the motion on the ground that a select committee could do no practical good, while the mere appointing of it might have a paralyzing effect upon trade and revenue. It would alarm the agriculturists who would regard the success of the motion as indicating another attack upon their interests, and a change in the existing law. Mr. Gladstone spoke in the embarrassed manner of an advocate, who has a strong suspicion that the other side is right, and that he himself is wrong. He "questioned" and "doubted," but was afraid to go to the jury lest his doubts might be removed. "I will prove what I say," declared Cobden, "if you will grant the committee." "I don't think you can," said Gladstone, "and I will not grant the committee."

The aim and effect of Cobden's argument was to show that while all the people were taxed for the benefit of agriculture, the men who did the plowing, and the sowing, and the reaping, and the mowing, got none of the proceeds, and that the luxurious landlords got it all. In "theory" the tax was a protection to industry; in practice it was a premium upon idleness.

The precursor of our inverted American statesmen who advocate a tariff for protection with incidental revenue appeared in the person of a dull nobleman, Lord Pollington, who was of opinion that a tariff should not be imposed for the purpose of raising revenue, but to insure our "independence of foreigners," and to give protection to our own producers. Mr. F. Scott maintained the principle of getting rich by taxing one another for the benefit of one another. He opposed the motion, and warned the manufacturers that they would sink themselves in sinking the agriculturists. In other words, if the manufacturers should cease to pay taxes to agriculturists, the latter would have no money with which to buy manufactured goods. Col. Wood thought he had made a good point against the Free Traders by mentioning the case of a bootmaker who was for a free trade in corn, but objected to a free trade in boots. The argument, however, counted against his own party, for it showed that the bootmaker was a protectionist, and that a selfish desire to promote our own interests at the expense of other people is the essential principle of the whole protective system. The bootmaker was willing that the law should make artificial high prices for the things he had to sell, but not for those that he must buy. He was a genuine protectionist. Many other members participated in the debate, and the Tories criticised the League with great severity. Mr. Newdigate charged the League with exciting the recent disturbances in the north, and its methods of agitation were bitterly condemned. The League, however, refused to stand on the defensive, and Mr. Bright, replying to the accusation that the League was exciting the people, admitted the fact, and promised that they would continue to do so. No evil, he said, had ever found redress until agitation had compelled it. Mr. Gladstone commanded the Protectionist forces, and he defeated Cobden by the triumphant majority of ninety-one—the Tory lucky number; for it was the exact majority that brought Peel into power in 1841.

On the 19th of March the Free Trade question came up again in another shape. An attack was made by Mr. Ricardo on the "reciprocity" excuse for the restrictive system. This excuse had been offered by the Government many times of late. They said, "shall we open our ports to nations who close theirs against us?" "Can we safely reduce the tariff on French boots so long as France maintains a tariff against English stockings?" "Can we admit American corn so long as the United States excludes English crockery?" This kind of argument had great weight, for it appealed to national prejudice, and suggested the tariff hostility of other nations. On this reasoning was built the doctrine that commerce between nations must depend on treaty. The principle of it was that whatever we imported was an injury to our own people, consequently the importation must be forbidden, unless the nation whence it came would consent to inflict a counter-injury on itself by importing something of ours in return. Mr. Ricardo made an assault upon the whole "reciprocity" theory as a useless and antiquated mistake. He moved an address to the Crown praying "that the principle of reciprocity might not be insisted on in our commercial negotiations, nor in the regulation of our customs duties." He showed the inutility of all the recent commercial diplomacy of England, and he contended that nations could much easier obtain desirable commercial objects by judicious legislation regarding their own imports rather than by intricate negotiations with other nations as to exports. He begged Sir Robert Peel not to continue a protective system injurious to the people, in the expectation that other nations might pay them for relaxing it. Mr. Ewart seconded the motion, and said that it was idle to wait until foreign governments should offer to purchase a mitigation of the English restrictive system, and that the time had come when the Government must adopt the principle recommended in the motion of Mr. Ricardo.

Once more Mr. Gladstone was chosen to answer the Free Traders. He opposed the motion, and declared that the principle of it was far too broad and sweeping. He maintained that there was an economic and philosophical distinction between duties for revenue and duties for protection, and that so long as that distinction remained foreign commerce must largely depend on treaty concessions regarding imports. The essence of Mr. Gladstone's argument was that so long as it is wise to exclude the products of a foreign nation by a tariff levied for the protection of our own people against the competition of those products, it must be unwise to admit them unless that nation will pay for their admission by a corresponding concession in regard to our productions; and that those mutual concessions must be made and guaranteed by treaty. Under those circumstances, he said, that it was not wise to fetter the Government by an abstract declaration.

Lord Howick answered Mr. Gladstone. He was the son of Earl Grey, the Prime Minister who carried the Reform Bill of 1832. Judging by the debates in Parliament, Lord Howick appears to have had a mental grasp of economic principles quite unusual in an English nobleman. He regarded the proposition as a practical, and not an abstract one. He said, "the word 'abstract' in the government sense of it, seems to mean something that is right in itself, but inconvenient to certain interests too strong to be offended by ministers. They have not yet shaken off the old mercantile theory, that the only valuable trade of a country consisted in her exports, whereas, in truth, her imports formed the most advantageous part of her commerce." Turning to Mr. Gladstone, Lord Howick said, "You ought to consider at once, and without reference to foreign countries, the means of reducing your import duties; and if foreign countries neglect to follow your example, their own commercial loss will be their punishment." So little was the principle contended for understood at that time, and so small was the interest in it, that the House was counted out in the middle of the debate, forty members not being present.

The doctrine of Reciprocity is a political makeshift, ready for service on either side. It is a "Jack in the middle" tilting impartially the see-saw plank with Protection on one end and Free Trade on the other. It is plausible as a tin peddler, and patriotic as the spread eagle. In America it is used by Mr. Blaine as a concession to Free Trade; and in England by Lord Salisbury as a sop to Protection. Thackeray makes fun of it in the Book of Snobs, where he describes the use made of it by Mr. Jawkins at the "No Surrender" Club:

"As I came into the coffee room at the 'No Surrender' old Jawkins was holding out to a lot of men, who were yawning as usual. There he stood waving the *Standard* and swaggering before the fire. 'What,' says he, 'did I tell Peel last year? If you touch the Corn-Laws, you touch the Sugar Question; if you touch the sugar, you touch the tea. I am no monopolist. I am a liberal man, but I cannot forget that I stand on the brink of a precipice; and if we are to have Free Trade, give me *Reciprocity*.'"

But old Mr. Jawkins never became Secretary of State.

CHAPTER XI.

AT THE ZENITH.

The moral power of the League in Parliament was shown in the June debate on the annual motion of Mr. Villiers for a total repeal of the Corn-Laws, and the physical power of the administration was shown in the vote upon the motion. It was as follows: "That it is in evidence before this House that a large proportion of her Majesty's subjects are insufficiently provided with the first necessaries of life; that nevertheless a Corn-Law is in force which restricts the supply of food, and thereby lessens its abundance; that any such restriction is indefensible in principle, injurious in operation, and ought to be abolished."

To that motion Mr. Ferrand offered this amendment: "That it is in evidence before this House that a large proportion of her Majesty's subjects are insufficiently provided with the first necessaries of life; that although a Corn-Law is in force which protects the supply of food produced by British capital and native industry, and thereby increases its abundance, whilst it lessens competition in the markets of labor; nevertheless, machinery has for many years lessened among the working classes the means of purchasing the same, and that such Corn-Law, having for its object the protection of British capital, and the encouragement of native labor, ought not to be abolished."

This amendment is now looked upon in England as a

curiosity, and people gaze upon it as they do upon the plesiosaurus or some other skeleton from the antediluvian world. We exhume it merely to show what fantastic doctrines British statesmen and members of Parliament believed in forty-seven years ago; and the amazing fact remains, that every bit of this crazy amendment, except the childish complaint against machinery, is orthodox Protection doctrine in the United States to-day. The obvious untruth that the exclusion of wheat, nails, or cloth from a country increases the abundance within that country of wheat, nails, and cloth, is as vigorously asserted by the protectionist party in America now as it was by Mr. Ferrand in the English Parliament forty-seven years ago. How familiar, too, is that hollow ding dong "Protection of British capital, and encouragement of native labor." There is also a large number of the American Protectionist party among the workingmen who believe in the whole amendment, and who regard the machinery dragon with superstitious dread as Mr. Ferrand regarded it in England.

This debate was notable for several reasons. During its progress the Whigs, in the picturesque language of American politics, "climbed on to the fence," and they stayed there for a year, Lord John Russell declaring as he led the way, that he could not vote to remove all protection, and he was not in favor of the existing law. Mr. Miles, a radical Tory, called upon the country gentlemen to listen to no compromise, but to maintain the law as it stood. This debate revealed a more important fact, which was, that the politics of the country was no longer a contest for office between the Whigs on the one side and the Tories on the other, but was a life and death struggle between the protectionist majority inside Parliament, and the League outside. It was significant that many of the Tories, instead of directing their arguments to the question before the House, spent their time in criticising the League and denouncing its methods.

Sir Robert Peel and Mr. Gladstone were the chief speakers on the Protection side. Mr. Gladstone claimed a longer trial for the existing law. He contended that the experience of its operation had fully vindicated the statesmanship of the Government, and had realized all their expectations. He condemned the agitation of the League as productive of the most mischievous consequences, and declared that if Parliament continued to argue the question it would unsettle business, and be injurious to every interest in the country, and especially to the public credit. Amid great cheering from the Tory side, he claimed stability for the decisions of Parliament, and trusted that the House would not disturb the settlement that had been arrived at after a fair examination and adjustment of conflicting interests, and which adjustment had been put into law by the compromise measures of 1842.

In parrot-like imitation, our American statesmen at Washington, defending the McKinley bill of 1892, repeat Mr. Gladstone's plea for the Peel bill of 1842. "Cease to agitate the Tariff question" they implore, "until the McKinley bill has had a larger trial; wait for a few years and see how it will work. 'Tread softly, and speak low,' or you will unsettle business, and injure the public credit. This is the best adjustment we could make of conflicting interests. *Stare decisis*, and preserve the compromise, leaving the stolen goods in our possession, while you wait."

Lord Howick was in favor of the motion. Referring to the unpleasant fact that the men who profited by the Corn-Laws were members of both houses of the legislature, he said, "The root of good government is sapped away when it is once discovered that those in whom political power is centered are perverting it to their own purposes. When the conviction seizes the people that the Corn-Laws exist only for the few, I warn you that the days of the law are numbered. The discontent of the people is the result of class legislation; that is what they say, and I think they are right."

Captain Layard made a strong speech in favor of the resolution. In the course of it he gave an amusing illustration of the protective system. He said that when he was in China he had been shocked at the barbarous custom of contracting the feet of the children. Expressing to some Chinese gentlemen of his acquaintance his surprise at the continuance of it, they apologized for it by explaining that there were certain old women who made their living by binding and contracting those children's feet, and that the welfare of the old women required the maintenance of the practice.

Mr. Milner Gibson defended the League. That there might be no misunderstanding of its objects he declared that it sought Free Trade not only in corn but in everything. He quoted from Paley that restraint of trade is an evil *per se*, and that the burthen of the argument in each particular case is on him by whom the restraint is defended. Those who interfered with the freedom of exchange were bound to show the advantages of their theories. In answer to the "home market" argument Mr. Gibson asked this question, "Do English purchasers give more for Manchester cotton goods than the American purchaser gives? If not, what is the advantage of the home market to the Manchester man?"

It may be a little humiliating to the English aristocracy, but the fact ought to be mentioned that the stupidest men that figured in Parliament were lords. In a debate where Peel, Gladstone, Cobden, Bright, Villiers, Gibson, and men of that character took part, it was extremely comical to see a lord jump up as Lord Rendlesham did, and maintain that high rents were an element of national prosperity, and that the fall of prices which would reduce rents would lower profits and wages. The rate of wages was regulated by the price of corn. To reduce wages he said was the object of the motion, and the purpose of the League. Of course it is equally humiliating to Americans that the same argument is repeated in the Senate and in the House of Representatives at Washington, but there is the difference between the cases that whereas Lord Rendlesham did not know any better, our American statesmen do.

Mr. Cobden having indorsed the broad platform just laid down by Mr. Gibson, reminded the House that it was not the League that was on trial, but the law. He said, "You cannot put down the League by calling names, nor by such childish displays as have been seen to-night. It was said that the agriculturists could not meet taxation without protection, but if the manufacturers were therefore to pay the taxes of the landlords who were to pay the taxes of the manufacturers, and how were you to requite those classes who are neither landlords nor farmers nor manufacturers?" "I am for Free Trade in everything," said Mr. Cobden, "and if the protection on corn is destroyed, the protection on everything else will break down with it." Then pointing straight at the seats where sat the ministers, he said, "The Treasury bench has evaded the question; Lord Stanley has never met it, and I now challenge him to satisfy the Lancashire manufacturers of the justice of Protection." As Lord Stanley's father owned a large part of Lancashire, and derived enormous revenues from his possessions there, this challenge was one of those *ad hominem* thrusts in which Cobden was more skillful than any other man in Parliament. Lord Stanley did not reply.

Sir Robert Peel then rose to answer Cobden. He accepted the broad issue presented by Milner Gibson, and agreed that the repeal of the protective duties upon corn meant the withdrawal of protection from manufactures, and from shipping too. This he said would be productive of disaster to the country, and of almost certain ruin to Ireland. He made some amusement, and was loudly cheered when he pointed to the empty bench on the front opposition side where Lord John Russell and the Whig leaders usually sat. He criticised Lord John Russell's course in declining to vote, and taunted the Whigs with dodging the question. Sir Robert adopted a rather exultant manner toward the League, and said that their mitigated tone indicated that they felt that they had outstripped the feelings of the people, and could no longer stand upon the ground they had so imprudently attempted to occupy. He declared himself in favor of Protection, not for the sake of the landlords, but from a conviction of the evils which the removal of prohibition would inflict upon the general interests of the country, domestic and colonial. He contended that the present law had worked well, and should have a further trial. Amid uproarious cheering from the "country gentlemen," he declared that it was the intention of the Government to adhere to the present law. There was a fatal weakness in his argument, and he gave away his party and his case together when he said that he would not contest the principles of Mr. Villiers in the abstract, "for they might in the abstract be correct, and justified by philosophical considerations."

The Tories did not worry themselves over the moral condemnation of "Protection" contained in those admissions. All they cared about was the promise of the Prime Minister that monopoly should not be disturbed. They were so exultant that when Mr. Bright rose to address the House they listened to him with much impatience, and finally coughed him down. Mr. Villiers in closing the debate made a remarkable prediction. After referring to the fact that nobody had dared to controvert his arguments, he told the "country gentlemen," who cheered the Prime Minister so vigorously, that Sir Robert Peel had made a similar speech to them in 1839, and had afterward thrown them overboard: The same thing would happen again. This prophecy was literally fulfilled within two years. The motion was lost by 328 against 124, a stolid majority of 204, enough to dishearten even Cobden, whose high spirits had never failed him since the organization of the League.

When the vote was taken at the close of the great debate of 1844, the dawn of the summer day was just peeping through the windows of the House of Commons. It was greeted by the boisterous cheers of the protectionist majority, stimulated not only by victory, but by wine. Those cheers smote Cobden like a blow. Five years of incessant labor night and day had told heavily upon him, and mind and body needed rest together. There was another man there, however, who was smitten harder than Cobden, upon whose conscience this noisy cheering struck with a mocking sound. This was the great minister who had led the exultant majority to victory. He, and he alone, heard in those cheers the knell of the noisy monopoly that was making them. He knew that the flushed men he commended that night were utterly besotted and selfish; that the wants of the people were nothing to them, so long as they could enjoy the unjust profits of "Protection." He knew that if they had constituted the "landed interest" in Canaan at the time of the dearth, they would have demanded a high protective tariff against the "pauper" corn of Egypt, and the rich alluvium of the Nile. In the argument he made for them he knew that he was wrong. The disputant who concedes that the position of his adversary is "correct in the abstract and justified by philosophical considerations," knows that he himself is in a false position; and if he is a conscientious man it will not take him long to reach the platform where his adversary stands.

While Cobden sat gazing at the dense majority of 204, and believing it to be solid, Peel knew that it was hollow; while Cobden was fearful that the League had failed, Peel knew that it had succeeded; that it was fast becoming irresistible; that ere long it would conquer all opposition, and that not even the British monarchy could safely stand in its way. We all know now, what nobody knew then, that the only arguments that made any impression upon Peel in that debate were not those of his own party, but only those contained in the speeches of Cobden, Villiers, Bright, and Gibson. In this hour of its triumph the Tory chieftain knew that the end of "Protection" was at hand.

Mr. Morley, in his "Life of Cobden," describes the struggle made by the Free Traders that night as a "very hollow performance." The correctness of that opinion may be doubted. It is based on the serious physical defeat inflicted that night upon the Free Traders, and the air of superiority and conquest assumed by the Protectionists. These airs were largely affectation and assumption, for they knew that the moral triumph of the debate was not on their side. The sneer of Mr. Gladstone that "the League is a thing of no practical moment now, its parade and ceremonial are the most important parts of it," was merely a bit of sarcastic tinsel ornamenting a "very hollow" defense of the protective system. He certainly was too wise to believe it. The fact that Mr. Gladstone and the Tories wandered from the question to attack the League is proof that they were overmatched in argument, and surely a "hollow performance" would not make the Prime Minister concede that his opponents had on their side all the philosophy of the question. Milner Gibson was very strong that night. He planted himself on the solid rock of the Creator's grand design, and man's adaptation to it. He declared that to help one another, to be friends with one another, and to trade with one another, is the very law of human civilization; and he demanded that those who imposed restraints upon trade should give good reasons why.

How did the Tories answer him? Why, they said

they had enjoyed protection so long that it had become "vested," an inheritance in fee simple, absolute. In other words, they contended that a wrong that had existed for a long time became, at last, a right. But Mr. Gibson showed that no length of time could sanctify a wrong, and that the privilege of the landlords had never been a quiet possession and undisturbed enjoyment; that it had always been protested against, and could never ripen into a good title.

How did Peel answer him? By advancing the popular American mistake that "Protection" is a system in which all parties are interested; that it had become woven into the political organization of the country, and that it gave to all industries an equal and mutual assistance; that the agriculturists were interested in "protection" to manufacturers; that the manufacturers were interested in "protection" to agriculture, and that both of them were interested in "protection" to shipping and commerce, and that all must stand or fall together, and that although the motion was only aimed at corn, yet, if protection should be withdrawn from that, it must be withdrawn from everything else, which would be disastrous to the country. But Mr. Cobden showed in that very debate that there cannot be any such thing as universal protection, because, if every interest in the community is protected equally, then nobody is protected at all. Protection being a tax levied for the benefit of certain trades and occupations, somebody has to pay it, or the object of it fails. To form ourselves into a circle, and each man take a tax from the pocket of his neighbor on the right and drop it into the pocket of his neighbor on the left, does no good because, when the starting place is reached again, nobody has made anything at all.

Shortly after this debate Parliament adjourned, and did not meet again until February, 1845. The temperament of the Free Traders was not of a character to remain despondent long, and, besides, there was no occasion for discouragement. The confession of the Prime Minister that Free Trade principles were right in the abstract had a great effect outside the walls of Parliament. Many men thought that if that were true they might possibly be wise in the actual also. During the recess there were great accessions to the League. To some people who looked only on the surface of affairs, it seemed as if there was a lull in the Corn-Law agitation, and that the better times had deprived the League of its strength. But the League might well claim, and did claim, that the improved condition of the country was due to the modification of the protective system in the tariff of 1842, and that if the country should discard "Protection" altogether, the good times would be better still.

CHAPTER XII.

A SURPLUS REVENUE.

One element of the Tory glorification in the session of 1844 was the good looking budget which the Chancellor of the Exchequer was able to show; and there was an immense crowd in the House of Commons on the 29th of April to hear his financial statement. The credit of the country, too, had been improving under Sir Robert Peel's administration. In April, 1844, the Government three-per-cents sold at par, for the first time since the year 1749, and the revenues for the year showed a surplus instead of a deficiency. There was an air of excusable exultation about Mr. Goulburn, the Chancellor of the Exchequer, when he laid his annual balance-sheet upon the table of the House of Commons, for the scrutiny of Parliament and the country. He had a surplus in the treasury of about fifteen million dollars, and the manner in which he proposed to deal with it is well worthy the examination of American statesmen, whenever they have also to solve the problem of a surplus revenue.

Although Mr. Goulburn was a high Tory and a protectionist, it never occurred to him that the wise thing would be to waste the surplus revenue in order to preserve the system of tariff taxation; that the duty of the party in power was to rob the exchequer, and invent schemes of bounty and loot, in order to absorb the surplus, and thus remove the reason for an amendment of the tariff. Strangely enough, the last thing that occurs to the mind of an American statesman under those circumstances, was the first thing that occurred to the English minister; and surplus revenue being only surplus taxation in visible form he accompanied his budget with a plan to reduce tariff taxation to the amount of the surplus. He also put his reductions where they would do the most good, chiefly on the necessaries of life, and the raw materials of manufactures. He proposed to reduce the tariff on coffee four cents per pound, and he made an experimental advance toward a "free breakfast table" by reducing the duty on sugar. He put vinegar on the free list. There were fools who sneered at this, and laughed at "cheap pickles," but Mr. Goulburn was not thinking of pickles at all. Vinegar was largely used in manufactures, especially in calico printing, and that's what he was thinking of. He made a reduction of seven shillings per cwt. on currants. To some persons this may seem like relieving the tax on luxuries; but those who know that plum-pudding is not a luxury to an Englishman, but one of the necessaries of life, will see in a moment the value of this reduction. In the manufacture of a genuine dyspeptic, indigestible plum-pudding, currants are only secondary in importance to plums themselves.

The most important article, however, which Mr. Goulburn proposed to strike out of the tariff was wool. The duty on this he would abolish altogether. The plan of encouraging "sheep husbandry" by a high tariff on wool had failed, while it had put the masses of the people on half rations of clothing, and had taken away from them the comfort of carpets altogether.

There were plenty of sentimental patriots who still maintained the principle of protecting the high-toned and expensive sheep of Old England from the competition of the "pauper" sheep of the United States and Brazil; but their theories had almost passed out of the practical statesmanship of the country. The spasmodical high prices made by the tariff on wool could not be permanent, because they reacted on the demand by a rule as rigid as the Rule of Three, that customers decrease as prices rise. They merely made woolen clothes a luxury for the rich, and drove the middle classes and the working classes to the wearing of rags, cotton, and shoddy. The attempt to make high prices on wool by law, and keep them up, had proved as futile as would an act of Parliament prescribing how many pounds of wool a ram should wear in his overcoat. The chief defect of Mr. Goulburn's plan was that in reducing the duties on sugar he had preserved the protective discrimination in favor of the sugar of the British colonies. He gave the old excuse for this, and said that his object was to prevent sugar, "the produce of countries tainted with slavery, from being imported into Great Britain and Ireland."

Lord John Russell ridiculed this pretension, and said, "Surely it is very new to erect a pulpit in the custom house, and convert all the tide waiters and appraisers into abolition preachers." It seems a little foolish now, but there were many good men in England, and wise men, too, men like Dr. Lushington and Mr. O'Connell, who long believed that the commercial code of Britain might be made to do missionary work among the heathen; and that it might be "so adjusted" as to reward good nations and punish bad ones. Lord

John Russell pointed out the inconsistency of Mr. Goulburn, who was discouraging slavery in Brazil by an abolition discrimination against her sugar, and encouraging it by a pro-slavery reduction in favor of her coffee. He bantered Sir Robert Peel a little about his tariff of 1842, wherein he had applied the principle of "buying in the cheapest market" to onion seed, spices and herrings, and he hoped that the time was not far distant when he would apply it to the essential food of the people. These criticisms were not very serious. They fell harmless on a public ledger that showed a favorable balance, and the "noble Lord" himself admitted in conclusion that nothing was proposed by Mr. Goulburn which was likely to be very dangerous to the financial interests of the country. There was no moral strength in Lord John Russell's criticism, for he himself was a protectionist to the extent of demanding a tariff tax amounting to eight shillings a quarter on the "essential food" of the people. Between him and Peel it was merely a quarrel about expedients, Lord John Russell claiming that his protection scheme was better than Peel's.

The year 1845 opened favorably for the Government and the people. Affairs both foreign and domestic looked bright and promising; and the tone of the press generally was cheerful and encouraging. A nonpartisan paper of great influence, in reviewing the past year, said, "As a nation, we have been prosperous; peace and plenty have blessed the land, and beneath their happy influence commerce has flourished. Nearly every branch of industry has been employed; the revenue has increased; and the abundance of capital seeking for investment created a competition that enabled the Chancellor of the Exchequer to dictate terms to the public creditor." *The Annual Register*, speaking at the end of the year, described the beginning of it thus, "The commencement of the year 1845 may be described as presenting on the whole a more than usually prosperous state of affairs. The harvest had been a productive one, trade was brisk, the manufacturing classes well employed. The revenue gave symptoms of continual advance. The question of the Corn-Laws formed the greatest exception to unanimity, the continued exertions of the Anti-Corn-Law League still occasioning disquiet to the agricultural interest."

Again the Government was confronted with the knotty problem of a "surplus revenue"; and again the Ministers must determine what to do with it. The problem was not an easy one to solve, on account of the rivalry of "interests," each clamoring to be favored in the anticipated reduction of taxation. As Sir Robert Peel had obtained from Parliament in 1842 the concession of an income tax to supply the temporary deficiency of the revenue for that year; and as it had been granted for three years only, the people who paid it naturally insisted that as the three years was about to expire, and there was a surplus in the treasury, the income tax should cease; but Sir Robert Peel had already made up his mind that it was a just tax, and that he would continue it three years longer. Strangely enough, although he was still the leader of the Protectionist party, he retained the income tax for Free Trade reasons. He had noticed that the protective import duties were a far greater tax upon the people and their industries than the amount that went into the treasury, and he had observed that the income tax relieved this burden in proportion to the amount it yielded; therefore what he had obtained in 1842 as a mere expedient, he determined in 1845 to keep on principle.

Although nobody knew anything about it, an early suspicion was abroad that the income tax would not be repealed; and as it was known from the quarterly returns of the treasury, that there was a surplus, the "interests" immediately began to agitate, each for a remission of the tax that pressed upon itself. The Prime Minister was overwhelmed with letters of counsel, advising him what duties ought to be lowered, and what ought to be abolished. The agricultural "interests" insisted on the repeal of the malt tax, which pressed heavily upon them. The glass-makers declared that the window tax ought to be abolished, because it was an unjust burden upon their industry. The glaziers went with them thus far, and a little farther; they required not only the repeal of the window tax, but also the removal of the protective tariff on glass; and right there, at the forks of the road, the glaziers and the glass-makers parted company. The grocery "interest" wanted a reduction of the duties on tea and coffee and sugar, for they had noticed that the slight reduction of duty on those articles made by the tariff of 1842 had greatly increased their business. Naturally enough, every "interest" wanted its own special burdens removed; and the Government found that it was more embarrassing to deal with a surplus than to supply a deficiency.

Mr. James W. Grimes, a Protectionist Whig, was United States Senator from Iowa during the war; and in 1861, when it became necessary to adapt our fiscal system to the exigencies of the hour, and when the

Confederate flag on Munson's Hill could be seen from the windows of the Capitol, he noticed that the protected "interests," greedy and selfish, raided Washington, demanding that they, and not the nation, be considered in the preparation of the new tariff; they cared nothing whether it produced any revenue for the country or not, so that it produced revenue for them. Their eager avarice was an object lesson from which Mr. Grimes learned that the protective system was utterly unpatriotic, and he thought that as it was morally wrong, it could not be politically right. Subsequent study and observation confirmed his doubts, and he became the advocate and defender of a radical Free Trade policy. No doubt a similar experience had great influence in the conversion of Sir Robert Peel, for he saw in the swinish competition of the "interests" in 1845, what he must have seen in preparing the tariff of 1842, that a protective system is in the nature of it unpatriotic, because the beneficiaries of it openly declare themselves jealous of the country, and insist that any revenue derived by the Government from the tariff is unjustly taken from the protected interests, and that they ought to have it all. Our own American protected classes now say with as much effrontery as *Blackwood's Magazine* said long ago, "Duties for revenue never formed any part of the restrictive system, and they were never considered by any one as anything but necessary evils."

Lord Beaconsfield, in his biography of Lord George Bentinck, expresses the opinion that the improved condition of the country in 1845 had rendered the League powerless to disturb the administration, and that Sir Robert Peel might have defied it if the bad harvest had not come; and that his government could have stood against even "the persuasive ingenuity of Cobden." But this is a superficial view of the matter, and is the opinion of the most spiteful Protectionist then in Parliament, every one of whose predictions was falsified by the event. The agitation may not have been so boisterous on the surface, but it was deeper down. The crowded meetings at Covent Garden Theatre showed that the League was still formidable; and a Ladies' Bazaar held there in the spring of 1845, netted over a hundred thousand dollars to the funds of the League. But the most convincing proof of all was furnished by Sir Robert Peel himself, as soon as Parliament convened. When the Queen opened Parliament in February, 1845, she said: "Increased activity pervades almost every branch of manufacture. Trade and commerce have been extended at home and abroad. . . . . I congratulate you on the success of the measures, which, three years since, were adopted by Parliament for the purpose of supplying the deficiency in the public revenue. . . . . The act which passed at that time for imposing a tax upon income will shortly expire. It will be for you in your wisdom to determine whether it may not be expedient to continue its operation for a further period."

Those remarks indicated that the revenue reform policy was to be persevered in, and they gave positive notice to the country that the income tax was not to be repealed. Scarcely had the usual address in answer to the royal speech been moved and seconded in the House of Lords, when up rose the Duke of Richmond, and began to plead like a mendicant for the "agricultural classes." These were the very " classes " that had been "protected " by the onerous taxation of other "classes" for many years; and now they came to Parliament asking for charity. This duke who was passing the hat around for himself and some other dukes, and pretending to be an "agriculturist" in distress, owned more than 250,000 acres of land in England and Scotland. He had a palace in the loveliest and most fertile part of England, and it took ten miles of wall to inclose the park around his mansion. To keep up the style and extravagance of a prince, he impoverished his tenants, and then asked Parliament to relieve them at the cost of other people. To maintain high rents, and a high tariff, he would subject his fellow-citizens by sentence of the legislature to hunger and privation. He would maintain the Corn-Laws at any cost, although as Mr. Justin McCarthy says in his History of our own Times, "The Corn-Laws, as all the world now admits, were a cruel burden on the poor and the working classes of England."

In the debate on the Address in answer to the Royal speech, some of the "landed gentry" talked in the House of Commons, in the tone adopted by the Duke of Richmond in the House of Lords, and they were severely stung by Lord John Russell, who, in criticising the royal speech because it said nothing about the Corn-Laws, declared that "Protection was the bane of agriculture, rather than its support." This caused Mr. Miles to ask him, "Why, if he thought so, he had proposed a protective duty of eight shillings a quarter upon corn? Had he found it convenient to alter his views, and ally himself with the League? From the tenor of his remarks, it looked as if the noble Lord had been suddenly converted to the principles of that organization." This was a fair hit, for his Lordship was not yet ready to join the League.

It is not certain that Lord John Russell was contemplating any Free Trade movement, but it is highly probable that Peel suspected him, and determined to anticipate him; for in the debate on the Address, he announced, that contrary to the usual precedents, he would not wait until April or May to make his financial statement, but would present it to the House early in the following week. This, of course, compelled Lord John Russell to postpone his contemplated movement, whatever it might be. Sir Robert Peel was a little exultant in his manner, especially toward Lord John Russell, to whom he personally addressed the last part of his speech. "The House will then have an opportunity," he said, "of determining whether *under us* the condition of the country has deteriorated, or whether we continue to possess that confidence, without which we could not usefully conduct its affairs, and without which—the noble lord will pardon me for saying—no government ought to remain in office." Mr. Villiers, however, was determined not to allow the Government to monopolize all the congratulations, and he reminded Sir Robert Peel that the prosperity of the country was owing, not to the Protective System, but to a relaxation of its tyranny in the Tariff of 1842.

Among Peel's political enemies was one for whom he had great admiration and respect, the stubborn and high-minded Scotchman, Joseph Hume; and because of that feeling the criticisms of Hume made a deep impression upon Peel. He listened with earnest attention when Hume said, "You congratulate us on the financial prosperity of the country, but you do not promise to mitigate the taxation that presses on the poor, the protective tariff on articles of prime necessity essential to the support and employment of the working classes. Combine your policy of economy and retrenchment with those principles of Free Trade which some honorable members think will prove ruinous to the country, but which are absolutely necessary for its welfare and the development of its resources."

The Government was somewhat weakened at the beginning of 1845, by the loss of Mr. Gladstone, who had withdrawn from the cabinet because of a difference with Sir Robert Peel on the proposition to make a grant of money to the Roman Catholic College of Maynooth, in Ireland. The difference was not so much a matter of present opinion as of an old opinion, which unfortunately was recorded against Mr. Gladstone in a book. In fact he had modified his opinion and was now willing to support the grant, but not as a minister of the crown. Here was more evidence that a politician should never write a book until his public life is closed. Mr. Gladstone had written a book in former days against granting money to Maynooth; and that book drove him from office. He could not retain office and support principles which he had condemned in his book, because that course might suggest mercenary motives, and the sacrifice of principle for place. He therefore chose to resign. Some people thought that he did not approve the contemplated reduction of the sugar duties, and that he was glad to leave the cabinet on the Maynooth question, rather than on a question of commercial policy. There is not much ground for this opinion, for the probability is that Mr. Gladstone was already a Free Trader.

Two days after the opening of Parliament there was a very excited and somewhat angry discussion caused by Mr. Cobden, who censured the Royal speech for not alluding to the Corn-Laws. It was a sort of rough and tumble affair between the extreme Protectionists and the extreme Free Traders, the others looking on. Mr. Bright made an emphatic speech, which Mr. Stafford O'Brien described as "bullying" the House. Mr. O'Brien was an English landlord with an Irish name; and with much animation he defied Mr. Bright. He told him that he could not "set the tenants of England against their landlords by any such interpretation as he had used that night." Mr. O'Brien believed in the Feudal system, and he thought that the relation of master and serf still prevailed between the landlord and the tenant. He regarded Mr. Bright as an incendiary striving to excite the serfs of England to rebel against their owners. Sir Robert Peel sat placid and serene throughout the whole affair, and when it ended he quietly remarked that the performance was all in vain, and that he would not be provoked at present into a discussion of the Corn-Laws.

CHAPTER XIII.

NEARING THE END.

The financial statement of Sir Robert Peel was anxiously awaited by Parliament and the country. The Free Traders anticipated it with hope, the Protectionists with fear. The latter were distrustful of their leader, because, in spite of the declarations made by the Government last summer, emphasized by the triumphant majority of 204 against the motion of Mr. Villiers, they could see that the success of the experiment made in 1842 was working on the mind of Peel, and swaying him in the direction of commercial freedom. They saw that his ambition was aroused, and they feared that in the desire to link his name forever to some splendid policy, beneficent and wise, he might be tempted to experiment still further in Free Trade economics. They had reason to fear, as we shall see.

The Protectionists mustered strong on Friday night, the 14th of February, to encourage their great leader as he unfolded his financial plans. To their amazement and dismay he opened a Free Trade budget. To be sure he had not touched the Corn-Laws, but it was feared that he had passed sentence on them, and had only respited them for the time. Although great expectations had been formed of what was coming, neither party was prepared for the bold and comprehensive measure introduced by Peel. He began by making a large reduction in the sugar duties, sufficient, he said, to reduce the price of it to the consumer three cents a pound. He next proposed to strike the protective duty from four hundred and thirty articles then on the tariff list; and this he had the coolness to tell his protectionist followers, "must be a great advantage to commerce." The suicidal duties on most of the raw materials of manufacturers were swept away, an example of financial wisdom well worthy the study of American statesmen. Among the raw materials made free, were silk, hemp, flax, yarns, (except woolen) furniture goods, manures, oils, minerals, (except copper ores), dye stuffs, and drugs. The people who made barrel-staves had been protected in that industry against the "pauper" barrel-staves of the United States. Sir Robert Peel said that the coopers had memorialized him to remove the duty on barrel-staves. He proposed to give them a chance now; and had struck from the tariff the duty on staves. The duty on cotton, he said, fell heavily on coarse fabrics, and of course upon the poor; he proposed to abolish it altogether. He also struck off the excise duty on glass.

This was not all. Every rag of the protective export duties was discarded, even the venerable export duties on coal, which had stood firm for centuries, and which even John Stuart Mill thought might wisely be retained. In the ignorant ages of Protective philosophy, men thought it would be dangerous to British manufactures if England should permit her coal to be bought by the Germans or the French, for they might use it in manufacturing articles to compete in their own markets, and in other markets with Great Britain. And now a protectionist ministry proposed to abolish this time-honored incubus. Sir Robert Peel plunged fearlessly into the deep sea of economics, and declared that in his opinion the repealed taxes, by the stimulus they would give to commerce, would so far increase the general prosperity of the country as to counterbalance the continuance of the income tax. "All classes of the country," he said, "whether agricultural, manufacturing, or commercial, and parties not engaged in any particular industry would be either directly or indirectly benefited by the plans he now proposed." There was great cheering when Sir Robert Peel sat down, but it came not from his own party, but from the Free Trade crowd who occupied the benches opposite. The country gentlemen, the "squires," who cheered themselves into apoplexy last June, now sat silent and enraged; and there were signs of mutiny.

The cheering done by the Free Traders was not so much on account of the reduction of duties proposed by the new tariff, or because its logical termination must necessarily be the complete overthrow of the whole protective system. Sir Robert Peel was a statesman of profound sagacity, and very great experience. It was impossible for him not to see that if the protective tariff had wrongfully increased the price of sugar three cents a pound, it could not rightfully increase the price of bread. From this dilemma there was no escape for him, as he must have known. So, the men who made barrel-staves were Free Traders in behalf of lumber in its rude state, but they were Protectionists against lumber when it was in the form of barrel-staves. In like manner the coopers were Free Traders as to barrel-staves, but Protectionists when barrel-staves were in the form of barrels. Now, the ethics and the politics that made the Prime Minister relieve the coopers from the extortions of the barrel-stave makers, must apply, and did apply to every other tariff extortion of every other trade and calling in the kingdom; and to this conclusion Sir Robert Peel was intellectually driven at last.

On Monday, the day appointed for their discussion, the Government proposals were subjected to a running fire of criticism from several members, many of whom, however, acknowledged that they could not vote against them. The chief debater on the opposition side was Lord John Russell. He objected to the income tax, because it led to vexation and fraud, and declared that nothing but a great emergency could justify its imposition. He then declared himself opposed to all protective duties of every kind. "It is the business of the Government," he said, "to make laws for repressing crime, preserving order, and defending the state, but not for meddling with the right of the citizen to dispose of his labor and the products of his industry in the best market." He was in favor of a short income tax, and a total abandonment of all monopoly.

Sir Robert Peel remarked that it would be ungracious in him to say much in reply to those who were about to support him in the most eloquent of all ways, namely, by their votes. Lord John Russell surprised him by denouncing the income tax, and then saying he would vote for it. Perhaps the noble Lord felt that he might be on the ministerial benches himself a couple of years from now, and that then £5,000,000 derived from the income tax would be a grateful sum to deal with. Little did Sir Robert Peel suppose that this banter contained a prophecy that was literally fulfilled. In a couple of years Lord John Russell actually *was* on the ministerial benches, and then he did find that the income tax was a very useful thing to have. The strength of Sir Robert Peel's command over both parties in the House is proved by this, that although nearly everybody condemned the income tax, only thirty members had the nerve to vote against it. The Prime Minister's demand that it be imposed for another term of three years was granted by a majority of 228 against 30.

Although a great reduction in the sugar duties was made by the new tariff, the discrimination in favor of the British West Indies was still preserved. The false reason given for this was the discouragement of slavery, the true reason was the "Protection" of the men who owned the plantations in the colonies. Lord John Russell and Mr. Milner Gibson each offered amendments to Peel's plan, in which they declared for an equalization of the duty on foreign and colonial sugar. They were easily defeated although they had the best of the debate. Lord John Russell and Mr. Labouchere exposed the inconsistency of the anti-slavery pretext, because the Government was very careful not to apply it to coffee, and cotton, and other things. Mr. Gladstone answered them, and although he was now out of office he defended the Government plan with his usual eloquence. He reminded the House of the great sacrifices it had made to obtain the extinction of slavery, and pointed out the inconsistency of placing cruisers on the coast of Africa to prevent the exportation of negroes to Cuba and Brazil, and at the same time giving by our fiscal policy such encouragement to the planters of those countries to produce a greater quantity of sugar as would induce them to obtain slaves at all hazards. Mr. Macaulay replied to Gladstone, and said he would not have two standards of right and wrong, nor strain at a gnat and swallow a camel. "This," he said, "is what you are doing." He then showed that Sir Robert Peel at the very moment in which he debarred the country from the importation of Brazilian sugar, because it was slave grown, took off all the duty on American cotton which was slave grown also. Sir Robert Peel defended the apparent inconsistency of the Government, and the opposition was overcome by a majority of ninety-four against Lord John Russell's amendment.

The exact period when Peel was first converted from the Protection faith will always be a matter of historical dispute, but there is evidence that he became dangerously sceptical as early as 1841, and perhaps before that. It is certain that in 1842 he had rejected Protection as a principle, and had retained it as an expedient only. On that subject *Frazer's Magazine*, a strong Protection journal, said:

We hope, and indeed believe for the sake of his consistency, that Sir Robert Peel imagined long before 1845 that the system of Protection had reached its extreme limits, and that the time was come for returning again to that order of things, which is at once the best in the abstract, and would be in practice the best also were all civilized nations to fall in with it.

It is no excuse for folly and injustice that other nations practice both. A truth in political science, as in moral science, remains true in every separate nation, whether all other civilized nations "fall in with it" or not. The nations that do not "fall in with it" are not yet civilized.

The memoirs of the Right Hon. John Wilson Croker, published not long ago, prove that Peel had a large assortment of Free Trade reasons in store as far back as 1842. Croker had been the intimate friend and political colleague and associate of Peel from his early manhood until the year 1846, when their friendship was dissolved, because when Peel abandoned Protection, Croker abandoned him. Croker supported the policy of Peel until that minister laid his hand upon that sacred monopoly of the aristocracy, the Corn-Laws, and then he notified Peel that their personal friendship was at an end. In 1842, Peel wrote thus to Croker:

The best thing we have done without exception is the reduction of the duty on timber. All species of shipbuilding, all parties concerned in fisheries, all public works, piers, harbors, and coffer-dams; all public buildings, and all repairs to farm houses will be benefited by the free access to Baltic timber. Hume of the customs said, and said justly, we have the command of coal and iron: give us the command of timber and we have every natural advantage. We cannot enter into deep sea-fishing in competition with other countries, from the dearness of timber, and the consequent fragility of our boats. .... The argument in respect to timber is, I assure you, conclusive. There is no one article that tends so much to confer a social improvement and to cheapness of production, as low prices of timber.

The policy of bringing cheap timber from the Baltic, was not only "best in the abstract," but the value of it was not in the least affected by the failure of other nations to "fall in with it." With all that experience before them, we have men in this country who pass for statesmen, who tell us that it would be mischievous for us to adopt the policy of cheap lumber, until all other civilized nations are willing to "fall in with it."

On the 10th of March, Mr. Cobden brought on his motion for a select committee to inquire into the causes of agricultural distress. He contended that the Corn-Laws were an injury instead of a benefit to the farmers and farm laborers, and this he would be prepared to show if they would grant him the committee. On the part of the Government Mr. Sidney Herbert, a young patrician of great fortune and family, was chosen to reply to Cobden. He was of the lineage of Sir Philip Sidney, and brother of the Earl of Pembroke. He was a high Tory, and was credited with more talent than usually belonged to men of his rank and fortune. He held office in Peel's Government as Secretary of the Admiralty. There was nothing remarkable about his speech except that it contained an honest and unlucky expression which greatly offended his party. After stating positively that Mr. Cobden's motion would be met on the part of the Government by a decided negative, he remarked that the agriculturists were a body of men with very susceptible nerves, easily excited to alarm. By granting the committee a notion would go abroad that the Government had an intention to alter the Corn-Laws. It was somewhat distasteful to him as a member of the agricultural body to be always coming to Parliament "*whining for Protection.*"

That last phrase was probably uttered by Mr. Herbert in a peevish moment, when his tongue was not well enough guarded. It gave great offense, and some alarm. Nothing that had fallen from Cobden had such a sting in it, for this was the language of contempt. The imperious demand of the landed aristocracy for protection to agriculture, was described in a patrician sneer as "whining"; and this, too, in a speech answering Cobden. It suggested more than it said; it indicated that the Tory Government itself had become tired of dry-nursing all the wheezy "interests" that claimed legislative charity. Had the insult come from any of the Free Trade party it might have been endured; but from one of themselves, a wealthy landlord, an aristocrat, and a Tory, it was a humiliation hard to bear, especially as Mr. Herbert had lately, at a public meeting, declared himself a firm adherent of the protective system, and had fiercely assailed the League. The phrase "whining for Protection," immediately passed into the colloquial slang of politics. Mr. Cobden's motion was defeated by a majority of 92.

The Tory mutiny broke out in the early days of March, but so strong was Peel, first, in the success of his ministerial policy; secondly, in the weakness and division of the Whigs; and thirdly, in the fears of his own party that if they lost him somebody worse would take his place, that the insurrection was easily suppressed. The revolt appeared in the shape of a motion by Mr. Miles to the effect "that in the application of surplus revenue toward relieving the burdens of the country, by reduction of taxation, due regard should be had to the necessity of affording relief to the agricultural interest." In his remarks upon that resolution Mr. Miles distinctly told his chief that if the Tories had known what was coming they would have driven him from office in 1842, by defeating the tariff measures proposed by the minister then. The loud cheering from the Protectionists which greeted this *ex post facto* threat, showed Peel that although by the duress of the situation they were compelled to give him their votes, their sympathies were with the mutineers, and not with the commanding officer. The resolution was seconded by the Earl of March, son and heir of the Duke of Richmond, and present possessor of that title. In supporting it, Mr. Disraeli made a showy and theatrical display. His speech was hailed with uproarious cheering by the Tories, and it really deserved the applause. There were many smart things in it, although they all smelt of the lamp, and bore evidence of careful study and preparation. The personal allusions to Peel were steeped in vitriol. That statesman had always underrated Mr. Disraeli, and still underrated him. He maintained his air of superiority all through, but the poisoned sarcasms wounded him like a shower of needles. In this philippic occurs the sentence that afterward became famous, and a Tory rallying cry; the sentence in which Mr. Disraeli denounced the administration as "an organized hypocrisy." Sir Robert Peel kept his temper, and in reply contrasted Mr. Disraeli's former flatteries with his present vituperation. With an air of disdain he said that he held his panegyrics and his attacks in the same estimation. The rebellion was crushed by a majority of 213 to 78.

In this passionate and spiteful debate the Government still proclaimed its adherence to the protective system. Sir James Graham, Secretary of State, while opposing the resolution of Mr. Miles, declared that the principle of protection should be and ought to be preserved in the economic legislation of the country, and Lord John Russell followed him with an emphatic declaration on the other side. He advised the protected classes to rely henceforth upon their energy, their industry, and their capital, as the true sources of prosperity and not upon the broken reed of "legislative protection." Sir Robert Peel made a very careful speech. He thought extreme protection wrong, and defended moderate protection as "necessary, not on principles of commercial policy, but as essential to a state of things where great interests had grown up, and whose injury would be that of the community at large."

The student of American politics may wisely study this apology of Sir Robert Peel. He will hear it often in the "impending conflict" in the United States between Protection and Free Trade. Sir Robert Peel himself stigmatized his own reasoning as unsound on "principles of commercial policy," but "great interests had grown up" under the stimulus of "Protection"; and if the artificial prop which supported them should be removed, they would fall to the ground; and the people who were living on protective taxes would receive injury. That the withdrawal of protection would be an injury to the protected classes was true, but that it would be an injury to the community at large was false. The community at large being taxed for the benefit of a class, Sir Robert Peel pretended that the removal of the tax would be an injury, not only to those who received it, but to those who paid it. This contradiction is flippantly proclaimed by the American protectionists now.

The claim thus impudently made by Sir Robert Peel would make injustice perpetual, for there never can come a time when the abatement of a wrong will not injure the man who profits by it. The claim is a lesson and a warning to us. It shows that no matter under what circumstances of pretended urgency "Protection" may be conceded, the protected class is never ready to surrender it. The rack-renting Morrill tariff of 1861, which Mr. Morrill himself declared at that time could only be defended as a "war measure" by the urgency of our situation, is now, twenty-seven years after the war, impudent and rapacious. Mr. Morrill will not permit a hair of its head to be injured. He was willing a few years ago to take it out of politics, and refer it to a "commission" of its friends with instructions to report in the language of Sir Robert Peel, that its preservation has become "essential to a state of things where great interests have grown up, whose injury would be that of the community at large." That commission, composed entirely of Protectionists, reported that the tariff ought to be reduced about twenty per cent, but that report made it more insolent and rapacious than before. It is an organized appetite that grows with what it feeds on. It is not yet satisfied; not even with the McKinley bill, although privileged by that measure to levy tribute and toll upon every bit of wages in the land.

Late in May Lord John Russell's plan was given to the country. It consisted of nine resolutions which the Whig leader presented to Parliament in a speech which was easily and successfully answered by Peel. These resolutions were intended to constitute a new platform for the Whigs. Had they been proclaimed before the opening of Parliament, they would have been regarded as very far advanced, and they might have embarrassed both the Tories and the League; but, coming after Peel's budget, they were of no more interest than nine old newspapers. Like some other political parties that might be mentioned, the Whigs came limping along behind their enemies. Of the nine resolutions this history is only concerned with two. The second resolution was, "That those laws which impose duties usually called protective tend to impair the efficiency of labor, to restrict the free interchange of commodities, and so impose upon the people unnecessary taxation."

It had taken the League six long years to pound those principles into Lord John Russell. He had adopted them at last, and it must be acknowledged that in making his confession to the House of Commons he had managed to condense a vast amount of economic truth into a very few sentences. The wonderful fact remains that he was not yet ready to apply those principles to corn. The third resolution was, "That the present Corn-Law tends to check improvements in agriculture, produces uncertainty in all farming speculations, and holds out to the owners and occupiers of land prospects of special advantage which it fails to secure."

And yet he was not ready to vote for a repeal of that law. He merely wanted to change the "sliding scale" for a fixed duty. He confessed, however, that after all the discussion which had taken place, he could not reasonably and fairly propose the eight shillings fixed duty which he had offered in 1841. He thought that a duty of four, five, or six shillings a quarter would be about right. The League had made him a Free Trader as to everything but corn, and as to that, it had crowded him back from eight shillings a quarter to six, or five, or even four. Lord John Russell had the Whigs and Free Traders with him on the division, but was easily beaten by a majority of seventy-eight.

In June came on the annual motion of Mr. Villiers for a total repeal of the Corn-Laws. It was in the form of three resolutions :

1. That the Corn-Law restricts the supply of food, and prevents the free exchange of the products of labor.

2. That it is, therefore, prejudicial to the welfare of the country, especially to that of the working classes, and has proved delusive to those for whose benefit the law was designed.

3. That it is expedient that all restrictions on the importation of corn should be now abolished.

The debate on the resolutions revealed the new position taken by Lord John Russell. He gave his unqualified support to the first resolution and the second, but was not ready to vote for the third. The Whig leaders were still beguiled by a fantastic will-o'-the wisp, seducing them into the slough of compromise. They cherished the delusion that in the break-up of parties which was coming many fragments might be cemented to the Whigs by a concession to Protection of a moderate duty upon grain, and by a concession to Free Trade of a tariff for revenue only as to all other things. But the time for compromise had passed, and principles now stood arrayed against each other in "irrepressible conflict." Lord John Russell echoed Villiers and Cobden. He charged that the legislators maintained the existing law, because it added to their own incomes; and he declared that they had failed in their attempts to prove that it was beneficial to the rest of the community.

The debate also disclosed the change that had come over Sir James Graham in three months. He no longer contended for protection as a principle, but merely for cautious and prudent legislation in dealing with it. He seemed to plead that the doomed culprit might have a long time to prepare for death. He admitted that by prudent measures they might bring the Corn-Laws nearer to the sound principles of commerce; but he hoped that no sudden step would be taken. He very much feared a "shock" to the agricultural interest, because it would convulse all other branches of industry. He feared that the free importation of corn would permanently reduce the price of wheat to about thirty-five shillings a quarter, thereby throwing land out of cultivation, and inflicting great injury on parts of England, and on the whole of Ireland. This injury, he thought, would not be compensated by the benefits resulting from Free Trade. Still, if it appeared that free importation was the only way in which to supply sufficient food to an increasing population, he would not oppose it any longer. Unfortunately, Sir James Graham was in the situation of Mr. Gladstone; he too had written a book, and its doctrines were continually tripping him up. The principles laid down by him in his work on "Corn and Currency" were very inconvenient to him now, and his opponents made the most of his embarrassment. He never flinched, however, but took his punishment in a very manly way. Wherever he differed from his book he courageously acknowledged that his opinions had undergone a change. Mr. Bright answered Sir James Graham. He accused him of dealing in fallacies, and referred to the Free Trade Bazaar at Covent Garden Theatre as evidence that the Free Trade agitation outside Parliament was vigorous and increasing.

The "fallacies" of Sir James Graham were the logical result of a popular mistake that the ultimate object of agriculture is the cultivation of land; but this is merely a way to achieve its final purpose, the production of something to eat. Food is the ultimate object, and the land which cannot produce it as abundantly as other land, throws itself out of cultivation by the law inexorable that the fittest shall survive. It ought to go out of cultivation because it is unable to yield a sufficient return for the work done in farming it. Sir James Graham himself was lord of "The Netherby clan." He owned a very large estate on the Scottish border, but it was poor land, and he had no right to claim that because his land was poor, the people of England should not have the benefit of the rich land of Illinois. He saw this afterward and yielded his own monopoly to the Free Trade principle, not because he was compelled to do so, but because he saw that it was right.

Several speeches were made by the partisans on either side. Lord Ebrington, a Whig nobleman of some importance, declared that he should vote for the resolutions. He had formerly opposed them because he hoped that a fixed duty would have formed a compromise between the two great interests of the country. He now despaired of any such compromise, and would give his hearty support to the resolutions. Mr. Cobden made a vigorous attack upon the existing system. He declared that the condition of the laboring classes was a disgrace to the country, and he maintained that it was an act of injustice to tax the food of the people. This question, he said, had never been fairly met with argument in the House of Commons, and he ventured to predict that it never would be fairly met.

The most remarkable thing about this debate was the towering air of superiority with which Sir Robert Peel lectured the pack behind him. With lordly patronage he told them that although he was about to lead them to victory once more, their arguments were unsound. He distinctly stated that although he must vote against the motion of Mr. Villiers, he could not agree in all the arguments adduced against it. He formally repudiated and laid aside the mistake of the protectionists, that dear commodities make high wages, and although some of his own followers had proclaimed the doctrine in that very debate, he told them it was not true. The protectionists bore this lecture with such patience as they could, but when their leader told them that he opposed the motion, not because it was not right, but because he desired to make "a gradual approach to sound principles with a cautious attention to the interests which had grown up under a different system," they could scarce conceal their anger. They very well understood that he meant by "sound principles" the doctrines of Free Trade. To be told, not only that their arguments were bad, but also that their principles were not sound, was more than they could bear. The division was taken mechanically, and the speaker announced that the "Noes" had it by 254 to 122, a little more than two to one. This was the last victory for the Protectionists in England. Parliament adjourned in August. When it met again in January, the Tory party had been disintegrated and broken to pieces by the League; the Protectionists were disorganized and routed so completely that they were never afterward known as a party in the politics of Great Britain.

CHAPTER XIV.

AT LAST, FAMINE.

And now the time was close at hand when that boasted Protective System which was to make Britain "independent of foreign countries" for its food supply, was to be subjected to a test it could not stand. In the summer of 1845 Mr. Cobden had ridiculed that precarious commercial system which was at the mercy of a shower of rain. "Three weeks rainy weather," he said, "will prove the danger of leaving the industrial scheme of such a country as England to stand or fall on the cast of a die." He had scarcely ceased to speak when the rainy weather came, and it lasted through the harvest time. The wheat crop was short, and its quality was poor. It was not so short, however, as to create any alarm, or affect the politics of the country. No uneasiness was felt until the middle of August, when it was rumored that the potato crop had been smitten with a strange disease, and that the potatoes in the south of England were rotting in the ground. While this occasioned some anxiety to the Government, and was the cause of some correspondence between Sir Robert Peel and Sir James Graham, it was not until the middle of September that the Ministers became alarmed; for although the reports were contradictory, as in all such cases, yet enough was known to satisfy Sir Robert Peel that the rot was extensive and even general throughout England; and there was a horrid whisper creeping about that the crop had also been smitten in Ireland. This was more alarming still, for the potato constituted the principal food of the Irish peasantry. In a letter written by Sir James Graham to Sir Robert Peel, from Netherby, in the north, and dated September 19th, 1845, he says, "I hope there may be some exaggeration in this report of the failure of the potato crop in Ireland; but there is no doubt that to some extent the disease has made its appearance in that country. We had again a great deal of rain yesterday; and the weather is broken and no longer favorable."

In October the reports grew worse, and men all over England were denouncing that governmental system which had made the Irish people dependent on a wretched root for food. So far from being "independent of foreign countries," the people of the British Islands saw themselves in the autumn of 1845 almost at the mercy of other nations for their coming winter's bread. Sir Robert Peel vibrated between hope and despair. In his own memoirs he says, "Even so late as the 6th of October the accounts from Ireland were not decidedly unfavorable, and on that day Sir James Graham, writing from Netherby, observes, 'the accounts of the potato crop in Ireland are more favorable than I had ventured to expect. The recent terrible rains will still do no harm. I am afraid that the price of food generally will be very high.'" Soon after the 6th of October the reports from Ireland became very unsatisfactory. On the 13th of October, Sir Robert Peel addressed a letter to Sir James Graham, in which he said, "The accounts of the potato crop in Ireland are becoming very alarming." The letter concludes with the following important paragraph, "I have no confidence in such remedies as the prohibition of exports, or the stoppage of the distilleries. The removal of impediments to imports is the only effectual remedy." This proves that Sir Robert Peel had made up his mind as early as the 13th of October. But he was the leader of a stubborn and stupid party, nearly all of it opposed to him; and he was at the head of a cabinet, every member of which was a protectionist, from education, from prejudice, and from self-interest. He seems to have had but one sympathizing friend in his own cabinet; but one man with whom he could hold confidential counsel amid the awful responsibilities and dangers which were rapidly closing around him. That was Sir James Graham, Secretary of State for the Home Department. Between Sir James Graham and his chief there appears to have been a kindred feeling of responsibility, and a mutual willingness to do whatever ought to be done, regardless of consequences merely personal to themselves.

In the middle of October Sir Robert Peel sent a commission of scientific men to Ireland with instructions to investigate and report upon the potato disease, so that he might act upon correct information. This must have been rather to influence and satisfy his colleagues than for his own information. He was already satisfied, and had determined what to do. On the 15th of October he wrote to the Lord Lieutenant of Ireland as follows, "The accounts from Ireland of the potato crop, confirmed as they are by your high authority, are very alarming. We must consider whether it is possible by legislation, or by the exercise of prerogative, to apply a remedy to the great evil with which we are threatened. The application of such remedy involves considerations of the utmost magnitude. The remedy is the removal of all impediments to the import of all kinds of human food—that is, the total and absolute repeal for ever of all duties on all articles of subsistence." On the 27th of October, in a letter to Sir James Graham, Sir Robert Peel said, "The Anti-Corn-Law pressure is about to commence, and it will be the most formidable movement of modern times. Everything depends upon the skill, promptitude, and decision with which it is met."

Sir Robert Peel was right. The League had now become almost irresistible. A large portion of the press which had long held aloof from it gave in their adhesion, not only to its doctrines, but also to its plans. It held great meetings and made many converts. It caused petitions to be circulated throughout the country demanding the immediate repeal of the Corn-Laws. These were signed by thousands. Mr. O'Connell, who had long been a member of the League, sent fearful accounts from Ireland, and demanded a cessation of party conflict in the presence of the calamity that was impending over the country. He called upon the Government to open the ports to the admission of foreign grain. Sir Robert Peel felt the fearful weight of his responsibility, and there were frequent meetings of the cabinet, but the people knew nothing of its discussions except that they were not harmonious.

The first cabinet council to consider the subject was held on the 31st of October. It met again the next day, and then Sir Robert Peel laid before it a memorandum of the situation, and of the remedies that he thought ought to be adopted. After explaining why the cabinet had been called together, and laying before it all the information he had received concerning the condition of the country, he proposed First, that the ports should be opened to the admission of foreign grain by an order in council, trusting that Parliament would pass an act of indemnity excusing the Ministers for this unconstitutional suspending of the law; Secondly, to call Parliament together not later than the 27th of November, and leave the whole matter to its decision. He gave the arguments for and against both plans, and frankly declared his opinion that if the ports were once opened, even for temporary relief, they could never be closed again. The cabinet separated without coming to any opinion, and agreed to meet again on the 6th of November, to determine what policy should be adopted.

On the 6th of November the cabinet met again, but not even the reasoning of Peel could move it from a stolid, selfish conservatism. The proposals of the Prime Minister were supported by only three members—the Earl of Aberdeen, Sir James Graham, and Mr. Sidney Herbert. "The other members of the cabinet," remarks Peel, "some on the ground of objection to the principle of the measures recommended, others upon the ground that there was not sufficient evidence of the necessity for them, withheld their sanction." This, he says, would have justified him then in relinquishing office, but fearing that the dissolution of the Government would excite the public mind, he determined to retain office for the present, and give the cabinet until the last of the month to consider the whole question. "In determining to retain office for the present," he said, "I determined also, not to recede from the position I had taken, and ultimately to resign office if I should find on the re-assembling of the cabinet that the opinions I had expressed did not meet with general concurrence."

The discord in the cabinet looked like an opportunity for the Whigs, and they thought to make some party capital out of it; and it is only fair to say that they also thought that it gave them an opportunity to be of real service to the country. Lord John Russell was in Edinburgh quietly watching the progress of events, and he saw that there was a division in the cabinet. How wide it was he did not know, but he thought that it was probably wide enough to let him pass through it, and return once more to power. All through November the political gloom grew deeper, and at last he thought that his time had come. He was member for the City of London, and on the 22d of November he wrote from Edinburgh a letter to his constituents on the condition of the country. It was written somewhat in the spirit of party, and it censured Peel; but the people did not notice that; all they saw was the more important fact that he had gone bodily over to the League, and declared himself in favor of Free Trade. He confessed that he had been converted from the errors of a lifetime. "I used to be of the opinion," he said, "that corn was an exception to the general rules of political economy." Observation and experience had at last convinced him of the expensive folly of the whole protective system. He said, "Let us, then, unite to put an end to a system which has proved to be the blight of commerce, the bane of agriculture, the source of bitter divisions among classes, the cause of penury, fever, mortality, and crime among the people."

This letter meant that the Whigs were getting off the fence; and presently they were seen tripping over one another in their haste to join the League. It precipitated the crisis, and broke up the Ministry. As soon as it appeared Sir Robert Peel called the cabinet together. He told his Ministers that he could not any longer assume the responsibility of continuing the Corn-Laws; he proposed to open the ports by an order in council, and declared himself in favor of Free Trade. On the 25th of November the council met, and on the 26th Sir Robert Peel laid before it a memorandum in which he said, "I, for one, am prepared to take the responsibility of suspending the law by an order in council, or of calling Parliament at a very early period, and advising in the speech from the throne, the suspension of the law." On the 29th of November he forwarded to each member of the cabinet another memorandum containing the whole argument on the case, but they were not convinced. In answer to it the Duke of Wellington said, "I am one of those who think the continuance of the Corn-Laws essential to the agriculture of the country in its existing state, and particularly to that of Ireland, and a benefit to the whole community." He thought, however, that a good government for the country was of more consequence than the Corn-Laws. He thought that the Government was safer in the hands of Peel than it would be elsewhere, and agreed to stand by him in any policy that he might think proper to adopt. He said, "In respect to my own course, my only object in public life is to support Sir Robert Peel's administration of the Government." The Duke of Wellington was never prone to indulge in cant, and he was not a hypocrite or a Pharisee. He meant what he said, and believed it, but his answer to Peel shows to what mental destitution the protection theory will bring a man if he cherishes it long. The Duke of Wellington, a naturally practical and sagacious man, had nursed the protection doctrine so long that he literally believed that a system which had reduced the people of England to half rations, and the people of Ireland to imminent starvation was "a benefit to the whole community."

Mr. Goulburn, Chancellor of the Exchequer, in his answer to Peel's memorandum, said, " I wish to consider protection to agriculture precisely as I would protection to manufactures; for agriculture after all is a manufacture, of which the raw material is earth, and the manufactured article is corn." As the American protectionist to-day makes the public debt an excuse for the imposition of protective taxes, so did Mr. Goulburn then. He said, "From the immense amount of our debt, and the charge imposed on every interest in the country in respect to it, every manufacturer in this country has in justice a claim to be protected as regards the supply of the home consumer against the competition of a foreigner, who, not having the same charges upon him, is, or ought to be able to supply articles at a cheaper rate." Here Mr. Goulburn concealed the fact, or else he did not know it, that this protection given to the manufacturer to help him bear the burden of the public debt, was given at the expense of other classes of the people, who, in addition to this protective tax, were also compelled to bear their own share of the public debt. This concession to the manufacturers, however, was only a pretext for demanding a larger protection for the agriculturists.

He goes on to say, "On this ground you give linen, cotton, and woolen manufacturers a protection of from 10 to 20 per cent., and to this extent on the same ground I see no reason why corn should not be protected." He then proceeds to argue that for peculiar reasons corn should have "an extra protection."

Lord Wharncliffe, in his answer to the memorandum, said that in his opinion no case was made out *as yet* that would justify the Government in taking the action proposed by Sir Robert Peel. He thought that the Government "could not consistently propose such measures to Parliament as in their conscience they must feel to be, not only an abandonment of the present Corn-Law, but of the principle of Protection." He argued strongly against a Free Trade policy. Lord Wharncliffe was an old man, scarcely able to endure the strain of the prevailing excitement, and ten days after writing that letter he died. Lord Stanley was firm in his resistance to the changes recommended by the Prime Minister. The discussions in the cabinet continued from day to day until the 5th of December. Some of the younger Tories were willing to go with Peel, but Lord Stanley and the Duke of Bucclough could not consent to overthrow the Corn-Laws, which in some shape or other had taxed the people of England for generations. The clamor of the League could be heard in the council chamber, and rather than endure it any longer the whole Ministry resigned. Sir Robert Peel, speaking of this last cabinet council, says, "Lord Stanley and the Duke of Bucclough, after anxious reflection, each signified his inability to support a measure involving the ultimate repeal of the Corn-Laws. All the other members were prepared to support such a measure. I could not, however, conceal from myself that the assent given by many was a reluctant one—that it was founded rather on a conviction of the public evil that must arise from the dissolution of the Government at such a time and from such a cause, than on the deliberate approval of the particular course which I urged upon their adoption." For these reasons the Ministry was broken up, and Sir Robert went down to Osborne, and handed his resignation to the Queen.

Lord John Russell was sent for to form an administration. He accepted the task, and there was a great deal of "mounting in hot haste," and "hurrying to and fro," and sending for this man and for that man. Although Lord John Russell had obtained the promise of Sir Robert Peel that he would support him in carrying out a policy in accordance with the measures advocated in the Edinburgh letter, he found himself unable to form an administration. After a couple of weeks' tinkering with the "crisis," he went down and told the Queen that he had failed in his attempt to form a government. He confessed in the language of *Punch*, who was making fun of him at the time, that he was not "big enough for the place."

When Lord John Russell was making up the "slate," he offered the greatest man in England, the author of the commercial revolution, a subordinate position as Vice-President of the Board of Trade, under a titled mediocrity, the Earl of Clarendon, who was to be President of the Board. This was a good deal like offering Oliver Cromwell a Corporalship under the Earl of Essex. So hard was it for the Whig aristocracy to understand that the democracy of England had at last become a power in the state. Cobden declined the offer, not because the office was not big enough for him, but because he never sought official distinction of any kind.

It was not to be regretted that Lord John Russell failed to form a government. Had he succeeded, he would probably have subordinated the mighty question of the hour to the exigencies of party. There was but one man who was equal to the occasion; who had the tact, ability, and temper, the scientific knowledge, the character, and the parliamentary following to carry England safely through. That man was Peel. Lord John Russell advised the Queen to send for him, and place the Government in his hands again. Sir Robert resumed his office, and proceeded to reconstruct his cabinet. Most of the old members agreed to serve under him again, and among the new members was Gladstone. Even the Duke of Wellington, whose Tory prejudices were so bitter and so strong, agreed to take office under Peel once more, and promised to stand by him till the fight was ended. It is proof of the confidence of the people in Peel's capacity, that as soon as it was known that he had consented to resume his office, the funds rose.

Paradoxical as it appears, the Duke of Wellington surrendered to a radical policy for conservative reasons. He saw that in the temper of the people it must be either a commercial revolution or a political revolution, and that in order to prevent the latter calamity, Protection must be given up. The Duke of Wellington was almost a dictator in the House of Lords, so completely under his influence was the Tory majority there; and he terrified "their lordships" into obedience to Sir Robert Peel by saying, " Would you compel the Queen to send for Mr. Cobden?"

The average estimate of Peel as a leader and a statesman, may be gathered from the following extract taken from a London journal of great popularity. The article was published immediately after the fall of the ministry, and before it was known that Peel would again be called to power. It contains a severe criticism on Peel's conduct in proposing measures directly antagonistic to the principles on which his government was formed. After showing that with the present Parliament a Whig ministry is impossible, it searches the Tory ranks for a new leader to take the place of Peel. It acknowledges that it cannot find one, and says:

If a Tory Cabinet cannot be constructed, it is a fatal sign for the party. It is in this respect that the prospects of the Tory party are the most unsatisfactory. It is impossible to say what men occasion and opportunity may not bring forth, but at present there is neither an equal nor a successor to Peel.

. . . . . Another of his fathom they have not
To lead their business.

Stanley would seem the approximate leader; but he is wanting in temper. Graham would not do, for he has been both a Whig and a Corn-Law repealer. Gladstone is beyond all question the most able man in the ranks of the party, but is implicated in the tariff, and committed to commercial liberality as deeply as Peel. Taking the many qualifications that Sir Robert Peel possesses, combined with his position and influence, the man does not exist who can supply his place completely.

That, from a hostile critic, is a fair criterion of the estimation in which Peel was held by his countrymen at that time. It must be remembered that he never was a popular man in the sense of popularity as we understand it in America. A man of great wealth and aristocratic education, owing nothing to the people, and absolutely independent, he neither courted them nor flattered them. He could say more truthfully than any man in England,

> I love the people,
> But do not like to stage me to their eyes,
> Though it do well ; I do not relish well,
> Their loud applause and aves vehement,
> Nor do I think the man of safe discretion
> That does affect it.

All this time the League was pressing its advantage; it faltered not. Immense meetings were held in London, Manchester and other places. At a great meeting in Dublin Mr. O'Connell proclaimed "every man an enemy who did not support Bright and Cobden." He said: "Why should we not support the abolition of the Corn-Laws? Do they make wages high ? Certainly not, but they give a fictitious value to land. In the county of Kilkenny he had inquired the rate of wages, and found that it was only one shilling and sixpence per week." He denounced the Government for not opening the ports. On the 15th of December a vast Free Trade meeting was held at Guildhall, the City Hall of London, which was presided over by the Lord Mayor himself, in his official character as chief magistrate of the city. The mighty giants, Gog and Magog, who had guarded London for a thousand years and more, were nearly shaken from their pedestals by the cheers that went up when Cobden rose to speak. He was in great spirits that day, for he knew that the end was near. One of the speakers at the meeting was Mr. Perkins, who, in proposing one of the resolutions, made the following remarks, which look very curious to us now: "The Peel administration," said Mr. Perkins, "is afraid to face the speech of the President of the United States, which will arrive in this country within the next ten days. The Western States of America have now a majority in Congress, and they never will meet this country on terms of amicable feeling and mutual interests until they have free access to the markets of this country."

Mr. Cobden was the chief speaker, and he was received with immense applause. He was in his most humorous and sarcastic vein. Referring to the breakup of the cabinet, he said: "The Protection societies tell us confidently that there is a sufficient supply of corn and potatoes in the country. If this is so, what is the matter at headquarters? If there is no potato rot, what is that murrain which we have got in the cabinet?" "It is easy," said Mr. Cobden, "for our dukes and squires, maundering like old women at agricultural meetings, to say there is no scarcity, and to attempt to arrest the opinion in favor of Free Trade. They can go out to hunt and shoot during the day, and when they come in they can regale themselves with venison, champagne and the like dainties. With them there is no scarcity; not so with the people."

Two days afterward there was a great meeting at Covent Garden Theatre. Thirty thousand tickets of admission were applied for. Mr. Villiers presided, and speeches were made by Mr. Cobden, Mr. Bright, and Mr. Fox. But London was excelled by Manchester. At one meeting there it was resolved to raise twelve hundred and fifty thousand dollars for the League, and three hundred thousand dollars was contributed that day. Twenty-three men subscribed five thousand dollars each as fast as the secretary could write their names. Nothing could stand against such earnest public opinion as that. The counter-meetings gotten up by the Agricultural Protection Society were so weak and spiritless that they only served to make more apparent the invincible power of the League. Badly educated and ill informed old dukes mumbled out complaints against the League, and scolded Sir Robert Peel for deserting them. At one of those Protection meetings, the Duke of Richmond, in spite of the fact that the League had mastered both Russell and Peel, said, "The Anti-Corn-Law League is of no power at all unless it be led by men like Sir Robert Peel and Lord John Russell." These old dukes displayed such deplorable ignorance, and made such comical blunders whenever they spoke, that they helped the League immensely, and furnished great sport for Cobden, who would rather go gunning for dukes than dukes would for pheasants. At one meeting the Duke of Norfolk brought the whole peerage into ridicule by recommending curry powder as a remedy for the public distress. He had discovered that an excellent thing to make the laborer warm and comfortable in a time of hunger was "a pinch of curry powder in a quantity of hot water," and the Duke of Cambridge made great amusement by innocently doubting the stories about the potato disease, because, "really he hadn't noticed anything wrong with the potatoes that were furnished his own table."

On the 20th of December, Sir Robert Peel in an interview with the Queen, at Windsor, consented to assume once more the office of Prime Minister. That evening he returned to London, and immediately summoned his old cabinet to a council in Downing street. It was late at night before they got together, and this time Sir Robert met them not as a colleague, nor even as their official chief, but as their master. He informed them at once that he had not summoned them for the purpose of deliberating on what was to be done, but for the purpose of announcing to them that he was again Prime Minister, and whether supported or not, was firmly resolved to meet Parliament as Minister, and to propose such measures as the public exigencies required. Failure or success must depend upon their decision; but nothing could shake his determination to meet Parliament, and to advise the speech from the throne. As their advice on public questions was not asked, there was nothing for them to decide upon but the personal question whether or not they would resume their offices as the ministers of Peel, and promise to support the changes in the revenue and economic systems of the country which he intended to recommend to Parliament. They all agreed to serve under his command again, except Lord Stanley and the Duke of Buccleugh. Lord Stanley positively declined to re-enter the cabinet, and the Duke of Buccleugh requested time to consider, which was granted him. At the end of two or three days he gave in his adhesion to his old chief and the new policy. He resumed his place in the cabinet, and agreed to support the measures of Peel. For fifteen years a superstition had prevailed among the Tories that nobody but Peel was competent to govern England. The strong hold it had upon them was now apparent when the Duke of Wellington, the Duke of Buccleugh, the Earl of Aberdeen, and men of that character yielded their individuality to him once more, and agreed to support measures they had always opposed, believing them to be essential to the welfare of the country, because Peel said so.

CHAPTER XV.

THE REFORMED SYSTEM.

At the beginning of 1846 the public mind of England was in a feverish condition. Business was good, but there was great anxiety about the anticipated scarcity of food. The contradictory reports on that subject increased the excitement instead of allaying it. Those in favor of changes and reforms were accused of exaggerating the reports about the failure of the crops, while the conservatives were charged with concealing the extent of the calamity. The relations between England and the United States were unfriendly because of the Oregon dispute; and the proceedings of Congress were watched with deep concern. The disruption of the cabinet excited the public nerves and although it was known that Sir Robert Peel would propose changes in the commercial policy of the country, nobody knew what the changes were to be. To create a public opinion strong enough to compel him to a radical repeal of the Corn-Laws became the object of the League, and to that end immense meetings were held in all parts of the Kingdom. On the other hand, the Protection societies held counter-meetings, and tried to create a rival agitation, in order to restrain the Prime Minister and keep him to a conservative policy. In this contest the League had a great advantage both in the largeness of its gatherings and in the vigor and ability of its orators. It was always on the aggressive while the protection speakers maintained a strictly defensive attitude. The League was eager for discussion, while the Protection societies avoided it. At a meeting of the "Protection Society," held at Wolverhampton, it was bravely announced that no discussion would be allowed, and the "noble chairman," the Earl of Sandwich, said that only on that condition had he consented to take the chair. It is easy to see that meetings like that did more injury to the protection side than to the other.

In this nervous condition of the country the Queen opened Parliament on the 20th of January, 1846. The speech from the throne foreshadowed what was coming. It contained these ominous words:

I have had great satisfaction in giving my assent to the measures which you have presented to me from time to time, calculated to extend commerce, and to stimulate domestic skill and industry by the repeal of prohibitory, and the relaxation of protective, duties.

I recommend you to take into your early consideration whether the principles on which you have acted may not with advantage be yet more extensively applied, and whether it may not be in your power, after a careful review of the existing duties upon many articles, the produce or manufacture of other countries, to make such further reductions and remissions as may tend to insure the continuance of the great benefits to which I have adverted, and by enlarging our commercial intercourse, to strengthen the bonds of amity with foreign powers.

In the House of Lords the mover and seconder of the Address in answer to the royal speech were listened to with the usual courtesy, and then "Sir Devon, the bull," as *Punch* pictorially described him, proceeded to butt the cars off the track. The Duke of Richmond condemned the anticipated policy of the Government, and called upon their lordships not to abandon the protective system. Referring to the mover of the address, who had asked the House to postpone discussion until they had heard the plans of the Government, he said, "I have heard enough to satisfy me what the Minister intends to do. He intends to withdraw Protection." He then paraded the ancient argument of the protectionists, that laws which gave them a power to tax their fellow-citizens were in the nature of a contract and a vested right that could not be repealed. He said, "This is getting rid of the compact which Sir Robert Peel made in 1842 with the agriculturists, and which Mr. Gladstone said was made for the purpose of securing to the agriculturists a permanent law. I hope this House will not so far abandon its duty as to be intimidated by the Anti-Corn-Law League, or by the money that body has raised." He then declared that everybody knew that the protection laws were not for the benefit of one class only, but were for the benefit of every class in the community.

The Duke of Richmond like many others of the English nobility, had plenty of courage, but little wisdom. He had proved his courage as a soldier in the Napoleonic wars, and in one of the battles had received a French bullet in his lungs; yet in spite of that, he had good lung power and plenty of courage left; and he was perfectly willing to fight the Free Trade locomotive. Wellington, his old commander, answered him. He told him it was no use trying to stop the train; that the Corn-Laws were sentenced, and that the sentence would be executed in a few days. Still the Duke fought desperately, until old Wellington thought, like Richard, that there must be at least "six Richmonds in the field."

Sir Robert Peel made a short explanation that same night in the House of Commons. In the course of it he said that his opinions on the subject of protective duties had undergone a change. He was yielding to the force of argument and more enlarged experience. He had closely watched the operation of protective duties during the past four or five years, and was now convinced that the arguments in favor of their maintenance were no longer tenable. He was convinced that low wages was not the result of low prices of food. Sir Robert supported this last statement by facts that could not be denied, the rate of wages and the rate of prices that had prevailed during the preceding six years. He said, "For three years preceding those last past, prices were high while wages were low, while during the past three years, prices were low while wages were high." This was a very uncomfortable statement for those political economists who had been trading on the fallacy that the protective tariff was necessary in order to secure high wages for the workingman; and that cheap bread, and meat, and clothes, meant low wages.

In the year 1884 the National Republican Convention at Chicago performed the paradoxical feat of adopting a high tariff platform, and placing upon it a candidate supposed to represent a "spirited foreign policy," which being interpreted, was said to mean a policy that would secure for the United States a larger trade with the South American republics and the empire of Brazil. Thus the candidate was to pull the wagon one way and the platform the other. The party meant by "trade" selling only, but not buying, and

Mr. Blaine himself, in the manifesto published by him in 1882, in explanation of his course as Secretary of State, says that the intention of his policy was "To cultivate such friendly commercial relations with all American countries as would lead to a large increase in the *export* trade of the United States, by supplying those fabrics in which we are abundantly able to compete with the manufacturing nations of Europe." The history of England and of our own country shows that this desirable object can be best accomplished in one way, and that is by a reduction of the tariff. This truth had forced itself upon the mind of Sir Robert Peel, by the result of actual experiment. In the explanation which we are now considering he said, "Since the year 1842, when the first invasion was made on the principle of protection, the *exports* of the country had risen from £42,000,000 to £47,000,000 in 1843, to £58,000,000 in 1844, and, leaving out the trade with China, the increase had been from £42,000,-000 in 1842 to £46,000,000 in 1844, and to £56,000,000 in 1845. The results of the revenue presented a similar picture. The state of morality was also a gratifying result of increased prosperity. The commitments throughout the country had enormously decreased." Against a stone wall built up from facts like these the taunts of the protectionists that Peel had "deserted" and "betrayed" them made little impression, and it was finally agreed that on the following Tuesday the Minister should present his new commercial plans. Peel's was a Free Trade speech, and, as Cobden wrote the next day to a friend, "it would have done for Covent Garden Theatre," the place where the League meetings were held. It was not the speech of a minister yielding to pressure, but of a man who had become convinced. As he said a few nights afterward, it was the declaration of a man who had become converted to a belief that the protective system "was not only impolitic, but unjust."

It is impossible to open the national gates to *imports*; and keep *exports* from escaping through the gap. Sir Robert Peel's experiment, made in 1842, timid as it was, proved this; but neither Peel, nor Cobden, nor the most sanguine Free Trader, could have anticipated that within forty-five years, under the stimulus given by free *imports*, the *exports* of merchandise from Great Britain and Ireland would amount in value to £248,000,000. This of British produce alone, excluding foreign and colonial produce amounting in value to £66,000,000—produce which England had bought from some outside countries and sold to others at a profit. The total value of *exports* from the United Kingdom in 1889 was £314,000,000.

In 1842, after centuries of protection, the *exports* of the United Kingdom amounted to £42,000,000. In 1888, after forty-two years of Free Trade, they amounted to £314,000,000. This, too, in defiance of the tariff blockades erected against England by nearly all the other nations of the world, not excepting her own colonies. This is a marvelous achievement, when we remember that Great Britain is not blessed with one-half as many nor one-half as valuable natural resources as belong to Pennsylvania alone.

In 1892 the Protectionists at Minneapolis, although they repudiated the patentee of the double-action wagon, gave it a new coat of paint, and hitched the "Reciprocity" horse to the front of it, to pull it forward, and the "Protection" horse to the rear of it, to drag it back. And England still perseveres, according to Governor McKinley, in the benevolent folly of paying the taxes of all nations, by exporting merchandise to them and paying the tariff tribute levied on it.

Tuesday, January 27, 1846, was an exciting day in London. It was known that the Prime Minister intended on that day to propose in Parliament a radical change in the commercial policy of England, but it was not known in detail what the change would be. Although Parliament did not meet until four or five o'clock, crowds of people began to assemble in the neighborhood of the House of Commons as early as one o'clock, and before four o'clock the house itself was crowded in every part. Westminster Hall had not seen so great a multitude since the trial of Warren Hastings, while the open street was densely crowded from Westminster Abbey to Whitehall. The Peers' gallery was full of dukes, and earls, and barons, anxious to learn the fate of those monopolies which their order had enjoyed for centuries. The Duke of Cambridge, the Queen's uncle, was there, and Prince Albert was accommodated with a seat inside the bar. A few nights afterward his visit there was criticised by Lord George Bentinck, who resented the presence of the Queen's husband in the House of Commons as an attempt of the Crown to influence the free debates of Parliament. Some sort of excuse was given by the Court, and the Prince never entered the House again. Many years afterward Queen Victoria apologized to the nation for the attendance of her husband in the House of Commons, and explained that he merely went there out of curiosity, and for the instruction to be derived from listening to a great debate, as her sons were always permitted to do. It was insinuated that Sir Robert Peel himself had contrived the attendance of the Prince, for theatrical effect, and for its influence on the House—a "smart" political trick of which he was quite incapable.

The members known to be in favor of Free Trade were loudly cheered, while the Protectionists were greeted with silence. The Duke of Wellington received a great ovation, for it was known that he had promised his assistance to Peel. Although he had opposed every popular movement of his time he was always forgiven because of Waterloo. Near five o'clock a roar of cheering rolling along the street announced the coming of Sir Robert Peel. As he alighted from his carriage he raised his hat in acknowledgment of the hearty greetings of his countrymen, and passed into the House. He carried a small box in his hand. It contained the death warrant of the protective system. In that little box were carefully arranged the details of the new commercial policy, the enlightened system of Free Trade.

About five o'clock Sir Robert Peel rose and moved that the House resolve itself into a committee of the whole on customs and corn importation. The House having resolved itself into committee, Sir Robert began his speech. For three hours the crowd listened to the Minister, as one after another each protected interest went down to its doom. He gave due notice that while he called upon the agriculturists to resign the protection they had long enjoyed, he should require the manufacturers to resign theirs also. With just and impartial hand he struck protection from the linen, the woolen, and the cotton manufacturers, from the ironworkers and the silk-weavers, from the soap-makers and the brass-founders, from the shoemakers and the tanners, from ribbon-makers and from hatters, from tin workers, and from button-makers, from tailors and from carriage-makers, from brewers and from clock-makers, from West India sugar planters and from— almost everybody.

With great candor, in what Lord Beaconsfield says was not a candid speech, Sir Robert Peel described the process of his conversion from the Protection to the Free Trade faith. He quoted some good doctrine from the American Secretary of the Treasury, who had lately said, "By countervailing restrictions we injure our own fellow-citizens much more than the foreign nation at whom we purpose to aim their force, and in the conflict of opposing tariffs we sacrifice our own commerce, agriculture, and navigation. Let our commerce be as free as our political institutions. Let us with revenue duties only, open our ports to all the world." Thus among the missionaries who had helped to convert Sir Robert Peel was the American Secretary of the Treasury. Let us hope that the time is not far distant when we shall see another Secretary of the Treasury equally wise.

At the very beginning of his speech Sir Robert Peel laid the foundation of his argument, First on the scientific wisdom of the Free Trade theory, and Secondly, on the practical results of the experiment of 1842. For three or four years he had patronized Free Trade as a "theory" which might be philosophically correct, but was so hampered and qualified by the accidents of government and actual business, by foreign relations, and local surroundings, as to be of doubtful utility in practical political economy. He had passed out of the region of doubt into the strong light of conviction and now advocated Free Trade as just and wise, not only in theory, but in practice, too. He said, "I am about to proceed on the assumption that the repeal of prohibitory and the relaxation of protective duties is in itself a wise policy—that protective duties abstractedly and on principle are open to objection—I am about to act on this presumption—that during the period of the last three years there has been in this country an increased productiveness of revenue, notwithstanding the relaxation of heavy taxation—that there has been an increased demand for labor; that there has been increased commerce; that there has been increased comfort, content, and peace in this country; and I say that the enjoyment of these benefits has been concurrent with the policy of repealing prohibitory and reducing protective duties."

This was a strong opening, and it was plain that if he could prove what he said by the facts of commerce, revenue, and wages, the Prime Minister had already made out his case against the protective system. That he felt confident of his ability to do so was plain from the challenge with which he accompanied his statement. He called upon the opposition to meet him with a counter-proposition, viz.: "that Protection is in itself a good." He justified the "horizontal" plan on the ground that whatever a man lost by the withdrawal of protection from his own interest was made up to him by the gain which he received by the withdrawal of protection from all other interests. He said, "I make no separate and isolated proposals. I have confidence that the proposal for which I contend is just, when I ask all protectionists to make the sacrifice, if it be a sacrifice, which the application of the principle requires of them." He then referred to the sacrifice he had made of revenue in admitting raw materials free, and said, "In 1844 we reduced altogether the duty upon wool; in 1845 we reduced altogether the duty upon cotton. There hardly remains a raw material imported from other countries upon which the duty has not been reduced. The manufacturers of this country have free access to the raw materials which constitute the fabrics of their manufactures. I am entitled, therefore, I think, to call upon the manufacturer to relax the protection which he enjoys."

Sir Robert Peel then criticised as unjust and unwise all the protective taxes on the clothing of the people. He said, "In dealing with the clothing of the great body of the people, I call on the manufacturers of the great articles of cotton, woolen, and linen to relinquish their protection." He then went into historical argument to prove that the protective system had originated with the manufacturers, and that the agriculturists had adopted it in self-defense. He quoted Adam Smith as saying, "Country gentlemen and farmers are, to their great honor, of all people the least subject to the wretched spirit of monopoly." This was received with loud laughter and derision by the Free Traders, but Sir Robert with admirable coolness and self-command repeated the quotation, and proceeded thus, "The manufacturers seem to have been the original inventors of those restraints upon the importation of foreign goods which secure to them the monopoly of the home market. It was probably in imitation of them, and to put themselves on a level with those who they found were disposed to oppress them, that the country gentlemen and farmers of Great Britain so far forgot the generosity which is natural to their station, as to demand the exclusive privilege of supplying to their countrymen corn and butcher's meat."

All that apparent flattery was probably ironical on Peel's part, but whether so or not, it was a fair commentary on the protective system, which is a competition of classes to get "level" with one another and something to boot. Lord Beaconsfield, in describing this remarkable speech, a dozen years afterward, insinuates that Peel was not ingenuous in making this comparison between the "country gentlemen" and the manufacturers to the advantage of the former, and that it was only a part of that consummate art by which he managed the House of Commons. Of this part of it Lord Beaconsfield says, "While the agitated agriculture of the United Kingdom awaited with breathless suspense the formal notification of its doom, wondering by what cunning arguments the policy of its betrayer could be palliated, the Minister addressed and pursued at considerable length to the wondering assembly, an elaborate and argumentative statement, the object of which was to reconcile the manufacturers to the deprival of protection. Considering that this protection was merely nominal, the sacrifice did not appear to be too severe, yet the orator seemed scarcely sanguine of inducing his audience to consent to it. With imperturbable gravity the Minister read to the House the passage of Adam Smith, in which that eminent writer acknowledges, that 'country gentlemen and farmers are the least subject to the wretched spirit of monopoly,' and fixing, with a sort of mournful reprobation, the manufacturers as the originators of the protective system in this country, the speaker declared, amid the titter of the Free Traders, which, however, was solemnly reproved, 'that it was but justice that they should set the example of relinquishment.'" Lord Beaconsfield evidently regarded the whole tribute to the country gentlemen as what the boys call "taffy," and had he known the word he would probably have used it. The whole comparison was a sort of soothing chloroform by which Peel endeavored to quiet the country gentlemen while he was pulling their teeth. Whatever import duties remained on the manufactures of cotton and woolen clothing under the proposed new tariff, were limited to the finer fabrics indulged in by the rich; on those used by the great body of the people the tax was altogether abolished.

As it is now in the United States, so it was in England then, each protected interest purchased the silence of a rival interest by protecting that also, leaving the great mass of the consumers to bear the burden of the whole tax accumulations; for instance, in order to protect the tanner, Government levied a high tariff on tanned leather, and then it bribed the shoemaker and the saddler into acquiescence by levying a similar tariff on saddles and harness, and boots and shoes. Of course, in returning to a correct system, the reverse plan must be adopted, and the reduction of the tax on one must be accompanied by a kindred reduction on the other. Recognizing the force of this, Sir Robert Peel said, "Having remitted the duty on almost every article connected with the tanning process, I propose to remit the duty on dressed hides. There will then not be one raw material which the manufacturer of leather cannot command without the payment of duty. Having done that, I propose to diminish the duty on foreign boots and shoes imported into this country." This was the "horizontal" plan, and it is difficult to see how any other could be either just or wise. To take the tax burthen from leather in one shape, and leave it upon leather in some other shape, would be unstatesmanlike and unfair; and all the taxes upon leather being removed, there was no longer any excuse for permitting the shoemaker to levy taxes upon everybody else, in order to protect his business. Sir Robert Peel applied this principle to hats and other things. Having remitted the duties on the materials of the hat manufacture, he then reduced the duty on hats. He still clung to the delusion that he could make a missionary pulpit of the custom house, and use the tariff schedule as an abolition tract, so, while he reduced the tariff on sugar, he limited the reduction to that grown by free labor. He proposed to punish Brazil, Spain, and the United States for preserving slavery by making a custom house discrimination against their sugar. At last he came to the Corn-Laws, and in the midst of breathless anxiety, he announced that the duties on Indian corn, and on all cattle, vegetables, and other provisions were to cease at once. On wheat, barley, oats, peas, and beans, a small duty would remain for three years, and on the first day of February, 1849, that duty also was to cease, excepting a nominal tax of about three cents a bushel on wheat, for procuring statistics of information; and even that was abolished in due time. It is not necessary to go into any further details of an argument which lasted three hours and a quarter, and which concluded amidst great excitement on his own side of the House, and immense cheering on the other.

This was the most important speech delivered in Parliament in modern times; it was fraught with greater consequences to Great Britain than any other, and it was answered by the Tories not with argument, but with personal denunciation of the Minister. Lord Beaconsfield, who was the most virulent and sarcastic of all Peel's enemies, and who came into parliamentary prominence through his poisonous assaults upon him, writing of the speech in 1858, attempts to throw contempt upon it while admitting its power. He says, "But no inability to endure the dread suspense on the part of his former adherents effected the slightest alteration in the tactics which the consummate master had arranged. He had resolved that a considerable time should elapse before they learned their doom, and that a due impression should be conveyed to the House and to the country that on this night of sacrifices the agricultural classes were not the only victims. And in this he succeeded so well, that, even to this day, controversies are continually arising as to the nature and degree of protection still retained and enjoyed by the staple manufactures of the country."

Lord Beaconsfield tries to account for the power of a speech he could not answer, by pretending that the success of it was due to the crafty tactics and management of Peel rather than to any merit in the production itself. He says, "This remarkable man, who in private life was constrained, and often awkward, who could never address a public meeting or make an after-dinner speech without being ill at ease, and generally saying something stilted, or even a little ridiculous, in the Senate was the readiest, easiest, most flexible and adroit of men. He played upon the House of Commons as on an old fiddle. And to-night, the manner in which he proceeded to deal with the duties on candles and soap, while all were thinking of the duties on something else, the bland and conciliatory air with which he announced a reduction of the impost on boot fronts and shoe leather, while visions of deserted villages and reduced rentals were torturing his neighbors, were all characteristic of his command over himself, and those whom he addressed." Here with incautious candor, the man who next to Lord George Bentinck was the chief leader of the Protectionists in Parliament, confesses that the opposition of the Tories to Free Trade was due to a vision of "reduced rentals." To maintain high rents for idlers the food and clothing of the industrious must be made scarce and dear by means of a protective tariff.

Again, trying to explain the success of Peel in presenting his new policy to the House of Commons, and the discomfiture of the Protectionists, Lord Beaconsfield, instead of admitting that it was too great for him and his party to answer, impudently pretends that it was too little. He remarks, "Some fine judges have recognized in all this only the artifice of a consummate master of the House of Commons, lowering the tone of an excited assembly by habitual details, and almost proving by his accustomed manner of addressing them that, after all, he could have done nothing very extraordinary. When a Senate, after a long interval and the occurrence of startling transactions, assembles, if not to impeach, at least to denounce a Minister, and then are gravely anointed with domestic lard, and invited to a speculation on the price of salt pork, an air of littleness is irresistibly infused into the affair, from which it seems hopeless to extricate the occasion." All this is ingenious, and contains within it a flavor of patrician contempt for details and vulgar things like lard and soap and leather, but the fact remains that the speech made a profound impression upon Parliament and the country, an impression which has never been removed, but which remains to this day.

CHAPTER XVI.

THE NEW POLICY.

The plan of Sir Robert Peel was a surprise to all parties. Although much was expected, the country was astonished at the bold and comprehensive sweep of the new policy. The Free Traders were literally dumb, for although the measure fell short of their extremely radical demands, it came so much nearer to them than was expected, that they thought it would be ungracious in them to criticise the Minister, who with a rebellious party on his hands, had the fortunes of a great empire in his keeping. They felt that Peel was bringing all the resources of patriotic statesmanship to the solution of a revenue and economic problem that was agitating the country, and unsettling the theories of ages; that he was actuated by a sincere desire to establish the prosperity of his country on a permanent and sure foundation, and at the same time avert an impending scarcity which might culminate in famine. They therefore said nothing in reproof, leaving the task of censure to his own party. The Tories immediately began to whimper and scold; they dwelt upon the perversion of the Government to the Free Trade heresy, but they did not attempt to refute the arguments of the Prime Minister, nor to contradict his testimony. Their oratory might have all been condensed into the painful exclamation of the Earl of March, son and heir of the Duke of Richmond, a baby statesman with no brains, who cried out, that "really he never in all his life was so horrified, so distressed, or so astonished, as when he heard the Prime Minister's plans that night." Visions of "reduced rentals" had horrified and distressed him. The speeches were all in support of a motion for a continuance.

Like a culprit under sentence, Protection made a pitiful appeal for a few days' respite. Its friends appealed for time to consider such important changes; and finally, two weeks was granted. Some demanded that the sense of the country should be taken by the dissolution of Parliament and a new election. Some were in favor of referring the whole matter to a "commission," and thus to obtain a reprieve; but it was of no use, their dilatory motions were all overruled, and on Monday, the 9th of February, the great debate began, the most important that had taken place since 1688. The feature of the night was the introduction of Lord Morpeth, who had just been elected from the West Riding of Yorkshire, where he was defeated in 1841. He brought with him no less than 103 petitions from Yorkshire asking for Free Trade. One petition from Leeds was signed by 19,000 men, and one from Bradford by 14,000. Some amusement was created by Mr. Ferrand, who challenged the signatures as not being the free and unbiased acts of the men who signed. He was prepared to prove, he said, that the workingmen in many factories in Yorkshire were obliged to come into the counting-houses of the owners and sign. Lord Morpeth silenced him by saying that in his belief the signatures were all the true and independent acts of the parties; and then, amid considerable excitement, the question having been put that the Speaker leave the chair that the House might resolve itself into a committee on the Corn and Importation acts, Mr. P. Miles, on the part of the Protectionists, moved as an amendment that the House should resolve itself into committee that day six months; and on that amendment the great debate began.

Mr. Miles was not regarded as a very able man, and his remarks merely served to open the discussion, nothing more. He repeated the usual Protection generalities, but brought no evidence nor attempted any proof. He declared that there should be a dissolution of Parliament before such momentous changes; he believed that in the mind of the Prime Minister the cause of protection had long been doomed, and that potatoes were the last pretext for sealing its fate. He repeated Peel's old argument about the danger which would arise if the country became dependent upon foreigners for grain. The country might now consider Free Trade to be the ruling principle of Her Majesty's Government. Mr. Miles was truthfully prophetic when he said: "Sooner or later every interest must bow to the operation of the Free Trade principle." He felt convinced that the shipping interest would, before long, be deprived of protection. "Of what use," inquired Mr. Miles, "are navigation laws, or reciprocity treaties, if protection is to be taken from our own productions?" He expressed his fears that the League would not dissolve as it had promised to do if the Corn-Laws were repealed. He feared that it would preserve its organization, and agitate for revolutionary changes in another direction. Sir W. Heathcote seconded the amendment in a speech wherein he declared that "domestic industry requires protection in proportion to the amount of manual labor necessary to carry it on;" and by force of this principle he tried to make it appear that agriculture being more "manual" than manufactures, ought to have more protection. In other words, that occupations having the advantage of machinery needed no protection, while those that used no machinery did. This curious doctrine did not strike the House of Commons as very profound, although, if "the lower wages in other countries" theory was correct, it was a good one, and Sir W. Heathcote sat down without having created any great sensation.

As the converts at a camp-meeting in relating their "experience," all say the same thing, so a half-a-dozen Tories followed Sir W. Heathcote, and echoed him in monotonous repetition. Then Lord Sandon startled the House by making a good, sensible argument against the measure, and at the same time declaring that he should vote for it. He foreboded great disaster from it, especially to farmers and farm laborers. His motive, he said, for voting for the measure was the conviction that it was impossible to maintain Protection against public opinion. "We may grumble and struggle," he said, "but the question is decided against us." The position in which Lord Sandon found himself shows how difficult it was for some Tories to separate themselves from Peel. They had so long looked up to his cool head for guidance that the habit of doing so had become an infatuation. They could not believe it possible that they themselves might be right and Peel wrong. They had leaned upon him so long that, without him, they were helpless. Even the Duke of Wellington talked in the House of Lords very much as Lord Sandon did in the House of Commons, showing that in spite of what they called his "desertion" of them, a large number of the Tory party had ceased to have any individuality of their own, but had permitted themselves to become absorbed in the personality of Peel.

The chief incident of the first night's debate was the speech of Lord John Russell. His position was peculiar, for he had been turned out of office by Peel in 1841, for proposing a small modification of the Corn-Laws, and he was now marshaling the Whig party to support a proposition of his rival and antagonist for their total repeal. Lord Beaconsfield, in his anxiety to point suspicion at Peel, asserts that Lord John Russell spoke in the tone of a man who had been wronged by Peel, and unfairly driven from office; that his manner was complaining, and justly so. The speech does not bear that interpretation. It is magnanimous and patriotic. True, Lord John Russell did criticise some of the details of the new plan, especially the three years' respite; and he also complained that when he had endeavored to introduce similar reforms he had been met by a party opposition, and finally driven from power; but it was all said in such a manly way as to elicit cheers from both sides of the House, and even from Sir Robert Peel himself. Lord John Russell said: "Considering the plan of the Minister as a great measure, a measure that is to lay the foundation of a completely new principle with regard to our commercial legislation—that principle being neither to foster one trade nor the other, but to leave them to 'flourish or to fade,' according to the energies and skill of the people, and believing that is the sound principle, I am prepared to give every support I can to the plan brought forward by the right honorable gentleman."

As party warfare goes, it would not have been especially unfair if Lord John Russell had taken advantage of the "crisis" to turn the Tories out, but in this instance he certainly put patriotism above party, and the relief of the people before official jealousy and personal recriminations. Referring in a dignified manner to Mr. Lascelles, who had just remarked that he supported the plans of the Prime Minister because he thought him more likely to succeed in passing them than Lord John Russell could, he said, "It is by the aid of the Whigs, and by the conduct that we shall pursue that the measure will attain its success." Then waiving all personal ambition, and ignoring private griefs, he generously said, "If the right honorable gentleman has the glory of adopting plans of commercial freedom which will benefit his country, which will enable the poor man to get a better reward for his labor, which will increase the demand for all the productions, and which, after these questions are settled, will, I hope, open the way to the moral improvement of the people of this country, hitherto prevented by their want of adequate means of comfort—if the right honorable gentleman has the glory of carrying a measure fraught with such large and beneficial results, let ours be the solid satisfaction that, out of office, we have associated together for the purpose of aiding and assisting the triumph of the Minister of the Crown."

It was important that the position of the Whigs should be declared thus early, and the speech of Lord John Russell was a great disappointment to the rancorous faction of Protectionists, who under the lead of Lord George Bentinck and Mr. Disraeli were seeking to obstruct and defeat the reformation. They had hoped that the Whigs would find partisan excuse for opposition, in revenge for 1841, and naturally enough, they could see no merit in the speech. Their vexation lasted long. A dozen years afterward Mr. Disraeli, describing it, said, "Lord John Russell, who followed in a speech which was not one of his happy efforts, agreed with Lord Sandon, 'that the Minister had not laid his grounds broadly and extensively enough in point of time.' Lord John was not very felicitous in point of time himself. Embarrassed by his engagement to support the measure of his rival, little anticipating the importance and duration of the debate then taking place, and anxious to free himself as soon as possible from the fulfillment of an awkward duty, he wasted his ammunition much too soon in the engagement, spoke inopportunely and ineffectively, and the future first Minister of the country was not heard of in the House of Commons for three weeks." The weakness of this criticism is apparent as the motive of it is suspicious. Mr. Disraeli's opinion is based upon the erroneous assumption that had Lord John Russell known that the debate was to last for three weeks, he would have dramatically drawn importance to himself during the whole of that period by concealing his intended action, until near the end of the debate, and then revealing it in a pyrotechnic shower of dazzling sparks. But Lord John Russell was far too dignified for tricks like that. He had made up his mind to support Peel's measures, and he believed that it was due to Peel, to the country, and to himself, that he should say so early in the debate.

The debate of the second night is valuable reading, as it exposes the economic error so firmly believed in by the American protectionists to-day, and so tenaciously held by the English protectionists forty-five years ago; that we should sell to other nations, but not buy of them; and that wise legislation should facilitate the exportation of our products, and forbid the importation of those of other countries. The debate was opened by Mr. Stafford O'Brien, a land-owner, and member for the county of Northampton. He ridiculed what he called "the maxims of political economy," and declared that they could not be applied to practical purposes. He dug up the ancient "pauper labor" scarecrow, and exhibited it again. He became pathetic over the sorrows of the workingman, after the maudlin fashion peculiar to the rich monopolists of that day—and this. He said, 'Suppose that acting upon the axiom of buying in the cheapest market and selling in the dearest, he, a wealthy man in England, furnished his house with paper-hangings from Paris; suppose that he traveled in a continental carriage—that he purchased all his earthenware in Germany; suppose all this; when he looked out of the window of his gaudy house, or his foreign-built carriage, what would he see? A vast multitude of unemployed, starving Englishmen. And what would they say to him? 'We are poor English paper-stainers; we are Birmingham hardware men; our trade has been taken away from us, what are we to do?'" This kind of talk still had some weight outside, among ignorant workingmen, whose prejudices against "foreign pauper labor" could be easily aroused, but it was laughed at in the House of Commons, as a detected imposture; it was tiresome twaddle there. Mr. O'Brien requested his countrymen to starve with patience so that he might obtain high rents for his land; and on those terms he was willing to promise that he would not buy his fine carriages in France, nor his crockery in Germany.

Sir James Graham followed Mr. O'Brien, and applied this principle to his argument, that no country can permanently maintain exportation without imports in some shape or other to balance it; nor can a nation maintain importations for any length of time, without exporting something to pay for them. He said, "The honorable member from Northamptonshire described a state of things where a certain person has the walls of his house covered with French paper-hangings, furnished with articles of German hardware, and who rides in a Brussels carriage, while workmen are crowding the market with nobody to hire them. How does he think those carriages are to be obtained? Whatever may be the form of the transaction by which they are obtained, that transaction of necessity resolves itself into a barter. Directly or indirectly there must be an exchange of commodities, and you must in the long run export some of your own productions to pay for what you have got from abroad." Sir James Graham in replying to the challenge of Lord Worsley that if the members of the Government had changed their opinions they should manfully own it, said, "I accept that challenge. I do frankly avow my change of opinion, and, by that avowal, I dispose of all the speeches." Next to Peel himself, Sir James Graham was perhaps the ablest debater in the Ministry, and his speech on this occasion was regarded as a successful defense of the Government. Speaking as a landlord, he said, "For one, sooner than it should be said of myself, or any of the class to which I belong, that our object was to secure for ourselves an increase of rent, and not to promote the welfare and happiness of the great body of the community—sooner than leave any room for such a suspicion, I should say, speaking for myself, that I would descend to a lower estate, and abrogate my inheritance."

That Sir James Graham really meant what he said there is no reason to doubt. That he would have made the sacrifice willingly is probable; but when he claimed chivalry of that kind as an attribute of "the class to which I belong," the landlords of England, he spoke with innocent and unconscious irony. That "class" was protectionist, selfish, and unpatriotic. It claimed the lands of England by right of conquest, and it would not surrender any of its baronial privileges though famine threatened the people. It was protectionist and rapacious to the end.

While this debate was proceeding in the House of Commons, another with more pathos in it, was going on outside. It was conducted at night by the "protected" farm laborers of Wiltshire. Its revelations were of a startling character, and the protectionists, both in Parliament and out of it, were greatly disturbed by them. The Tories were thrown upon the defensive; while apologies and explanations came thick and fast. It may be doubted whether the skillful oratory and logical argument of Peel, and Graham, and Bright had so much effect as the rude pathos of those rustic hinds, who had been "protected" to starvation by a false and selfish economic system, the relic of a barbarous age. Their simple statements constituted eloquence of a very exciting kind. They could not be answered by argument; they could only be denied, and denial was useless, for the facts were too plain. Some of the speakers were women, and the stories they told of suffering made the protectionists appear to be the mere apologists of poverty and injustice. One man said, "My friends—I be a laboring man; I have a wife and seven children in family, my wages at the present time is eight shillings a week." Another said, "For the last fortnight I have received only six shillings a week. I know many men with four children who have only six shillings a week. I expect to be discharged when I get home for coming to the meeting. It be them Corn-Laws—them cursed Corn-Laws—that make bread dear. I have been employed like a horse in drawing a cart. I was one of five men yoked to the cart." Many others talked in the same way, but the speeches of the women were more pathetic and sorrowful than those of the men. One woman said that she was compelled to feed her children upon nettles and weeds, and this, they said, is "Protection." This exposure of the condition of the "protected" English peasantry was a powerful weapon in the hands of the Free Traders, and the protectionists were not able to soften down the indignation which it caused among the people.

On the fifth night of the debate, Sir Robert Peel addressed the House. He spoke for three hours, and gave a full explanation of the break-up of his Government in December, and his resumption of office. He defended himself from the imputation of unfairness to Lord John Russell, and read a letter which he had sent to the Queen on the 8th of December, two days after his resignation, and when he expected that Lord John Russell would succeed in forming an administration.

In that letter he had promised Her Majesty that he would support Lord John Russell in any measures he might bring forward for a repeal of the Corn-Laws, not inconsistent with the spirit of his lordship's letter from Edinburgh to the electors of the city of London. He then gave his reasons for introducing the measures before the House, and defended them on principle and on grounds of expediency. Even Lord Beaconsfield admits the strength of this important speech. He says, "The speech of Sir Robert Peel was one of his best; indignant and vigorous, free from the affectation of fairness, and that too obvious plausibility in which of late years he had somewhat luxuriantly indulged; he threw off the apologetic tone, and was uncompromising, both in his principles and demeanor. The peroration was in the high League style, though, of course, adapted to the more refined taste of the House of Commons." This is a great concession on the part of Lord Beaconsfield, but the speech deserved it.

Some of Peel's facts and arguments coming from the towering height occupied by an experienced Prime Minister and statesman fell with crushing weight upon the protectionist resistance, and absolutely broke it down. For instance, he made this challenge, "Show me," he said, "one relaxation, one removal of prohibition, which has not contributed to the advantage of the great body of consumers. I will go farther, I will show you that these removals of prohibition have contributed not merely to the general weal and advantage of the consumers, but that they are perfectly consistent with the permanent benefit and increased wealth of the producer." He then enforced his challenge by some startling statistics, showing the increased importation of timber under the reduced tariff, which increased supply had stimulated ship-building and every trade of which wood was the raw material. A reduction of the tariff on silk and its materials had been followed by the increased prosperity of the silk trade. For centuries the English silk manufacturer had been protected by a high tariff against the "pauper labor" of France. With an air of triumphant superiority that almost shrivelled up the protectionists, he exclaimed, "Look at the state of your silk trade at this moment. The French have long been accustomed to plume themselves upon their silk manufactures. But it may, perhaps, surprise not a few of those who are now listening to me, to learn that last year, with our relaxed tariff, we actually exported to France more silk than we exported to the whole universe in any year of the protective system. And there is no branch of manufactures in which the same improvement is not observable."

Those magnificent realties were only a "theory" in 1842, but they had become cannon-ball facts in 1846, battering down the ramparts of "Protection," and crumbling that old rapparee "theory" into ruins grim and hated as those of the old Bastile. Proceeding with his argument, in the self-confidence of a man who knows what he is talking about, he turned upon the angry crowd behind him, and said, "I am prepared to prove all this," but there was not one of them bold enough to call for the evidence. Referring to the dread of foreign competition, he pointed to the immense resources of England, her coal and iron, her freedom, the skill of her artisans, the physical and mental strength of her people; and then with the haughty pride of an Englishman looking down upon surrounding nations, and scorning to believe that they were able to compete with his own countrymen in manufactures or in anything else, he inquired, "What have you to fear?" Some day a triumphant statesman standing in the Capitol at Washington, and pointing to the resources of our country, a hundred-fold greater than England ever had, and to the activity, intelligence, and the industrial skill of our people, will silence our own protectionists by repeating the question of Peel, "What have you to fear?"

The debate went on for three weeks, and was greatly enlivened on the last night of it by a speech from Mr. Cobden. He was good-natured, and indeed, rather patronizing to the Tories, and he assured them that their fears of Free Trade were foolish. He told them that they themselves had lost confidence in the soundness of the "Protection" principle, and that their actions proved it. "You wish for an appeal to the country," he said, "and you will abide by its decision. If you could depend upon your principles you would not take such a course. You would say that you would not yield to one defeat or many, but you have no confidence in your doctrine." Referring to the threat that the bill should be defeated in the House of Lords, he said with great significance, "Recollect there is no cotton-spinner nor manufacturer there." Like a kind father talking to a lot of children, Mr. Cobden lectured the protectionists; and so amiably was it all done, that they bore it with good humor, if not with pleasure. Once, when he told them that in case of a new election they would lose every town containing as many as 25,000 inhabitants, they interrupted him with loud cries of

"No," "No," but he replied quickly, "I tell you that you have neither Liverpool nor Bristol." He made much ridicule of the old arguments about "dependence on the foreigner," "land going out of cultivation," the "drain of gold," etc., which, he said, although knocked in the head long ago, had come out again in this debate as fresh as ever. "You would know better," said Mr. Cobden, "if you lived in the world, and not in a charmed circle. Recollect," he continued, "I want no triumph; but I want us all to confer together to see if we cannot carry out something better for our country, and when this great measure is passed we will dissolve the League—but not till then." The hopeful, modest, and sunshiny tone of Cobden's speech lifted the debate into a more friendly atmosphere, and then Lord George Bentinck closed it. He had lately been chosen leader of the Protectionist party, and for three hours he made an obstinate struggle against a hostile tide; and when he finished his remarks there were loud calls of "Divide," "Divide."

More than a hundred speeches had been made, and it was thought that the debate would end on Friday night, the 27th of February. Great crowds of people waited in Parliament street all night long, anxious to hear the result. It was three o'clock in the morning of Saturday, February 28, 1846, when the debate ended; and when the division was had there appeared to be—for the Government proposals, 337; against them, 240. The revolution was accomplished. The cheers of the Free Traders inside and outside the House waked up London. The Protectionist Parliament of 1841 had, in the beginning of 1846, established Free Trade as the commercial policy of England by a majority of ninety-seven votes. The great struggle was ended, and the industry of Britain was free. In the year 1436 the first law was passed restricting the importation of foreign grain. It had been altered for better and for worse many times since then, and now at the venerable age of four hundred and ten years, it was slain on the spot where it was born. As the League had proclaimed from the very beginning, it carried down with it the whole system of protection. The schedule of import duties yet remaining was based on the principle of a tariff for revenue only.

A fine illustration of the bigotry of good, old fashioned, protection Toryism was furnished during the progress of this debate by the Duke of Newcastle. He owned a great part of the county of Nottingham, and in that county his will was law. He directed who should be elected to Parliament, and who should be defeated. Now, it so happened that his eldest son, the Earl of Lincoln, was member for South Nottingham shire, and he was also a member of Sir Robert Peel's administration. He had changed his opinions on the subject of Protection, and had become a supporter of the Free Trade measures of the Government. He had resigned one post in the administration to accept another, that of Chief Secretary for Ireland. The acceptance of this new office vacated his seat in Parliament, and required him to go before his constituents for a reelection, and before them he accordingly went. The Duke of Newcastle, however, had become so angry and indignant because Lord Lincoln supported Peel, that he gave orders that his son should be defeated, and defeated he was. Mr. Hillyard, a Protectionist, was elected in his place by a majority of 700 votes. The Duke of

Newcastle was a representative specimen of what Sir James Graham called, "the class to which I belong," a class which he thought would make sacrifices, rather than have it said that "our object is to secure an increase of rent, and not to promote the welfare and happiness of the great body of the community." The Duke of Newcastle furnished convincing evidence that a man who is privileged by a Protective Tariff to levy toll and tribute upon his fellow-citizens cares nothing about the welfare and happiness of the community. All he cares about is the welfare and happiness of himself.

CHAPTER XVII.

A TARIFF FOR REVENUE ONLY.

THE vote of February 27th was merely for going into committee; the measures approved by it were not yet law. Every separate clause and item in the new tariff could be debated and amended in committee of the whole. This offered to the Protectionists a chance to delay the bill, and they spitefully resolved on a policy of obstruction. They hoped, in a bewildered sort of way, that if they could gain time something might "turn up" to help them. They did not know exactly what, but, like the doomed criminal, they looked upon even a respite as including within it the chance of ultimate escape. Lord Beaconsfield confesses this with a simple fatuity not excelled by Mr. Micawber himself. In his "Biography of Lord George Bentinck" he says: "The great object which Lord George now proposed to himself was to delay the progress of the Government measures, so that they should not reach the House of Lords before Easter. He believed that time still might insure their discomfiture. The majority of the 27th of February was only in favor of going into committee. Before, therefore, any bill for the repeal of the Corn-Laws could be brought forward the principle of every projected alteration of the tariff must individually be sanctioned by a particular vote. The opportunities for resistance, therefore, were considerable and encouraging."

Rarely have statesmen pursued an object so microscopically "little" as this, which Lord Beaconsfield calls "great." Hunger was general throughout England and Scotland, while actual famine was impending over Ireland. The ministers offered relief to the starving people by repealing the "Protective" tariff on food, and this horse-racing son of a duke employed all the opportunities which the rules of Parliament gave him to resist this beneficent measure; and these, remarks Lord Beaconsfield, were "considerable and encouraging." This policy of delay was adopted, and, in fact, it was not until May that the bill passed its third reading and went up to the House of Lords. But all this was mere formality, after the vote of February 27th,—the mere ceremonial of nailing on the coffin-lid and preparing the deceased for burial. The funeral might be delayed, but it could not be prevented.

When the bill went up to the House of Lords the Tory peers made a fussy pretense of throwing it out, but they were at last afraid to do so. They had only one man among them of really great ability. That man was Lord Stanley, who had lately resigned his place in the cabinet rather than consent to a repeal of the Corn-Laws. The hopes of monopoly centered on him, and every protectionist in England was cheering him with the ancient slogan, "On, Stanley, on!" He made a great speech, which, for a moment, gave a little courage to his party. He opposed Free Trade with the same vehemence that his father and his grandfather had opposed railroads, and for the same antiquated reasons. The old earl used to employ a lot of people whose duty it was to shoot railroad surveyors when they came upon his lands. Lord Stanley paraded over and over again the ancient heresies of the protective system as if the steam engine and the printing press had not yet come. Shut out from the light of the nineteenth century, in the gloomy grandeur of the House of Lords, his speech might have been the speech of his ancestor fresh from the fight at Bosworth field.

On the same day that the bill passed its third reading in the House of Commons the Duke of Buccleugh, on the part of the Government, moved its first reading in the House of Lords, which was instantly opposed by the Duke of Richmond, who passionately denounced the measure as "an unauthorized abandonment of the great principle of Protection to British industry." Lord Monteagle replied to the Duke of Richmond, and said that "the doctrines of Free Trade recognized a clear distinction between protective duties and a tariff for revenue only." Earl Grey made the ablest speech on the Free Trade side. He had lately been transferred to the House of Lords by the death of his father. As Lord Howick, he had, in the House of Commons, proved himself, next to Mr. Villiers, the most philosophical and consistent Free Trader among all the members of the aristocracy who took that side; and in his new position he was pronounced and clear as he was in the Lower House of Parliament. He said that "he could only accept the scheme of the Government as an installment, not a perfect measure of Free Trade. He was still, as he had ever been, against all duties for protection; and he could answer for the great body of the manufacturers that they desired not a particle of protection for themselves when they asked for the removal of all protective and differential duties on every article of consumption." It is a pleasant coincidence that Earl Grey and Mr. Villiers are still, at the age of ninety, active statesmen, attending to their parliamentary duties—one of them in the House of Lords, the other in the House of Commons.

Lord Ashburton of the house of Baring, was one of the few peers who belonged to the commercial classes, and he insisted on preserving the plan of "Reciprocity." "The Germans," he said, "had their Zollverein, and France her restrictive system, and England required a similiar system to counteract them." Replying to Earl Grey, he said, he did not believe that the manufacturers would redeem the promise that had been made in their name. Lord Ashburton showed a very good knowledge of human nature when he said that "he believed the magnanimity of the manufacturers to be of the kind that would like Free Trade for every commodity except that which they themselves supplied." He did not see that this very sarcastic opinion, while intended to apply specially to persons, contained within it a general application to the whole protective system, which offers a legislative temptation stimulating greed, and seducing men to prey upon one another. All men desire Free Trade in the articles which they must buy; and laws are mischievous, and corrupting, which tempt them to ask protection on the products they have to sell. The selfish genius of the protective system was responsible for it, that the manufacturers were "of a kind that would like Free Trade for every commodity except that which they themselves supplied."

Lord Stanley reserved his great speech for the debate on the second reading of the bill. It was strong in oratory, but weak in argument, and its ignorant denial of the famine impending over Ireland must forever exclude Lord Stanley from the galaxy of great statesmen. Although the approaching scourge was as plainly visible as the funnel-shaped cloud which portends a hurricane, he spoke of it as "an utterly baseless vision haunting the imagination of Sir Robert Peel;" and he declared that "no country of eminence had ever ventured upon the rash experiment of leaving corn unprotected by restrictive duties on foreign importation." He said that reducing the price of wheat in order to relieve a scarcity in potatoes would produce no more effect than a law to reduce the price of pine-apples. He also denounced the League and said that the Government had mistaken the brawling torrent of agitation for the calm, still current of public opinion. The Anti-Corn-Law League, he said, had obtained a victory over the ministers of the Crown, and the ministers of the Crown had obtained a victory over their own political supporters, and he might also say over the independence of Parliament itself. Explaining his conduct in the cabinet, he admitted that he had agreed in November to a temporary suspension of the duties on the importation of foreign corn, "provided it were merely temporary." This declaration was inconsistent with the opinion expressed by Lord Stanley a moment before, that cheap wheat could no more supply the failure of potatoes than cheap pine-apples could. It was unstatesmanlike in this, that he was willing to admit foreign grain to stay the hunger of the people, but only for a time, and on the express condition that as soon as their hunger was relieved the protective tariff should be re-imposed, to make them hungry again.

Lord Stanley then claimed that the large exports of British manufactures proved the value of the protective system, but this was merely the old sophistry that two conditions being shown, one must be the cause of the other. Large exports of manufactured goods being possible under the protective system, Lord Stanley pretended that they would be impossible without it. This assumption is adopted by the American Protectionists now. They claim that all the prosperity of the country is due to the protective system, totally forgetting the ten thousand means of wealth that compel prosperity in spite of the tax laid upon our internal resources by the protective policy. The fallacy of Lord Stanley's argument was apparent in the fact that every reduction of tariff duties had been followed by a larger *export* trade, and it ignored the probability that exports would be multiplied still more should protection be abandoned altogether. That this probability was well founded was subsequently demonstrated by the test of actual experiment. Lord Stanley was afterward twice Prime Minister of England, but this speech proves that he was deficient in that broad wisdom and penetrating foresight so essential to the character of a statesman.

At last he appealed to the selfish landlord feeling, and warned the House of Lords that should the Corn-Laws be repealed, their wealth and influence, and standing in the country would be gone. He said, "Whatever may be the difficulties of reconciling the action of our mixed constitution—of keeping the balance even between a proud aristocracy and a reformed House of Commons—depend upon it those difficulties will not be less if, instead of a proud aristocracy you substitute a pauper aristocracy." In all this there was a patrician insolence towering and haughty as a castle on the Rhine. Here was an "order" of professed idlers, who by conquest, confiscation, and all manner of injustice, had possessed themselves of the land, claiming special privileges as the reward of usurpation, insisting that they formed a superior caste whose prerogative it was to live in luxury on the toil of others, and whose vested right it was to make the food of the people dear in order to increase the wrongful rent of lands. The sacrilegious idea that Norman barons might have to earn their own living like Saxon peasants, went through the House of Deadlocks like a cold wave, and gave most of the lords a chill. The mere suggestion of it they resented as a wrong. Referring to the rack-renting body of British and Irish landlords, Lord Stanley pathetically said, "My Lords, these are the true aristocracy of the country. If you reduce these men in the scale of society you will inflict an irretrievable and irreparable injury upon the country." He patronizingly invited the Plutocracy to maintain Protection, and promised that they too should come into the sacred order. "God forbid," he exclaimed "that our successful manufacturers and our princely merchants should not take their places among our aristocracy." The speech of Lord Stanley is proof that class legislation must produce classes, and that special privileges in the way of taxation will create a Plutocracy, which in due time will become an Aristocracy, narrow, selfish, and oppressive as the House of Lords.

Lord Brougham replied vigorously to Lord Stanley and at the end of his remarks he paid a fine tribute to "the public virtues, the prodigious powers of mind, and the immense courage," of Sir Robert Peel, who, he said, "had cast away all private and personal considerations—had disregarded his own interests—had given up his right to power and superiority—and had exposed himself to the most tempestuous and troubled sea that the political world had in modern times ever exhibited—who had given up what to an ambitious man was much—the main security of his power—he had surrendered what to a calculating man was much—his influence and authority with his party—and he had given up what to an amiable man was much, viz., private friendship and party associations. All these sacrifices he had made voluntarily and with his eyes open, in order to discharge what he deemed a great public duty."

It was an ironical freak of politics that the man who as Mr. Robinson, had moved, when a member of the House of Commons, for the enactment of the Corn-Laws in 1818, was the very man, who, as Earl of Ripon, moved in the House of Lords the second reading of the bill for their repeal in 1846. He confessed in a straightforward way that he had been converted; and anticipating the charge of inconsistency, which he knew would be fired at him, he said: "I know you can extract from the records of this House, language and sentiments of mine different from those I utter here to-night; but I take no shame to myself because the only time to regret any change of opinion is when it proceeds from a bad motive." He then moved the second reading of the bill. After two or three nights of peevish and feeble debate the second reading was carried by 211 to 164.

Punch in its merriest mood never caricatured the House of Lords with such effect as the "noble peers" themselves unconsciously did in their childish resistance to Free Trade. While the nineteenth century, just introducing the age of steam and electricity, was demanding freedom for its energies in the name of nearly all the industrial forces of England, the thirteenth century, represented by a meeting of coroneted nobles, was protesting in behalf of the feudal system against railroads, telegraphs, and steamships, the mercenary agents of a Free Trade policy. While the intellectual Free Trade agitation was dissolving the mercantile superstitions of medieval England, and breaking cabinets to pieces, and while its Titanic palpitations throbbed like an earthquake under the British monarchy, a meeting composed exclusively of peers was held at the Clarendon hotel to protest against the development and exchange of God's bounties, and especially to protest against the abolition of the old stage coach "Protection," which, they pretended, had carried England in triumph through a great and prosperous career.

This quaint and curious meeting, which resembled the fifth act of a burlesque play, was the anti-climax of the aristocratic resistance to the new era. There is a scene in one of Gilbert and Sullivan's comic operas where a select set of nobles wearing their barbarian coronets, dance a comic dance and sing a comic song; and this comes nearest in character and appearance to the meeting of dukes and earls and barons held at the Clarendon hotel to protest against Free Trade. The Clarendon was a "grand, gloomy and peculiar" hotel in Bond street, where the mutton was supposed to have a finer patrician flavor than it had elsewhere, as indeed it had; and certainly the Clarendon was the most fit and appropriate place in London for the meeting. The Duke of Richmond was in the chair, supported by the Duke of Cleveland, and the ancient Gothic style of talk indulged in by Lord Stanley, Lord Beaumont and some other Norman Lords there present, gave those finishing touches of exaggeration to a caricature of the House of Lords from the contemptuous effects of which it has never yet recovered. These Don Quixotes and Sancho Panzas "unanimously resolved" that they would charge with lance and saber upon Free Trade whenever that form of modern civilization should appear in the House of Lords. Unlike the chivalrous Don, their courage failed them at the last, and, although they had the power to defeat the Free Trade measures on the third reading, they sat in sulky silence, afraid of the nineteenth century, and they did not even vote.

Almost as ludicrous as the meeting of the Lords at the Clarendon was the meeting of their tenants at Willis's rooms, a genteel place at the West End for concerts, lectures, dances, and the like. This meeting was heralded as a meeting of the "farmers," and so far as the men there present actually farmed the land they were entitled to be called farmers; but they were not farmers in the sense of independent yeomen, and therefore their meeting had no moral weight. It was notorious that they were only tenants and actual dependents of the barons who met at the Clarendon, farmers who voted and spoke at the bidding of their landlords. For this reason their protest against Free Trade counted nothing. The fact, also, that they chose little rooms to meet in, so that they might call them "crowded," raised a laugh against them, and forced a comparison with the great meetings of the League at Covent Garden theatre and elsewhere; a comparison humiliating to the farmers at Willis's, and to the Lords at the Clarendon. The Duke of Richmond took the chair in one room, and the Duke of Buckingham in the other, while Mr. Disraeli and Lord George Bentinck spoke to the farmers, promising them that the House of Lords would reject the Free Trade measures, or so mutilate them by amendments as to compel a dissolution of Parliament.

The last appeal for protection came from the Duke of Richmond, who presented a petition from some ribbon-makers praying that their contemptible monopoly might be spared from the general wreck. Once more Richmond and Buckingham called upon their lordships to fight for their ancient order, and have no fear of the League. This was Quixotic advice, and useless, for the baronial courage of the peers who met at the Clarendon hotel had already "oozed out at their finger ends," like the bravery of Bob Acres, and they feared that if they threw out the bill, and thereby compelled a dissolution of Parliament, the excitement of the people would add such power to the League that, in its rage, it might sweep away, not only the Corn-Laws, but the House of Lords itself. They therefore allowed the Free Trade measures to pass; and they were so disheartened that on the 25th of June the Corn and Customs bill went through the House of Lords on its third reading without even a division.

CHAPTER XVIII.

THE FALL OF PEEL.

It was dramatic that on the very same night that the Free Trade measures passed the House of Lords, the Government of Sir Robert Peel was overthrown. On the Irish Coercion Bill, the irreconcilable Tory faction in the House of Commons, led on by Lord George Bentinck and Mr. Disraeli, took revenge upon the Minister for his Free Trade policy by voting with the opposition. Although both of them approved the Coercion bill, and had voted for it in its early stages, they saw in the defeat of it a chance for unstatesmanlike revenge, and Lord George in the classic dialect of the race-track called upon his faction to go over to the enemy, and "kick out the bill and the ministers together." His orders were obeyed, and the administration was defeated by 292 to 219. Sir Robert Peel immediately resigned. On the following Monday night he announced his resignation in a speech of much good temper, pathos, and dignity. In the hour of his fall his political sky was at its brightest. On that very day came an official dispatch from America announcing that the United States Government had settled the Oregon question on the terms proposed by him, and thus had dissipated the war cloud which for some time had darkened the relations between the two countries. He said that he would offer no factious opposition to the government of those who had thrown him out of office.

He promised to support Lord John Russell's administration in carrying out the new commercial policy. He said, "If that be the policy which will be pursued, I shall feel it my duty to give to his government my cordial support. I presume that Her Majesty's government will adopt that policy—and that if other countries choose to buy in the dearest market, it will be no discouragement to them to permit us to buy in the cheapest." He then advised Lord John Russell to abandon the "treaty," "retaliation" and "reciprocity" system in his foreign commercial policy. "I trust," he said, "that the new Government will not resume the policy which they and we have found so inconvenient; namely, haggling with foreign countries, instead of taking that independent course which we believe to be conducive to our own interests."

Of course much of his speech was a review of his Free Trade policy, and to the leader of the Free Trade movement he paid this magnanimous tribute. He said, "The name which ought to be associated with the success of the Free Trade measures, is not the name of the noble Lord, the member for London, nor is it my name. It is the name of a man, who, acting as I believe from disinterested motives, has, with untiring energy, by appeals to reason, enforced their necessity with an eloquence the more to be admired because it was unaffected and unadorned;—the name which ought to be associated with these measures is the name of Richard Cobden." This roused the Free Traders to enthusiasm, and the cheering was loud and long. Many Tories joined in it, for everybody respected Cobden. At last in the midst of deep silence, he said:

"Sir, I shall leave office, I fear, with a name severely censured by many honorable gentlemen, who, on public principle, deeply regret the severance of party ties; I shall surrender power severely censured, I fear again, by many honorable gentlemen, who, from no interested motive, have adhered to the principle of Protection as important to the welfare and interests of the country; I shall leave a name execrated by every monopolist, who, from less honorable motives, maintains protection for his own individual benefit; but it may be that I shall leave a name sometimes remembered with expressions of good will in those places which are the abode of men whose lot it is to labor, and to earn their daily bread by the sweat of their brow—a name remembered with expressions of good will, when they shall recreate their exhausted strength with abundant and untaxed food, the sweeter because it is no longer leavened by a sense of injustice."

As he took his seat nearly the whole House rose, and cheered him for several minutes; the sulky Protectionist faction alone sat silent. Since the time of Wolsey no Prime Minister of England had fallen with greater dignity. When the cheering had subsided he again rose, and moved that the House adjourn until Friday, to give Lord John Russell time to form the new administration. Then taking the arm of a friend he left the House. In order to avoid the vast concourse of sympathizing citizens in the streets, he left by the side door that leads into Westminster Hall, and tried to escape that way, but the crowd heard of it, and headed him off. Hundreds of men formed a circle around him, and with rude but respectful courtesy, they escorted him to his home. Never in the history of England was the fall of a minister so like a triumph.

That Sir Robert Peel regarded the downfall of his ministry as affording him a grateful relief from the cares of office, is shown by the following letter to his friend, Lord Hardinge, Governor-General of India, written immediately after his resignation:

DRAYTON MANOR. July 4, 1846.
My Dear Hardinge:
You will see that we are out—defeated by a combination of Whigs and Protectionists. A much less emphatic hint would have sufficed for me. I would not have held office by sufferance for a week.

Were I to write a quire of paper I could not recount to you what has passed with half so much accuracy and detail as the public papers will recount it. There are no secrets. We have fallen in the face of day, and with our front to our enemies.

There is nothing I would not have done to ensure the carrying of the measures I had proposed this session; but the moment their success was ensured, and I had the satisfaction of seeing two drowsy old Masters in Chancery mumble out at the table of the House of Commons, that the Lords had passed the Corn and Customs bills I was satisfied.

Two hours after this, intelligence was brought that we were ejected from power; and by another coincidence as marvelous, on the day on which I had to announce in the House of Commons the dissolution of the Government, the news arrived that we had settled the Oregon question, and that our proposals had been accepted by the United States without the alteration of a word.

Lady Peel and I are quite alone here—in the loveliest weather—feasting on solitude and repose, and I have every disposition to forgive my enemies for having conferred upon me the blessing of the loss of power.

Most truly and affectionately yours,
ROBERT PEEL.

That Peel would have been called again to power is reasonably certain, for he was a vigorous man, only sixty-two years old, when, in the summer of 1850, he was killed by a fall from his horse, while riding in St. James's park; an event that filled the land with profound and unaffected sorrow; an event that, it may be confidently said, affected injuriously, and perhaps disastrously, the politics of England. Had he lived, the Crimean War folly might have been averted. On his monument, erected by the workingmen of England, is chiseled this immortal tribute, "He gave the people cheap bread."

This history ends here. Although the application of the new commercial system to all the conditions of the empire; to its agricultural, manufacturing, mining, colonial, shipping, and other interests was the work of a series of years and many acts of legislation, yet the struggle to establish the Free Trade principle as the policy of England ended with the triumph of Sir Robert Peel's measures in 1846. The repeal of protection to shipping, known as the "Navigation Laws," did not take effect until 1850, and it was not until some years later that all traces of the protective system were eliminated from the revenue policy of England, and the tariff on imports made for purposes of revenue only. The protective duty on sugar lingered along for some time on the plea of discouraging slavery and encouraging the free labor of the British West Indies. Some duty on timber survived for awhile on the theory that in return for the allegiance and trade of the colony of Canada, the Canadian forests ought to be protected against the "pauper forests" of the United States, while the Navigation Laws resisted reform because Adam Smith had said that they were an exception to the Free Trade theory, for they developed a mercantile marine from which native sailors could always be obtained to man the royal navy in time of war. The protectionists, of course, offered a mechanical resistance to the removal of these restrictions, and they declared that the repeal of the Navigation Laws was the death knell of England, the transferring of her shipbuilding industry to the United States, the disappearance of her flag from the ocean, the decay of her fighting power, and the end of her naval superiority. These arguments were strong, and the protectionist forebodings had much weight; so much weight, indeed, that in 1850, Lord John Russell's bill for the repeal of the Navigation Laws passed its second reading in the House of Commons by a meager majority of only fifty-six. Still, it was felt that the Free Trade experiment, having been entered upon, and the principle of it solemnly sanctioned, all protection exceptions to it were illogical and inconsistent; and, under the pressure of this reasoning, all commercial restrictions of every kind were finally swept away.

As a fortune-teller never goes out of business because his predictions fail, so the Protection soothsayers who had prophesied national ruin as the inevitable consequence of repealing the protective tariff, started again with the same old stock of dismal omens as soon as a proposition was made to repeal the Navigation Laws, and they began foreboding again with as much impudence as if all their former portents had not failed. I cannot resist the temptation to quote a few specimen auguries from our old friend, *Blackwood's Magazine*, because they have such a comical appearance now:

> The act of Navigation is not favorable to foreign commerce, or to the growth of that opulence that can arise from it. As defense, however, is of much more

value than opulence, the act of Navigation, perhaps, is the wisest of all the commercial regulations of England.

The fanaticism of political economists, who, like all other fanatics, are inaccessible to reason or experience, is, without doubt, a main cause of the disastrous policy to which the nation seems now irrevocably pledged.

Shipbuilding and ship-navigating are twice as costly in Great Britain as they are in Norway or Denmark. How could it be otherwise when they have the material of ships and rigging at their doors, while we have to transport them to the British shores from Canada or the Baltic?

That the system of Free Trade, the universal preference of foreigners for the sake of the smallest reduction of price, to our own subjects—must, if persisted in, lead to the dismemberment and overthrow of the British Empire, cannot admit of a moment's doubt.

What made the Roman power steadily advance during seven centuries, and endure in all a thousand years? The protection which the armies of the legions afforded to the industries of mankind. . . . . Free Trade in grain at length ruined it; the harvests of Lybia and Egypt came and superseded those of Greece and Italy, and thus this fall.

It is evident that the decline of British and foreign shipping will be so rapid under Free Trade in ships that the time is not far distant when the foreign tonnage employed in conducting our trade will be superior in amount to the British.

In all probability, in six or seven years that desirable consummation will be effected.

The awful warning which goes by the name of the "Roman Empire" was *Blackwood's* favorite example. If a little boy at the dinner-table asked for a second piece of pie, he was gravely and solemnly admonished by *Blackwood's* that "luxury caused the downfall of the Roman Empire"; and that venerable false prophet religiously believed not only that the repeal of the Roman Corn-Laws brought about the downfall of Rome, but also that buying corn in Egypt caused the downfall of Israel. And *Blackwood's Magazine* is prophesying still.

As soon as Great Britain was freed from the incumbrances of what is improperly called "Protection," that aspiring nation bounded forward to a prosperity greater than it had ever known before. The object of this history has been to avoid statistics as much as possible, for they are dry reading; but a few argumentative statistics may not be out of place. In 1840 the foreign commerce of the United Kingdom, exports and imports, not including bullion and specie, amounted to 665 millions of dollars; in 1880 it was 3,485 millions, and in 1889 it was 3,716 millions. Within those figures may be included all other statistics of every kind. A few more details, however, will not tire the reader, and will be found valuable. In 1840 the imports into Britain amounted in value to 310 millions of dollars, in 1880 they amounted to 2,055 millions. In 1840 the exports from Britain, of British produce, amounted to 255 millions of dollars, in 1880 they amounted to 1,115 millions. Fractions are excluded here, and a pound is called five dollars. The foreign and colonial produce exported from Britain in 1840 amounted to 50 millions of dollars, in 1890 it amounted to 315 millions.

The above figures show a wonderful increase in the wealth and material prosperity of the country; a growth out of all proportion to the increase in the population, but they do not show how that increased prosperity was distributed among the people. Nor is it necessary that they should, for the laws that govern, or ought to govern the distribution of wealth among those who have produced it, belong to another branch of political science, and need not be discussed here. We are not without assistance, however, in determining this question. The statistics of average annual consumption of the principal imported and excisable articles per head, for the total population of the United Kingdom, from 1840 to 1880, show the most surprising and beneficent results of the Free Trade policy. It may be stated in one sentence that in 1840 the working people of England, Ireland and Scotland were always hungry. This, of course, is not literally true, but it is true enough. In 1880 the hunger had not entirely ceased, but it was the exception, not the rule. In 1840 there was imported into Britain of corn, wheat and wheat flour 42 lbs. per head, for all the population; in 1880 the quantity was 210 lbs. per head. In 1840 the quantity of butter imported was 1 lb per head; in 1880 it was 7 lbs. Of cheese 1 lb. in 1840, 5 lbs. in 1880; of bacon and hams one-tenth of a pound in 1840, 15 lbs. and nine-tenths in 1880; of potatoes one one-hundredth of a pound in 1840, 31½ lbs. in 1880. It may be said that this table is fallacious because it only shows the increase to the people from importations, but does not show the loss they have sustained from decreased home production resulting from the repeal of the Corn-Laws; but the reply to that is that there has been very little decrease, for nearly as large a quantity of those articles is raised in England now as was raised then, so that the people have all the home production for their use and comfort, and this enormous importation also. The increased wealth of a country, stated in terms of money may be misleading as a test of the average wealth of the people; but the increased wealth of a country, stated in terms of eggs and bacon, may be accepted as evidence of increased average comfort, for those articles are consumed by the working classes; and that they are able to buy so much more of them than they formerly could, is evidence of increased employment and higher wages. The increase has continued up to the present time.

We have another test, and a fair one. In 1840 there was imported into the United Kingdom one-quarter of a gallon of wine per head for all the population; in 1880 it was less than half a gallon per head. Wine is the luxury of the rich, and these figures all show that the increased consumption of bread and meat was by the people at large. Another fair test, which will apply to both the objections above mentioned, is furnished by tea and sugar. These are not raised in England, and, of course, all that was used of them in 1840 was imported, the same as that used in 1880. The returns prove that in 1840 there was imported into the United Kingdom $1\frac{1}{4}$ lbs. of tea per head for all the population, while in 1880 the quantity amounted to $4\frac{1}{2}$ lbs. per head. In 1889 it was 4.90 lbs. per head. Of raw sugar the quantity imported in 1840 was $15\frac{1}{4}$ lbs. per head, in 1880 it was $54\frac{1}{4}$ lbs. Of refined sugar none was imported in 1840, in 1880 the importation was $9\frac{1}{2}$ lbs. per head. In 1889 the ration of refined sugar for the year was at the rate of 26 lbs. for every man, woman and child in the Kingdom. Of course, every man, woman and child did not get exactly that quantity, but the extra allowance taken by the rich of the increase was an insignificant quantity, when compared with the extra allowance taken by the poor.

Between 1840 and 1890 the wages of the working people of England largely increased, but it is not necessary to mention that, because the increased consumption of food shown by the above figures proves that the people must have had more wages to buy those comforts with, or they could not have been imported at all. They prove that the Free Trade policy has given to the people of England more to eat, more to wear, and better houses to live in. It has given them higher wages with less hours of labor. It has given them more holidays, more books, and more enjoyments, and their moral advancement has grown with their material prosperity. The man who sees the English now, and remembers the England of 1846, can scarcely recognize the people, so great has been the improvement in one generation.

A word or two about shipping, because the United States tenaciously clings to the Navigation Laws borrowed from England, which the people of that country unanimously believed for centuries were absolutely necessary to establish and maintain her shipbuilding industry at home, and her mercantile interests abroad, without which she could not have a nursery of sailors to man the royal fleet in time of danger. In the debate of 1849, on the bill for the amendment of the Navigation Laws, English statesmen had got no farther along in their political education than to talk like this, Mr. Drummond looked upon the measure as one of a series, "the end and intention of which was to discharge British, in order to give employment to foreign workmen." Mr. Bankes agreed with Mr. Drummond that the whole scheme was part of a policy for the "depression of the British laborer." Mr. Hillyard said that the effect of it would be "to draw capital from England, and make it dependent on foreign countries for shipping." Mr. Thompson said that "the United States could not, even if so disposed, give anything to us in comparison to the great advantages it was now proposed to surrender to them. America, from her geographical position, possessed many advantages over us. She had Free Trade with China; and, the Navigation Laws destroyed, American goods would displace British manufactures in that market." Mr. Robinson said that without protection, "it was impossible for the British shipbuilder to compete with the foreigner. The present tonnage of the United States was now nearly equal to that of England, and the difference would soon dwindle away if the Navigation Laws were repealed." The Marquis of Granby said that "our naval supremacy depends upon the maintenance of the Navigation Laws." On the final passage of the bill Mr. Drummond made another attack upon it, and declared that it came from the "Satanic school of politics."

Let us see how nearly the forebodings of those gentlemen came to pass. In 1849, the number of British sailing vessels engaged in the home and foreign trade was 17,807, with a tonnage of 2,988,021 tons. In 1880, the number of sailing vessels was 16,183, with a tonnage of 3,750,442 tons. In 1849, the number of British steamers engaged in the home and foreign trade (not including river steamers), was 414, with a tonnage of 108,321 tons. In 1880, the number of British steamers engaged in the home and foreign trade (not including river steamers), was 3,789, with a tonnage amounting to 2,594,135. In 1889, the number of steamers had increased to 5,585, and the tonnage to 4,664,808 tons. In 1849, the number of sailors employed on those vessels (not including masters), was 152,611. In 1880, the number was 192,972. In 1889, it was 230,263. In 1840, when the Navigation Laws for the protection of British shipping were in full force, the excess of British tonnage over the foreign tonnage entering the ports of the United Kingdom was 3,541,303 tons. In 1880, the excess was 23,961,905 tons. In 1840, the total tonnage of all the vessels entering and clearing at the ports of the United Kingdom was, British, 6,940,485 tons; foreign, 2,949,182 tons. In 1880, it was as follows: British, 41,348,984 tons; foreign, 17,387,079 tons.

On the impartial protectionist seeking to know the truth, those facts and figures may have some weight; on the selfish protectionist, interested in the preservation of monopoly, they will make no impression. On him reason, argument, facts and figures are all lost. To him the instructive numbers just given are unsubstantial and unreal, a vagary of Free Trade, a theory and a delusion. To him a barn, or a ship, or a grain elevator is nothing but a cloud, and "very like a whale"; to him the demonstrations of geometry are only the fanatical theories of Euclid, the doctrinaire. He is outside the courts of reason.

Every Protectionist argument is entitled to respectful treatment, except one—that which consists in a sneer at England for her Free Trade policy, a policy which has been so largely beneficial, not only to the people of Great Britain, but to the people of America. It is difficult to keep down an expression of contempt when we hear men who inhabit the fertile plain between the Alleghanies and the Rocky Mountains speak with derision of a policy which offers them a free and open market for everything they raise, and for everything they are able to manufacture, a policy which has not only multiplied the comforts of life to all the people of Great Britain, but which has given an added value to every acre of land in that exuberant American valley.

THE END

INDEX.

A

Agricultural protection 101, 158 seq. 184.
Agricultural protection meetings 220, 222.
Agriculture, foreboded ruin of —by free trade 54.
Albert (Prince) presence of —in House of Commons resented 228.
America, natural advantages of, 25.
American bacon 79.
American barrel-staves 190.
American cotton, removal of duty on 194.
American grain, duty on 97.
American produce, importation of 153.
American protectionists, arguments of 41, 64, 66, 68, 95, 109, 135, 137, 167, 168, 170, 175, 183, 195, 199, 213, 227, 246, 261.
American reformers 118.
American Secretary of the Treasury on Free Trade 230.
American statesmen 177.
American system of protection 10, 14, 76.
American wheat 107.
Annual Register on the Corn Law Agitation 145.
Annual Register on the prospects for 1845, 181.
Anti-Corn-Law League 9, 25, 29 seq. 30, 48, 58, 73, 88, 106, 126, 129, 145 seq. 168, 181, 184, 209, 218, 222.

Apparel, regulation of—in England 18.
Aristocracy and Plutocracy 202.
Ashburton, Lord 259.

B

Balance of trade 110.
Baring, Mr. 42.
Beaconsfield, Lord, on Free Trade Debate 233, 236, 243, 245, 250, 256.
Bentinck, Lord George 253, 256.
Big-loaf (the) argument 144.
Blackwood's Magazine 15, 90, 121, 135, 139, 272.
Blaine Mr., tariff policy of 165, 226.
Boston, protest of—against Protection 13.
Brazil, commerce with 157.
Bright, John 28, 89, 130, 145, 146, 162, 188, 203.
British Colonies, discrimination in favor of 79, 80.
Brougham, Lord 37, 87, 262.
Buckingham, Duke of 59.
Burdett, Sir Francis 71.

C

Cattle, importation of —discussed 77, 79, 83.
Charter, the Chartist 131.
Chartist riots, 89.
Chartists, 129 seq.
Cheap bread—cheap wages, argument 52 seq. 74, 134, 205, 225.

282   INDEX.

Cheap commodities and independence 138.
Cheap goods, alarm at the idea of 107.
Class legislation 143.
Clothing, duties on 232.
Cobden, Richard 28, 50 seq. 55, 74, 86, 101, 116, 126, 145, 158, 170, 196, 204, 215, 219, 226, 253.
Cobden, Richard, Sir Robert Peel on 268.
Commerce, supposed timidity of 106.
Community, artificial prosperity of special classes an injury to the 20, 199.
Consumption ruled by price 179.
Contract, protective tariff as a 109, 113, 118.
Contradictory protective laws 16.
Corn, meaning of term, in England 25.
Corn Laws (of 1815) 23.
Corn Laws, abolition of the 235.
Corn Laws, cruelty of the 185.
Corn Laws, debates on the. *See* "Debates"
Corn Laws, distress caused by the 90 seq. 248.
Corn Laws, operation of the 113.
Corn Laws, Lord J. Russell's Resolution on the 201.
Croker, John Wilson 134, 195.

D

Debates in Parliament 33 seq. 39 seq. 42 seq. 53 seq. 62 seq. 73, 75, 78 seq. 84 seq. 94 seq. 105, 108 seq. 117, 158 seq. 166 seq. 192 seq. 196, 198 seq. 223, 229 seq. 240 seq.
Destruction of property as an economic blessing 123.
Disraeli, Mr. 98, 198. *See* "Beaconsfield, Lord."

Distress caused by the Corn-Laws 90 seq.
Distress of the country, debate on motion as to the 94 seq.
Douglass, Sir Howard 114.
Dukes, comical blunders of old 220.
Duty, reduction of—to increase revenue 42.

E

Ebrington, Lord 204.
Economic principles, education in 15, 126, 143.
Edinburgh Review, on protective legislation 22.
Edinburgh Review, on relation between prices and wages 142.
Elliott (Ebenezer) the Corn-Law Rhymer 24, 142.
England, Protection laws of 16 seq.
Englishmen, insular prejudices of 120.
Exchange of commodities, the basis of trade 247.
Export duties, abolition of 190.
Export trade and tariff reduction 226.

F

Famine (threatened) Peel's proposed remedies for 209.
Farm laborer, condition of the 127.
Ferrand, Mr. 93, 97, 166.
Flail, for thrashing grain 130.
Food, the ultimate object of land cultivation 204.
Foreign competition, dread of 251.
Foreign commerce of Great Britain 274.
Foreign pauper labor, ghost of 121.
Fraser's Magazine 15, 82, 91, 134, 194.
Free breakfast table 178.

INDEX.

Free Trade, a live issue 27.
Free Trade, American Secretary of the Treasury on 230.
Free Trade, as now viewed by Mr. Gladstone 96.
Free Trade, beneficent effect of 65, 275.
Free Trade budget 189.
Free Trade, effect of—on exports 227, 257, 261
Free Trade, Lord J. Russell's conversion to 211.
Free Trade movement, early insignificance of 36.
Free Trade, growth of 23 seq. 145 seq.
Free Trade, Peel's arguments in favor of 230 seq.
Free Trade, Peel's conversion to 194.
Free Trade, petitions by workingmen in favor of 240.
Free Trade policy, value of 15.
Free Trade, resolution in favor of 201.
Free Trade Speech of Sir Robert Peel 230 seq.
Free Trade struggle, meaning of 9.
Free Trade, true principles of 149.

G

Gibson, Mr. Milner 115, 169, 193.
Gladstone, Mr. W. E. 79, 81, 95, 109, 118, 158, 160, 162, 163, 168, 174, 187, 193, 217.
Gold, drain of 110.
Goulburn Mr. 177, 213.
Government, supposed creation of prosperity by 20.
Granby, Marquis of 71.
Great Britain and Pennsylvania compared 227.
Great Britain, prosperity of 274.
Graham, Sir James 198, 202, 207, 208, 247.

Grey (Earl) 258. *See* "Lord Howick."
Grimes, Mr. James W. 182.

H

Heathcote, Sir W. 241.
Herbert, Mr. Sidney 196.
High prices, conditions of—according to Cobden 64.
High tariff platform 225.
Home industry, protection of 10, 16, 21, 31, 114, 213, 246.
Home industry, supposed injury of—by Free Trade 135, 161.
Home market, value of 139.
Horizontal plan of tariff reductions 77.
House of Commons, lords by courtesy in the 155.
House of Commons. *See* "Debates."
House of Lords, Free Trade caricature of the 265.
House of Lords, feudal ideas of the 85.
House of Lords. *See* "Debates."
Howick (Lord) 94, 111, 164, 169. *See* "Grey (Earl)"
Hume, Joseph 79, 118, 155, 186.
Huskisson, Mr. 10, 16.

I

Ignorance of economic principles 124.
Illustrated London News 52, 153.
Import duties, burden of 181.
Import duties, payment of 228.
Imports, the most advantageous part of commerce 164.
Improvements (public) opposition to 124.
Income tax 181, 192.
Independence and cheap commodities 138.
Industry, protection the paralysis of 15.

Interests (protected) competition among 182.
Ireland, failure of potato crop in 207.
Ireland, famine in 259.
Irish Coercion Bill 267.

K

Knatchbull, Sir Edward 112.

L

Labor, comparative value of 74.
Labor (native) protection of 167.
Labouchere, Mr. 38, 157.
Land cultivation, food the ultimate object of 204.
Landed interest, peculiar burdens supposed to affect the 105, 112.
Landed interest, protection of the 22, 30, 105, 196.
Landed interest, selfishness of the 248.
Latitudinal protection 13.
Layard, Captain 169.
Leather manufactures, duties on 234.
Leather monopoly in England 19.
Liberal press, protectionist feeling of the 153.
Lincoln and Cobden, comparison of 51.
Liverpool, Lord 11.
Local protection 19, 100.
London merchants, free trade petition of 10.
Longitudinal Free Trade 13.
Lords by courtesy only 155.
Lords, meeting of—at the Clarendon Hotel 264.
Lower classes, jealousy of 122.

M

Macaulay, Mr. 75, 194.
Machinery, effect of introduction of 54, 86, 87, 93, 97.
Machinery, effect on wages ascribed to 166.
Machinery, opposition to 123.
Manchester, Chamber of Commerce of 29, 34.
Manchester, Free Trade feeling at 219.
Manchester, Free Trade meetings at 88.
Manual Labor, protection for 241.
Manufactures, beneficial effect of Free Trade on 251.
Manufacturing interest, protection of 148, 213.
Maynooth College, grant of money to 187.
McKinley bill and Gladstone's Reciprocity 95.
McKinley Bill and wages 200.
Mediæval sentiment as to trade 112.
Melbourne, Lord 40, 85.
Mercantile system of protection 10.
Miles, Mr. P. 197, 241.
Monopoly, at the expense of the consumer 21.
Monopoly, effects of leather 19.
Monopoly, strength of—in England 32.
Monopolies, opposition of—to Free Trade 39.
Monopolies, protests of—against the New Tariff 82.
Moral results of material prosperity 226.
Moral Science, universality of laws of 12.
Morpeth, Lord 240.
Morrill tariff 200.
Morrison bill, debate in Congress on 113.
Muntz, Wm. 114.

N

National Republican Convention of 1884 225.
Navigation Laws, repeal of 271.

Navigation Laws, supposed effect of 272, 277.
Newcastle, Duke of, protectionist, bigotry of 254.
New Tariff Bill, debate on the 75, seq.
New Tariff Bill, questionable good faith of Peel and Gladstone in relation to 81.

O

O'Brien, Mr. Stafford 246.
O'Connell, Mr. 43, 54, 64, 131, 150, 209, 218.
Oregon question, settlement of 267.
Organized hypocrisy 198.
Overproduction, fear of 28, 123, seq.
Overproduction, misleading name for under-consumption 126.

P

Parliament, form of opening 32.
Parliament, opening of, in January, 1846, 228.
Parliamentary debate of 1842 61, seq.
Palmerston, Lord 36, 69.
Patrician insolence 261.
Patriotism and protection 28.
Pattison, Mr. 156.
Pauper labor (foreign), ghost of 121.
Peel, Sir Robert 27, 33, 36, seq., 51, 37, 60, seq., 76, 86, 106, 118, 142, 150, 171, 186, 189, 192, 198, seq., 205, 207, seq., 216, 221, 225, 229, seq., 249, seq., 267.
Peel, Sir Robert, confidence of Tories in 212, 216, 221, 242.
Peel, Sir Robert, death of 271.
Peel, Sir Robert, downfall of 267.
Peel, Sir Robert, Free Trade Speech of 230.
Peel, Sir Robert, letter of—to Lord Hardinge 270.

Peers, protest of—against the Free Trade policy 264.
Pennsylvania and Great Britain compared 227.
Penny Magazine 37.
People, sufferings of the—due to protection 55, 109, 116.
Petitions by workingmen in favor of Free Trade 240.
Plutocracy and Aristocracy 262.
Potato disease 204.
Potatoes and patriotism 80.
Political Economy, universality of laws of 13, 194.
Political prophecy fulfilled 193.
Price, affected by buying power 159.
Price (normal), a secondary consideration 137.
Prices rule consumption.179.
Principle, valueless concession to 11.
Protected interests, selfishness of 182, 191, 259, 261.
Protection against slave labor 43, 156, 179, 194.
Protection in favor of Colonies 271.
Protection laws of England 16, seq.
Protection of classes 199.
Protection, Mr. Gladstone's excuse for 95.
Protection, stimulus of 199.
Protection, the paralysis of industry 15.
Protection to local industries 19.
Protection to native industry 10, 13.
Protection to special trades 19, 22, 175.
Protection, Tory Journals on 15.
Protectionist feeling, grounds of 120.
Protectionist jugglery 66.
Protectionist principle (the) 96.
Protectionists, selfishness of 172.

Protective policy of Middlesex farmers 14.
Protective system 9.
Protective system, a competition of classes 233.
Protective system, Cobden's argument against the 55, 67, 101.
Protective system, death warrant of 229.
Protective system, downfall of the 253.
Protective system, effect of 35, 115, 213.
Protective system of the United states, effect of 55, 115, 161. See "American Protectionists."
Protective system, origin of 232.
Protective system, Peel's argument for 64.
Protective system, supposed compensator, character of 105.
Protective Tariff, considered as a contract 109, 113, 118.
Provisions, increased importation of—under the New Tariff 81.
Public houses, places of resort 129.

Q

Quarrel between Cobden and Peel 102.
Quarterly Review 133.
Queen's Speech, reference in—to Free Trade principles 223.
Queen's Speech, reference to public distress in the 92.
Queen Victoria, apology of 228.

R

Rain and Protection 206.
Raw materials, removal of duty from 78, 190, 232.
Reciprocity, doctrine of 96, 99, 116, 162, 164, 227.
Rent and wages 136.
Resolutions, Lord John Russell's Whig 200.
Restraint of trade, evil 169.
Retaliation, childish policy of 115.
Revenue, increase of, by reduction of duty 42.
Revenue, tariff for 113, 148, 254, 258, 271.
Revolutionary, all opposition to monopoly, said to be 40.
Ribbon-makers, petition of 266.
Riches, consist of other things than money 19.
Ricardo, Mr. 162.
Richmond, Duke of 85, 184, 223, 258, 266.
Ripon, Earl of 40, 263.
Roebuck, Mr. 111.
Rogers, Mr. Thorold, on protection in the United States 76.
Russell, Lord John 34, 36, seq., 69, 80, 93, 112, 117, 164, 179, 192, 198, 200, seq., 211, 215, 243.

S

Sandon, Lord 38, 43, 242.
Scottish people, intelligence of the 145.
Shipping, British 278.
Slave labor and protection 43, 156, 179, 194, 235.
Sliding scale for duty on foreign grain 38, 117.
Smith, Adam 10, 138.
Soothsayers, Protectionist 272.
Speculation, economic value of 118.
Speculative guesses, 136.
Stanhope, Lord 84.
Stanley, Lord 44, 214, 257, 259.
Statute of limitations in favor of Protection 68.
Stump oratory not peculiar to America 129.
Subsistence, standard of 141.
Sugar duties 156, seq., 193, 235.

Sugar duty, effect of 42.
Surplus revenue, applications of 177, 181.

T

Tariff for revenue only 113, 148, 254. 258, 271.
Tariff reduction, material and moral effects of 224.
Tariff reductions, with surplus revenue 178.
Tariff Reformer, Lord Palmerston as a 70.
Tariff Reformers, as opposed to Free Traders 119.
Taylor, Mr. James 130.
Tenant farmers, meeting of—at Willis' Rooms 265.
Thackeray on reciprocity 165.
Thompson, Colonel Perronet 24.
Timber, importance of cheap 195.
Times (the), on Mr. Cobden 160.
Tories, alarm of the 37, 38.
Tories, influence of Peel over 212, 216, 221, 242.
Tories, surprising victory of the 49.
Tory party, the 217.
Trade based on exchange of commodities 247.
Trade, improvement in 151.
Trade, mediæval sentiment as to 112.
Trade (restraint of) evil 169.
Trade statistics 274, seq.
Treaty concessions regarding imports, Gladstone on 163.
Tweedledum and Tweedledee 117.
Tyler, Mr., on reciprocity 116.

U

United States, benefit to the— of English Free Trade policy 279.

United States, free access of the—to English markets 218.
United States, protective system of 55, 115, 161. *See* "American Protectionists."
Universal protection, impossibility of 175.

V

Victorian era, commercial policy at commencement of 26.
Villiers, Hon. M. Pelham 28, seq., 73, 100, 108, 117, 166, 172, 186, 202.
Vincent, Henry 130.

W

Wages and McKinley bill 200.
Wages and rent 136.
Wages, increase of 277.
Wages, increase of—with cheaper food 53, 152.
Wages, laws of 140.
Wages, protection to 113.
Wages, supposed aim of the Leaguers to reduce 130, 133.
Wages, supposed effect of Free Trade on 42.
Wages, supposed reduction of— through cheap food 134, 140, seq., 205, 225.
Walpole, Sir Robert 11.
Wealth, what it consists in 110.
Weaver, condition of the 120.
Wellington, Duke of 54, 214, 216, 224, 229, 242.
Westminster Review 126.
Wharncliffe, Lord 214.
Whig government, perplexity of the 37.
Whig party, overthrow of the 46, 53.
Whigs and Tories 26.
Whigs (the) and Free Trade 167, 171, 200, 212.
Whigs (the) on Peel's Free Trade Policy 244.

Wiltshire laborers, pathetic arguments of the 248.
Wood, Mr. G. W. 33.
Wool, duty on 178.
Wool-grower, protection to 17.
Woolen manufacturer, protection to 17.

Workingmen, comparison between town and country 127.
Workingmen, improved condition of 130, 275.
Workingmen, petitions of—in favor of Free Trade 240.
Workingmen (town), intelligence of 128.

MAKING SCARCITY

BY

"WHEELBARROW"

CHICAGO:
THE OPEN COURT PUBLISHING COMPANY
1892.

This article, with others, written in a similar vein, on the labor question and on various topics of political economy, and finance, was originally published in *The Open Court* (No. 34). All the essays thus included, are now to be obtained in book-form in the work entitled "Wheelbarrow," published by The Open Court Publishing Co.

MAKING SCARCITY.

SOME time ago I made a few remarks upon that "competition" hobgoblin, which makes the hair of workingmen stand up in fright, "like quills upon the fretful porcupine." From my boyhood, it was a terror to me, but it does not scare me now. As I grew older I grew bolder, and at last I walked close up to it and examined it. I found it was a hollow pumpkin, with eyes, nose, and mouth cut in it, and stuck on a stick clothed in the drapery of a white sheet. I see that the President of the Federation of Trades Unions has exhibited this venerable old ghost to the Senate Committee on Education and Labor. Whether it scared the committee or not I cannot say. Since then I have noticed that some other gentleman has appeared before the same committee, in company with the same spectre, and demanded that convict labor shall not be put in competition with the mechanic trades, but shall be exclusively devoted to the business of "working on the roads."

I have tried to analyze the principle of non-competition, as enforced by the trades unions, and so far as I have been able to resolve it into its constituent elements, its chief ingredients appear to be monopoly and selfishness, with some very foolish dread of the evils of abundance. Take this convict labor question for example. Convict labor is not opposed on

MAKING SCARCITY.

any ground but that of "competition." It competes with outside labor, that is, it produces something, and this production is the injury complained of. Let us reduce the question to a concrete form. Suppose that the two thousand convicts in the penitentiaries of Illinois are all compelled to work at the shoemaking trade, and suppose that they each make a pair of shoes a day, or 62,400 pairs a year, will it be contended that the addition of this number of shoes to the common stock is an injury to the people of Illinois? There is no one who will claim that; but the President of the Federation will say: "It is an injury to the shoemakers' trade, and therefore it ought to be prevented."

Very well, then make tailors of the convicts. This plan doesn't solve the difficulty either, for the tailors won't agree to it, nor the tinkers, nor the tanners, nor the masons, nor the carpenters, nor any other trade. As the butcher, and baker, and candlestick-maker all refuse to work in competition with the convicts, and as none of these economists are daring enough to require that the convicts live in idleness, an easy solution of the problem is found by compelling them "to work upon the roads." But really this is only shifting the difficulty, and is no solution at all. At school I have solved many a hard problem in long division, which is as far as I went, by getting some other boy to do the sum for me, and the President of the Federation adopts the same plan with the convict labor difficulty. He dumps it on the "laborer" class, and says: "Here, you man with the wheelbarrow, work this hard sum." But I am not able to work it, because I find that I cannot set the convicts at any useful employment without putting them in competition with somebody. They must either live in idleness at the expense of the community, or they must earn something to pay for their board ; to earn something they must produce something, and that is an addition to the aggregate wealth of the people, at which we all get a nibble at last.

If adding to the wealth of a country is an injury, then subtracting from that wealth must be a benefit, and therefore the destruction of shoes and clothes, and houses and furniture, must be a desirable thing ; the Chicago fire, instead of being a great calamity, was a great blessing. This fallacy is firmly cherished by workingmen ; it is the guiding principle of trades unions, and is productive of want and poverty incalculable. It was instilled into me in my very childhood, and it was late when I got rid of it. I never ate a meal when a boy, that was not somehow or other complicated with the everlasting consideration of "work." When I got a good dinner I knew that my father was "in work" ; when the meal was scanty I knew that he was "out of work." In our home all human affairs whirled round and round the image of "work" forever. A big fire devoured a street—"It will make work," I heard my father say. A ship was lost at sea laden with silk, and leather, and cloth—"It will make work," said my father. A reservoir broke jail and swept the heart of the town away—"It will make work," my mother said ; and so all human calamities were softened as blessings to me ; they made work, and work made wages, and wages made bread and potatoes and clothes for me. God bless the shipwreck, and the fire, and the flood ; they make

"Work, work, work, till the eyes are heavy and dim,
And work, work, work, till the brain begins to swim."

MAKING SCARCITY.

Oh, comrade of the trowel, the needle, and the awl ; oh, toiler at the anvil and the loom ; oh, brother of the jackplane and the shovel ; oh, chivalry of toil by land and sea, it is not work we need so much as rest! Let us make all the wealth we can, and destroy nothing ; let us not be jealous of each other's talent, but teach each other everything we know! Let us make plenty in the land, and then let us try to shape our social system and the laws so that a fairer share of it will come to us after we have made it.

Last fall I picked up a newspaper and read in great black headlines this alarming news : "A Heavy Frost. It spread over various sections of the Northwest Friday night. Early planted corn escaped with little injury ; the late crop practically ruined." It requires no great skill in political economy, as they call it, to understand that the blighting of the corn crop is a great calamity ; it means less food the coming winter, and less food means less of clothes, and coal, and wood. And yet there are a lot of workingmen who would regard a blight of the hat crop, or the shoe crop, or the coat crop as a blessing to labor ; but in truth they are all equally injurious as the blighting of the cattle and the corn. Food, and clothes, and furniture, and all necessaries of life, are so intimately related, that the blight of one is the blight of all, and it means less of each to the workingman.

It is easy to prove by the doctrines of the anticompetitionists that this disaster to the corn crop is a good thing, because it removes from the farmers living south of the frost line the competition in the corn market of the farmers living north of it. And it is also a good thing for the people who have old corn in the bins ; but this is a narrow and selfish way to look at it, and if the doctrine be carried out to its logical end it elevates to the rank of a moral principle the unnatural dogma that the prosperity of one man depends upon the adversity of another. Once upon a time I had a job of "work on the roads" not far from an Indian agency. The tribe had just been paid off, and the Indians were trading at the store up at the agency, where I happened to go for some tobacco. They were buying some needles, for which the trader charged them fifty cents apiece. They complained of the price, but when the trader assured them that the needle-maker was dead, and the needle-making industry thereby terminated, they appeared satisfied. This lying excuse for the high price of needles presented to me a tough problem in economic science, and I went up to the shanty to work it out.

I lighted my pipe, and tried to read the solution of the problem in the clouds of smoke. The first question to be answered was this: Suppose the needle-maker was really dead, and his art lost forever, would that be a good thing? I had no trouble with this question at all. I could readily see that although it might be a good thing for the man who happened to have a large stock of needles on hand, it would be a bad thing for everybody else. The next question was not so easy. It was this: Suppose that one-half of the needle-makers in the world should die to-night, would that be a good thing in an economic point of view? It took several pipes of tobacco to answer this question, and I am not sure that I got it right even then. The answer involved so many collaterals. It was very clear that if every needle-maker was a master, and not a journeyman, those who survived, being relieved of competition to such a great extent, would make good profit out of it by raising the price of needles, but the community would still be losers. But suppose that of the survivors 95 per cent. were journeymen, and 5 per cent. masters, where would the new profits go? Labor being a marketable thing, the masters would still want to buy it at the old figures, and the jours would get but a trifling raise of wages, while the increased value of needles would nearly all go into the pockets of the masters. But even supposing that the increased profit were fairly divided between them, the community would still have to pay it, and, therefore, the sudden removal of so much competition in the trade would be an injury, and not a benefit. Applying this rule to every other trade and occupation, it appeared to me that the loss of wealth, or of wealth-producing capacity, is injurious to the community, that the workingmen cannot be benefited by such loss, and that all attempts to create a scarcity of competition by crippling talent, or forbidding the industry of anybody, can only be of local or personal benefit here and there, and the pursuit of such false systems of relief is a sad waste of the moral strength of the workingmen.

"Nature abhors a vacuum," is a maxim in physics, and in moral philosophy also. So nature tries forever to preserve an equilibrium in the moral and material universe. The very earthquakes and volcanoes are efforts in this direction, and men can no easier keep trades unbalanced than they can disturb the level of the sea. Create a vacuum in any trade and nature rushes in to fill it. If I should give paralysis to every shoveler to-night, how long should I enjoy my monopoly? In a week I should see shovelers galore. The telegraph operators made a vacuum,

WHEELBARROW.

but only for an instant; it at once began to fill; in a month the hole was almost gone. We may think we have destroyed competition by excluding a brother craftsman here, but he or somebody else has slipped in over there, for the struggle of life goes on. We must liberate labor, and exalt it by grander schemes than these.

PUBLICATIONS OF THE OPEN COURT PUBLISHING CO.

THE MONIST.

A QUARTERLY MAGAZINE OF
Philosophy, Science, Religion, and Sociology.

Single Numbers, 50 Cents. Two Dollars per Year.

THE OPEN COURT.

A WEEKLY JOURNAL
Devoted to the Work of Conciliating Religion with Science.

Single Numbers, 5 Cents. Two Dollars per Year.

THREE INTRODUCTORY LECTURES ON THE SCIENCE OF THOUGHT. By F. MAX MUELLER.
1. The Simplicity of Language; 2. The Identity of Language and Thought; 3. The Simplicity of Thought. Cloth, 75 Cents.

THREE LECTURES ON THE SCIENCE OF LANGUAGE. By PROF. F. MAX MUELLER.
With a Supplement "MY PREDECESSORS." Cloth, 75 Cents.

THE PSYCHOLOGY OF ATTENTION. By TH. RIBOT. Authorised translation. Cloth, 75 Cents.

THE DISEASES OF PERSONALITY. By TH. RIBOT. Authorised translation. Cloth, 75 Cents.

THE PSYCHIC LIFE OF MICRO-ORGANISMS. By ALFRED BINET. Authorised translation. Cloth, 75 Cents.

ON DOUBLE CONSCIOUSNESS. New Studies in Experimental Psychology. By ALFRED BINET. Price, 50 Cents.

EPITOMES OF THREE SCIENCES.
1. COMPARATIVE PHILOLOGY. By PROF. H. OLDENBERG.
2. COMPARATIVE PSYCHOLOGY. By PROF. J. JASTROW.
3. OLD TESTAMENT HISTORY. By PROF. C. H. CORNILL. Cloth, 75 Cents.

DARWIN AND AFTER DARWIN. An Exposition of the Darwinian Theory and a Discussion of Post-Darwinian Questions. By GEORGE JOHN ROMANES. Elegantly Bound, $2.00.

THE ETHICAL PROBLEM. By DR. PAUL CARUS.
Three Lectures Delivered at the Invitation of the Board of Trustees before the Society for Ethical Culture of Chicago, in June, 1890. Cloth, 50 Cents.

THE SOUL OF MAN. An Investigation of the Facts of Physiological and Experimental Psychology. By DR. PAUL CARUS.
With 152 illustrative cuts and diagrams. 474 pp. Cloth, $3.00.

THE IDEA OF GOD. By DR. PAUL CARUS.
A disquisition upon the development of the idea of God. Paper, 15 Cents.

FUNDAMENTAL PROBLEMS. By DR. PAUL CARUS. Second Edition. Revised and Enlarged. Cloth, $1.50.

HOMILIES OF SCIENCE. By DR. PAUL CARUS. Gilt Top. Elegantly Bound. $1.50.

THE LOST MANUSCRIPT. A Novel. By GUSTAV FREYTAG. Authorised Translation. Elegantly Bound, $4.00. In one volume bound in cloth, good paper, $1.00.

THE OPEN COURT PUBLISHING CO.
169-175 La Salle St., CHICAGO, ILL.

THE OPEN COURT

A WEEKLY MAGAZINE

Devoted to the Conciliation of Religion with Science.

THE OPEN COURT does not understand by religion any creed or dogmatic belief, but man's world-conception in so far as it regulates his conduct.

The old dogmatic conception of religion is based upon the science of past ages; to base religion upon the maturest and truest thought of the present time is the object of *The Open Court*. Thus, the religion of *The Open Court* is the Religion of Science, that is the Religion of verified and verifiable truth.

Although opposed to irrational orthodoxy and narrow bigotry, *The Open Court* does not attack the properly religious element of the various religions. It criticises their errors unflinchingly but without animosity, and it endeavors to preserve of them all that is true and good.

The current numbers of *The Open Court* contain valuable original articles from the pens of distinguished thinkers. Accurate and authorised translations are made in Philosophy, Science, and Criticism from the periodical literature of Continental Europe, and reviews of noteworthy recent investigations are presented.

TERMS: Two dollars a year throughout the Postal Union. Single Copies, 5 Cents.

THE OPEN COURT PUBLISHING CO.,

CHICAGO, 169-175 La Salle Street.

The Monist

A QUARTERLY MAGAZINE OF

PHILOSOPHY AND SCIENCE.

THE MONIST discusses the fundamental problems of Philosophy in their practical bearings upon the religious, ethical, and sociological questions of the day.

Among its contributors are: Charles S. Peirce, Prof. Joseph Le Conte. Dr. W. T. Harris, Prof. E. D. Cope, M. D. Conway, Prof. F. Max Müller, Prof. G. J. Romanes, Prof. C. Lloyd Morgan, James Sully, B. Bosanquet, Dr. A. Binet Prof. C. Lombroso, Prof. E. Mach, Prof. F. Jodl, Prof. Ernst Haeckel, Prof. H. Höffding, Dr. F. Oswald, Dr. Emil Hirsch, Prof. J. Delbœuf, E. de Roberty.

Per Copy, 50 Cents; in Cloth, 75 Cents. Yearly, $2.00; in Cloth, $3.00. In England: Per Copy, 2s. 6d; Cloth, 3s. 6d. Yearly, 9s. 6d; in Cloth, 13s. 8d.

CHICAGO:	LONDON:
THE OPEN COURT PUB. CO.,	MESSRS. WATTS & CO.,
169-175 La Salle Street.	17 Johnson's Court, Fleet Street, E. C.

WHEELBARROW

ARTICLES AND DISCUSSIONS

ON THE

LABOR QUESTION

INCLUDING

The Controversy with Mr. Lyman J. Gage on the Ethics of the Board of Trade; and also the Controversy with Mr. Hugh O. Pentecost, and others, on the Single Tax Question.

Elegant cloth binding, portrait of the author, and autograph letter, $1.00.

PRESS NOTICES.

"We heartily recommend this volume to every reader interested in the problems of labor and capital, money, trusts, and monopolies."—*Chicago Herald*.

"This book is worth reading by any person interested in human welfare and in the problem of labor."—Boston *Investigator*.

"The book is rich reading. The style is bright, forcible, and clear. It sparkles with wit, and drives a point home with the highest skill."—*Public Opinion*.

"On the essentials of the matter he is solid, and a master of the art of putting things for plain men."—*Independent*, New York.

"Suggestive and forceful. The best part of the book is the all too brief autobiographical note by the anonymous author."—*Lippincott's Monthly*.

"The articles are clear, strong and logical from his standpoint. He is no demagogue, but stands for the immutable principles of justice."—*Toledo Blade*.

THE OPEN COURT PUBLISHING CO.,

169-175 La Salle Street,

CHICAGO, - ILLINOIS.

www.ingramcontent.com/pod-product-compliance
Lightning Source LLC
Chambersburg PA
CBHW022105230426
43672CB00008B/1288